LPM 57291 · MARCH AROUND THE BREAKFAST TABLE · EDDIE BALLANTINE

LPM-1002 MUSIC FOR READING ~ MELACHRINO STRINGS

MERCURY MG 20072 · JAN AUGUST · COCKTAILS AND CONVERSATION

BOBBY SHORT
SF·33·13 SOUNDS IN SPACE
ON THE EAST SIDE

VG-50003

VG-50000

LPM-1938 MUSIC FOR AN ITALIAN DINNER AT HOME ~ ROMANO FERENZIO AND...

Verve and Esquire present SOUN

Verve and Esquire present SOUND

MUSIC FOR DINING ~ DAVE BRUBECK QUARTET

THE MELACHRINO STRINGS AND ORCHESTRA
COUNTDOWN—TIME IN OUTER SPACE

LPM-1000

KL-1238

ANIMALIZATION ~ THE ANIMALS

LES ELGART

JOSÉ JIMENEZ—THE ASTRONAUT · The First Man In Space

8103

ON TOUR

JAZZ IMPRESSIONS OF EURASIA

THE DAVE BRUBECK QUARTET

THE WORLD OF TRAVEL

S-0656

IT'S ALASKA—FEATURING THE HARRY SIMEONE CHORALE—MUSIC COMPOS...

STEREO 3004 · MAN ON THE MOON · OFFICIAL NASA VOICE TAPES N...

LPM-1656 COFFEE TIME ~ MORTON GOULD AND HIS ORCHESTRA

MERCURY RECORD MG 20068 · MUSIC FOR A RAINY NIGHT ~ KOSTY DRAPER

OX VXL 4 · 33⅓ RPM · 'ROUND THE WORLD—'ROUND THE CLOCK

DAVE BRUBECK QUARTET · TIME CHANGES

T SLP 2249

IT TO HAWAII

THE GREATEST OF STAN G...

WIRI 100.4

MUSIC FOR CARDS, CONVERSATION AND CUDDLING ~ HOLIDAY IN NEW YORK

SAIGO!

SPACE SONGS

LUTHER IN TROPICAL ORBIT · HARRY HERMANN

DESIGNED FOR HI-FI LIVING

DESIGNED FOR HI-FI LIVING

THE VINYL LP IN MIDCENTURY AMERICA

JANET BORGERSON

AND JONATHAN SCHROEDER

FOREWORD BY DANIEL MILLER

THE MIT PRESS
CAMBRIDGE, MASSACHUSETTS
LONDON, ENGLAND

This book was set in ITC Century Std and Helvetica Neue by the MIT Press. Printed and bound in the United States of America.

Library of Congress Cataloging-in-Publication Data

Names: Borgerson, Janet. | Schroeder, Jonathan E., 1962–
Title: Designed for hi-fi living : the vinyl LP in midcentury America / Janet Borgerson and Jonathan Schroeder ; foreword by Daniel Miller.
Description: Cambridge, MA : MIT Press, [2017] | Includes bibliographical references and index.
Identifiers: LCCN 2016041020 | ISBN 9780262036238 (hardcover : alk. paper)
Subjects: LCSH: Sound recordings—Social aspects—United States—History—20th century. | Sound recording industry—United States—History—20th century.
Classification: LCC ML3917.U6 B68 2017 | DDC 306.4/842097309045—dc23 LC record available at https://lccn.loc.gov/2016041020

10 9 8 7 6 5 4 3 2 1

CONTENTS

FOREWORD

DANIEL MILLER

It is hard not to be intrigued by the question of what is evoked in us by music. We can't actually see the music we hear. Many classical music compositions have titles that claim to convey something such as a mountain, a stream, or an ethnic identity. But mostly I can't picture that scene when I hear the music. Yet this seems to make no difference at all to whether I appreciate the music or not. I am still just as likely to find the sounds memorable, pleasant, irritating or moving. The best attempt I know at trying to get at this problem was that of the philosopher Susanne Langer in her 1942 book *Philosophy in a New Key*. Her concern was with issues of representation and the emotions. Not everyone agrees that this works for music, though it seems a pretty good bet that it works for LP covers.

Today I mainly listen to Spotify; I do not bother to look at the cover art of whatever format this music otherwise may have come in, and often I have no idea what the musicians look like. I do not believe this has made the slightest difference to my relationship to music. I am addicted to modern music, mainly pop. I can't go more than a day or two without hearing some, but given my current experience, I have no nostalgia for album covers as something that enhanced my experience of or relationship to music. If the point was the music, the covers seem, in retrospect, pointless.

Yet that is exactly why this book is important. In a way, trying to think about album covers just as a secondary reflection of music, as though music was the real thing and the covers mere shadows, was a mistake. Album covers as a visual form stand in their own right as creative work that we may have neglected. They are a genre of material culture, and as objects of observation, reflection, and conversation offer the ground for instruction, as well as relationships and personal and group identity. When we defocus from the music and instead focus directly on the covers we gain the insights found within this book.

We probably come closer to understanding why these album covers matter if we see them more as part of the history of consumer culture and advertising than of music, as, after all, that was their point: they promoted their contents in a lifestyle context. As such we have many tools for their investigation, and the authors are greatly respected for their expertise in this field. An example of the payoff of their approach here appears in the chapter on modern art and design. The authors zero in on a fabulous selection of LP covers featuring abstract art and modernist furniture, including iconic midcentury chairs, that contributed to establishing US postwar visions and values. By elaborating on the material details and aesthetics of the chair itself rather, in this case, than on the gendered stereotype of the woman lounging on the chair, they reveal not only the insidious sexism of the 1950s but also insights into the global concerns of US Cold War cultural diplomacy. This is a shift from the more typical tropes of identity to midcentury materiality, in which the story of the furniture is as revealing as identity politics. To me the LP cover looks to be an example of what Michael Schudson called "advertising as capitalist realism," which is by no means any simple kind of realism.

To go deeper we might acknowledge the work of Robert Marchand in his book *Advertising the American Dream Making Way for Modernity, 1920–1940.* During the first half of the last century we see the development of modern life, an increasing rapidity of change that could have caused anxiety as well as excitement. Marketing communications and advertising art were not primarily about having a particular cultural impact; they were there to sell goods. Vinyl records as durable forms in material culture made their way into homes and living rooms and onto hi-fi turntables. But in order to achieve that purpose, as a by-product, vast amounts of images were created, letting people feel comfortable and at ease with new goods, new services, and new times, rather than anxious. We are a long way before the Rolling Stones' infamous *Sticky Fingers* cover.

Selling a lifestyle may be the backdrop to what we see within this volume. There is certainly aspiration here, ranging from the new Technicolor palette to the suburban patio and the cosmopolitanism of travel. But the LP covers present these pleasures and adventures in relatively familiar comforting forms. This was a shoehorn style of art and design that helped reassure people while experiencing the new. We see this clearly in the book's Capitol of the World, Honeymoon, and Space chapters, which highlight unknown realms of potential anxiety away from home. The travel and tourism albums in particular produce ideals of peaceful, culturally rich exotic lands to explore; a caring, consumer-first travel industry; and healthy, financially independent travelers who can begin expanding their understanding of the world by buying vinyl LPs. The authors give us the rich and textured details that allow us to be transported back into that time and feel how this was done—which is why I want to end on the opposite point from which I began.

I don't think the album cover is required to appreciate music, but in this case we have an instance in which the music clearly does play its analogous role in shaping cultural identity. Many covers were designed for a particular kind of mood music, soothing and constantly repeated popular tunes that gave some hint of the wider and wilder fields of jazz and pop, but in such an attenuated fashion as to eliminate the anxiety. This might be said as well of the travel and Capitol of the World albums' foray into a wider and wilder world away from home. At least in this instance it seems that the music was doing pretty much the same thing as the covers, as Marchand puts it—making way for modernity, very gently. So we have come full circle, by refusing to see the cover as mere reflection of the music and focusing on the cover itself, this volume helps us to understand not only the point of the cover but in many cases also of the music in the context of this influential era.

PREFACE

Vinyl records are popular again. The collectible market is booming, sales of new vinyl eclipses compact discs, and Record Store Day has established itself as an international retail phenomenon. In short, vinyl is back.

We have been collecting records together for more than twenty years. We are partners—we live together and frequently write together. Unlike many of our friends and colleagues, we never got rid of our vinyl. We have always had a working turntable, and we have never given up the habit of seeking out and buying records. For a while, new records were few and far between. Maybe for this reason, every LP we touched seemed to be a used LP, and they were often obscure and inexplicable, from another era, but still attractive, and a bargain at fifty cents or a dollar. Over time we discovered a couple of kinds of albums that particularly attracted us—those LPs that fit into what we now call the home and away genres, often focused on making the most of your new kitchen and entertaining friends and also leaving home, and traveling, say, to Hawaii. After looking at, playing, and living with thousands of vintage albums, we began to reflect on how midcentury records like those in Columbia Records' Music for Gracious Living series and many other wonderful examples, fit in. What were they for? Why were they made? Who bought them?

In 2013, we gave a talk on our vinyl records at an academic conference; and our colleagues helped us realize that they deserved more attention. One reaction stands out: an international colleague living and working in the United States was amazed—after viewing an album focused on how to have a particularly American dinner party, a backyard barbecue—that Americans needed to be taught how to do such American things. Our records were a revelation to her—they showed that traditional US customs weren't as "natural" as they seemed. Even Americans needed to be taught how to barbecue.

Our title, *Designed for Hi-Fi Living: The Vinyl LP in Midcentury America*, pays homage to an evocative midcentury LP series, Music for Hi-Fi Living, a twelve-record set from RCA. These records embody many of the themes we develop in the book, which focuses on neglected LP genres. We found that a closer look at these vinyl artifacts revealed fascinating aspects of postwar consumer culture. And the colorful cover photographs and revealing liner notes provided unanticipated inspiration for reflecting on design, media, visual culture, and history. Throughout the book, we try to maintain a delicate balance between celebration and critique, and between enthusiasm and evaluation. We like our records—they have taught us a lot.

ACKNOWLEDGMENTS

A special thanks goes to many record stores, past and present, including Schoolkids, Encore, and P.J.s in Ann Arbor; Full Moon in Traverse City; Car City Classics in Detroit; Bonanza Jellybean and Ace in Flint; Rasputin's in Berkeley; Asta's in Oakland; Amoeba and Aquarius in San Francisco; B-Side in Madison; Twist & Shout and Wax Trax in Denver; Round Again, Olympic, and In Your Ear in Providence; Cheapo Records in Cambridge; Nuggets in Boston; Jerry's in Pittsburgh; Dusty Groove in Chicago; Pet Sounds in Stockholm; Piccadilly Records in Manchester; Real Groovy in Auckland; the Bop Shop, the Hi-Fi Lounge, and Record Archive in Rochester; Norman's in Brooklyn, and of course innumerable Goodwill, Salvation Army, and St. Vincent de Paul stores across the United States, and Oxfam stores in the United Kingdom.

Early aspects of this project were presented to various audiences in various places, including Cooley Law School; Brown University; Wellesley College; Stockholm University; Dublin City University; Konstfack-University College for Arts, Crafts, and Design; Rochester Institute of Technology; Linnaeus University; Stockholm School of Economics; and the Association for Consumer Research, Consumer Culture Theory, Critical Management Studies, and Ethics in Popular Culture conferences.

At Rochester Institute of Technology, we thank Hinda Mandell, Pat Scanlon, Jamie Winebrake, Cassandra Shellman, Israel Brown, Amit Ray, Jessica Lieberman,

Michael Laver, Bruce Meader, Roger Remington, Juilee Decker, Greg Decker, Grant Cos, Molly Cort, Bruce Austin; and the staff at RIT Production Services, especially Elizabeth Lamark, director of photography services, and Danielle Del Plato, assistant studio manager, for their work scanning the album covers, as well as the staff at the Wallace Center and the RIT libraries.

Deep appreciation goes to the enthusiastic and helpful staff at the LaBudde Special Collections at University of Missouri–Kansas City, including Marr Sound Archive director Chuck Haddix, Andrew Hansbrough, Kelly McEniry, Stuart Hinds, and Scott Gipson.

Thanks to Penny Milliken, Arlene Fishbach, and Barry Samson for assistance with reproduction rights. We thank Ilene Bellovin for picture research, and Daniel Gallagher for assistance with images and editing. Thanks to the team at the MIT Press, including our editor Doug Sery, Roger Conover, Pamela Quick, Deborah Cantor-Adams, Susan Clark, Colleen Lanick, David Ryman, Noah Springer, and Susan Buckley, as well as the manuscript reviewers. Thanks also to Kevin Morosini at Olympic Records; Tom Kohn at Bop Shop Records; Andreas Nutz at Vitra Design Museum; Toby Silver and Ana Way at Sony Music; Adrien Cadiuex, Nathalie Girard, Simon Frost, Lane Cooper, Robert Hoffman, Delphine Felisa, Karen Leisten, and Pam Kunick-Cohen at Technicolor; Alisa Coleman and Emma Smith at Abkco; Angela Hoover at the Chicago History Museum; Todd Waxler, Teresa Hale, Scott Ravine, and David Iscove at Universal Music Group; Polly Haas at mptv; Jenling Norman at Hedrich Blessing Photographers; Jan Wauters at the Consulate General of Belgium; Bruce Barnes and Jared Case at the George Eastman Museum; and Laura Zigarowicz and Lynne A. Shannon at Kodak.

Finally, we thank many colleagues and friends for their interest and insight over the years, including Fleura Bardhi, Dana Countryman, Phil Prygoski, Haidy Geismer, Daniel Miller, Larry Fagin, Lewis Gordon, Jane Anna Gordon, Jean and John Comaroff, Alexander Tochilovsky, Nitsan Hermon, Jennifer Trontz, Ken Corey, Pushi Prasad, Anshuman Prasad, Alexander Marr, Zeynep Arsel, Jonathan Bean, Giana Eckhardt, Worth Wagers, Markus Giesler, Stephen Brown, David Hardenbrook, Bruce Watson,

Gus Rylander, Jane Burchfield, Jonathan Avery, Kristin Avery, Brandon Artz, Robert Foster, Jacob Paulson, Alex Reed, Meredith Collins, Pierre Guillet de Monthoux, Morris Holbrook, Regenia Gagnier, John Dupré, Sir Steve Smith, Jeannie Forbes, Jonathan Gosling, Andrea Prothero, Pierre McDonagh, Martin Escudero-Magnusson, Natasha Slutskaya, Alladi Venkatesh, Sidney Levy, Ashlee Humphreys, John Schroeder, Ian Woodward, Alan Bradshaw, Doug Holt, Tuba Üstüner, Alex Thompson, Eminigül Karababa, Lindsay Stringfellow, Ron Weinstein, Rebekah Modrak, Katie Nix, Meredith Davenport, Victoria Cherry, Bruce Lindsay, Sean Wilentz, Cele Otnes, Peter Moruzzi, Saara Taalas, Erika Saaristo, Mehita Iqani, Cobus van Staden, Susan Genco, Joonas Rokka, Carol Summerfield, Arnold Weinstein, Sleiman El Bssawmai, Charlotte Birnbaum, Richard Popp, and Claudia Pretelin.

This project was supported by the William A. Kern endowment at Rochester Institute of Technology. We also gratefully acknowledge the support of an RIT College of Liberal Arts book club grant.

INTRODUCTION

Record albums from the 1950s and 1960s were only partly about the music. Indeed, while Frank Sinatra, Elvis Presley, and the Beatles were selling millions of albums, thousands more were released in unheralded categories such as mood music, instructional, and travel that never reached the charts. These often-overlooked vinyl LPs stood apart from the crooners, pop stars, and rock 'n' rollers that dominated the era. Today, they offer fascinating glimpses into lifestyles, listening habits, and longings at midcentury.

In this book we consider the contributions of midcentury record albums to the postwar imagination and their relevance for contemporary consumer culture. We have selected illustrative examples from a large, privately owned record album archive, and discuss album cover photography and graphic design, along with liner notes and music, to illuminate how LPs provided listeners with guides for becoming more culturally confident, cosmopolitan, and sophisticated. For example, home-entertaining records and travel records often included content dedicated to achieving a "modern" lifestyle, developing good taste, and becoming familiar with new sights and sounds. And, by taking a visual and vinyl approach, we hope to show how minor, even peripheral, objects—often moldering in basements, gathering dust at Goodwill and Salvation Army, or in more recent times, sold as campy or exotic collectibles on eBay—reveal powerful, yet relatively unnoticed, lessons in learning popular culture. In sum, we explore how these records helped to shape the imaginings of modern US identity and global citizenship at midcentury. Not just decorated cardboard that protected the vinyl disks within, vintage record album covers from the 1950s and 1960s served commercial, pedagogical, and rhetorical purposes.

Indeed, this book aims to change the way people understand record album covers. Yes, album cover images provided clues to a record's musical style or sensibility, but these carefully crafted covers, often photographs, also offered visual instruction for achieving aspects of contemporary, and aspirational, lifestyles that included backyard garden patios, adventurous dinners at home, as well as travel to places far away.

Pioneering American photographers, before they were well known, helped create visions for what we call the being-at-home genre, their striking depictions appearing in trickled-down form on our record album covers. For example, Edward Steichen worked for publishing house Condé Nast in the 1920s, helping to picture, in vibrant color, lifestyles that became more widely accessible some decades later.[1] Nickolas Muray's *Ladies Home Journal* "Bathing Pool Scene" from 1931 and Victor Keppler's "Housewife in Kitchen" from 1939 share a visual aesthetic we see in Columbia Records' Music for Gracious Living series albums, particularly *Buffet* and *After the Dance*.[2]

Interestingly, it was an architectural photography studio, Hedrich Blessing, "associated with documenting the modern architecture movement,"[3] that took on the challenge of depicting the Music for Gracious Living suburban scenes that we feature in chapter 3. In the 1950s, Hedrich Blessing worked with modernist architects such as Mies van der Rohe and Eero Saarinen, who profoundly influenced prominent midcentury designers, including Charles and Ray Eames, George Nelson, and Harry Bertoia. As modernist notions entered into the lives, lifestyles, and landscapes of postwar Americans, Hedrich Blessing became known as a "communicator" of related spaces and ideas, and their conceptualizations leap out, in brilliant hues, from the Music for Gracious Living album covers.[4] As historian Greg Castillo observes, "Idealized domestic settings lent physical and emotional immediacy to abstract ideological concepts. The cozy intimacy of the staged household obscured the mechanics of pedagogy."[5]

Photographs depicting iconic views of the world away from home had already been around for some time when 1950s LPs began to draw upon these visions for a mass American audience. In the mid-1800s, for example, Maxime du Camp's photographic images of the Sphinx and the Egyptian pyramids provided exotic scenes for the armchair traveler that find an echo on *Cairo!: The Music of Modern Egypt*, an LP from the Capitol of the World series. American modernist photographer Alvin Langdon Coburn's 1905 "View from Notre Dame" features the close-up gothic architecture of the cathedral's rooftop with Paris stretched out below—a view that influenced how generations of Americans imagined the great French city. And, in 1915, the Lumière brothers' autochrome glass-plate images of Switzerland's towering Matterhorn provided a still recognizable image for anticipating a picturesque trip abroad.[6] Travel agencies relied on such destination identities in their own promotional materials, such as posters, and album covers imitated them.

In addition to the cover art, the small print that filled an LP's back cover created a story for the recording within. These liner notes produced historical knowledge, not just about the featured music but also around the related cultural contexts deemed relevant to the listener's enjoyment and education. Indeed, in attempting to make the unfamiliar more palatable and the culturally sophisticated more accessible, album notes often became opportunities to teach record buyers not only about musical traditions, popular performing artists, and recording technology advances but also cosmopolitan lifestyle choices, unfamiliar rituals, and foreign lands—all aimed at developing a modern American consumer. For example, the phenomenon of commentary beyond the recording per se was particularly common on albums of unfamiliar musical styles such as Columbia's *Caribbee: Songs of the Indies* and Capitol's *Mexico: Its Sounds and People*. In this way, midcentury record albums played the role of advice column, cultural guide, and travel brochure, as they promoted postwar consumer lifestyles and celebrated iconic sites, sounds, and tastes of featured locations. And, travelers, whether actual or armchair, were offered a comforting position from which they might enjoy a sense of belonging, rather than exclusion, in otherwise unfamiliar places and spaces.

Clearly, the music found on these vinyl LPs is only one element of a package designed to introduce midcentury Americans to a host of consumer choices and experiences, helping them to navigate through new situations and destinations and gain access to the specific pleasures of each. Indeed, in the midcentury era, the LP record emerged as a central information technology and an information distribution format. As media theorist Jacob Smith reminds us: "From the 1940s to the 1970s, the phonograph industry experienced phenomenal growth in sales and cultural influence, producing recordings that were meant to serve a multitude of functions in the American home above and beyond the reproduction of popular music."[7] Smith writes that in the postwar period, "phonograph records frequently provided a 'segment-making' home media alternative to the dominant 'society-making' media of network broadcasting. ... Records convened audiences around shared interests that were often underrepresented in the broadcast media, making them a powerful vehicle for the formation of group identity during the postwar decades."[8] These LPs were generally aimed at adults, as opposed to teenagers—who remained the key market for 45 rpm singles.[9] Most were intended to appeal to middle-class audiences,[10] and in some cases to those in various kinds of transition—moving from small town to urban landscapes, from urban apartments to suburban houses, or from single to married lifestyles. Further, the target audience for most albums presented here was probably imagined to be white, but not exclusively, especially given the "away" records' potential appeal to different domestic ethnic and international audiences.

Vinyl albums included sound, text, and imagery. Indeed, we find that these albums offer a distinctive blending of the aural, visual, and pedagogical. As Norwegian visual theorists Asbjørn Grønstad and Øyvind Vågnes contend, a record album constitutes a unique "composite medium" that although often understood to center on music, "in transmitting that art form, simultaneously engenders a semiotic configuration and an aesthetic experience that is not reducible to music alone."[11] Nor are the covers merely decorative in their ability to communicate, entertain, and instruct. We examine the cultural work of these albums—as material objects, graphic design icons, as well as sound recordings—at midcentury. Of course, these LPs continue to circulate today as coveted collectibles and treasured artifacts of a golden age of album cover design, valued as retro icons as well as musical soundtracks.[12]

In the technology department, after Audio Fidelity released the first commercial recordings with stereo sound in March 1958, a "tone-arm race" was on for the highest fidelity sound.[13] Decca offered "Full Frequency Stereophonic Sound," RCA promoted "Living Stereo," Columbia presented "360 Sound," and Mercury chimed in with "Living Presence."[14] Album notes brimmed with technical information about advances in recording technology, admonishments to use high-fidelity needles, and expansive explanations of how stereo worked. Vinyl records required their own technologies and regimes of care and protection, of course, from the retail environment's plastic packaging to home storage methods. Liner notes, aside from detailed descriptions of needle diagnostics, often included tips on vinyl cleaning: dip in warm water with dishwashing detergent; wipe with soft cloth; and dry in dish drainer. Numerous hi-fi and stereo demonstration records from the mid-1950s revealed the wonders of modern technology. Hi-fi living had arrived.

We think aspects of these LPs offer a window into influential imaginings and reveal roots of contemporary US culture. Writing about midcentury design, journalist Dominic Bradbury suggests that "in many respects, the patterns and expectations of American and Western consumers in the midcentury period laid down the template for modern living itself and formed a foundation for our own lifestyles in the twenty-first century.[15] The 1950s and 1960s were decades during which postwar affluence contributed to changing lifestyles. Expanded audiences for interior decorating, home entertaining, and travel abroad enlivened notions of cosmopolitan cachet. As "vinyl archaeologist" Jennifer McKnight-Trontz observes, "In the 1950s, American homes, especially in the new suburbia, became full-service temples with new appliances, television, a state-of-the-art sound system, and the music you wanted anytime you wanted it. A simple LP could put your life in order (such as

Columbia's *Music for Gracious Living* series), help you relax, even make you feel good. Why leave home?"[16]

At the same time, of course, the development of international tourism for a mass US population united the marketing of hi-fi sets, exotic motifs—Afro-Cuban rhythms, Hawaiian honeymoon, Latin dancing—and packaged tours to create a vision of the rest of the world and how to travel through it. As well, consumers saw the marketing of Broadway shows, movies, and soundtracks, such as *Flower Drum Song*, *The King and I*, and *South Pacific*, that showcased international themes. Record labels developed new offerings: In the mid-1960s the respected jazz label Verve Records collaborated with *Esquire* magazine to release several "sound tour" albums that included gatefold sleeves, color photographs, and "insider" information for the continental connoisseur. Capitol Records producer Dave Dexter's Capitol of the World series featured albums representing at least twenty-five countries, including Argentina, Egypt, and Italy. For historical context, the war in the Pacific was still recent memory when Capitol released *Japanese Sketches* in 1958.

In concert with others, we have recently noted an increased interest in material culture, particularly in the objects that surround us and engage us and make us who we are. As sociologists Dominik Bartmanski and Ian Woodward found in their study of vinyl in the digital age, "What makes tangible objects like vinyl important to humans is that, being relatively unchanged, they give perceptually stable form to our feelings that often get dimmed by the passage of time and changes within ourselves. They lend that feeling of reassuring concreteness to the dreamy quality of our memories."[17] This certainly rings true regarding the development of consumer goods and consumer culture in the United States, and in the way US citizenship engages with the stuff of the world. Further, the place of the United States in the global economy is being challenged, and surpassed, by China and India, and a generalized identity anxiety may be emerging as many people in the United States begin to notice cracks in what had been perceived as normal and enduring, rather than historically situated and contingent. A pressing interest, then, in the building blocks of "our" society, "our" culture and history—and looking to the postwar period—is growing.

THE ALBUM COVER

It might seem natural that album covers should be square, reflecting practical qualities for flat edged shelf storage and efficient coverage for the circle within, but the square format itself has a graphic design history and is still seen to be "a symbol of uncompromising modernity."[18] Alex Steinweiss invented the album cover while working for Columbia Records during the 1940s and 1950s.[19] Steinweiss's innovation provided a package that both protected and promoted LPs as it associated sound recordings with images. As designer Paula Scher remarked: "When you look at your music collection today," for example, the small identifying album icons on iTunes, "you are looking at Alex Steinweiss's big idea."[20]

The word album derives from the Latin *albus*, white, and also *albho*, white ghostly apparitions. By definition, an album is a book with blank pages for the insertion and preservation of collections, such as photographs or other keepsakes. Alternatively, an album has been defined as a blank tablet on which records or notices were inscribed, registered, or listed.[21] Recorded music albums are albums within albums. The black vinyl disks are inscribed with a collection of musical pieces held within another album form: two covers containing liner notes (which evolved from concert program notes), illustrations or photographic images, and the index of songs, composers, and performers. Record album images are visual and aural: the photographs or designs on the covers collaborate with the music and lyrics inside. Albums, liner notes, and song lyrics instruct and inform through their representations of place, history, and culture.

Album cover design quickly emerged as an important arena for graphic design, and soon after, photography. Graphic artists such as Steinweiss and Jim Flora at Columbia, Reid Miles at Blue Note, as well as Bob Cato, Alvin Lustig, Ben Shahn, and Andy Warhol, participated in the early art of album cover design.[22] Following designer S. Neil Fujita's innovative ideas, photographers such as William Claxton, Lee Friedlander, W. Eugene Smith, and Francis Wolff contributed to the burgeoning genre, as the album cover came to represent a significant forum for design and cultural expression.[23] Examples from this book include Roy DeCarava, who came to prominence in the 1940s and 1950s photographing jazz musicians and everyday life in Harlem, giving us the lonely blue room on Big Bill Broonzy's *Big Bill's Blues* in our "Adventures in Sound" chapter. Also, the energy-evoking cover of West Side Manhattan–based nightclub jazz album, *Jumpin' at the Left Bank*, by the John LaSalle Quartet, features a photo by Friedlander, well-known for capturing contemporary life on the street.

For instrumental jazz and classical albums, cover design could provide important cues and clues about the musical style, tone, and overall feeling of an LP.[24] The Blue Note label, in particular, became respected for its vinyl album covers, which often featured striking black and white photographs of its jazz performers, as they developed a visual identity to match their sound.[25] In this context, midcentury vinyl LP covers invoked an ethics of representation that in some cases supported wider cultural visibility and artistic recognition of African Americans and other minorities. As Grønsted and Vågnes suggest, "A genre just a little over half a century old, the record cover has always been an indissoluble part of the larger realm of popular culture, often epitomizing vital trends or offering a visual shorthand for the cultural zeitgeist."[26] Thus, in a short period, a new design icon emerged.

Capitol, the first major record company in Los Angeles, brought a vibrant use of color photography to album cover design. In their celebratory fiftieth anniversary book from 1992, they boasted,

> Trends were spotted early by discriminating designers and applied to record covers to grab the attention of the consumer as far back as Capitol's history extends. Innovative concepts in photography, illustration and graphic design led potential buyers to judge music by its covers. When drab album art was the norm, Capitol introduced color, graphics and … sex appeal![27]

Of course, there are many contexts for considering the relationship between album covers and the recorded music within. Marvin Schwartz, longtime Art Director for Capitol Records (and credited with designing the Grammy award statuette), thought LPs that did *not* feature portraits of the performers led to creativity with album cover design: "Capitol has a policy of allowing the recording artist to approve any photography or art that displays their likeness … so it's in the non-likeness areas where the design opportunities occur."[28]

Other record companies began to reproduce imagery by visual artists, created outside the album design department, for their album covers. Numerous albums from the 1950s and 1960s featured abstract art, which fostered sympathetic connections between visual and musical expression. Modern art seemed especially apt "to illustrate the spontaneity, call-and-response rhythms, and dynamic energy of jazz—avant garde sounds were paired with avant garde imagery."[29] For example, Jackson Pollock's abstract expressionist painting *White Light* appears on the front cover of Ornette Coleman's LP *Free Jazz* from Atlantic Records. The absence of any image of Coleman himself resonates with our interests in the interaction of the LP and midcentury ideologies: "In replacing his image with one of contemporary art, Atlantic removes jazz from its club environment, and evokes instead the cultural currency of 'Western art' forms and modernist aesthetic values."[30] Much midcentury album design heralded progress, technology, and modernity.[31]

CONSUMPTION AND MODERNISM AT MIDCENTURY

Record albums, as popular, mundane, and mass culture artifacts in postwar America, were designed to teach US citizens about ideal lifestyles, including family bonds and how to entertain at home, as well as how to travel the world. So, it wouldn't be surprising to find that events overseas, after World War II and during the Cold War, influenced what our record albums communicate, especially given our sense that vinyl LPs of the time served as an essential information distribution format. And, indeed, in small and grand ways, from details of kitchen design to voices of the lunar landing, our records express, making subtle arguments for, the superiority of democratic capitalist freedoms in contrast with Soviet life.

Consider the American National Exhibition, held in Moscow in 1959: the trade fair, "designed by George Nelson, was intended to promote the comforts and contentment of a materialistic society as a contrast to the communist regime and lifestyle."[32] A film, *Glimpses of the USA*, by American design team Charles and Ray Eames, was shown on giant television screens. During the fair, the "rituals of family life were enacted four times a day with a wedding, a honeymoon, the backyard barbecue, and the country-club dance."[33] In these rituals, one finds notions of romance, love, individual freedoms, and family values, each of which figured in attempts to articulate and visualize aspects of US superiority over the gloomy communist alternative—often portrayed as disregarding aspects of individual attachment, desire, and welfare in favor of political and cultural ideology.[34]

These "rituals of family life" that were "enacted four times a day" at the forty-two day Moscow exhibition appear frequently among our Home section LPs: albums from the series Music for Hi-Fi Living contain titles focused around a country club dance, as well as two weddings and a honeymoon scenario. The Dinner Music series includes a barbecue album, and the Music for Gracious Living series features a guide to backyard barbecuing and bringing guests home for a party *After the Dance*. In fact, there were so many "honeymoon" albums, we turned this theme into a chapter, which overlaps with the chapters on New York and Hawaii, as well as with chapters on airlines and Capitol of the World—with post-nuptial, and also wedding anniversary, travel a key motivation for going "away."

Historian Lizbeth Cohen has argued that the postwar rise of the "consumer republic" profoundly changed "America's economy, politics, and culture, with major consequences for how Americans made their living, where they dwelled, how they interacted with others, what and how they consumed."[35] In particular, at midcentury, new forms of entertaining, listening, and watching emerged:

The legendary white middle-class family of the 1950s, located in the suburbs, complete with appliances, station wagons, backyard barbecues, and tricycles scattered on the sidewalks, represented something new. It was not, as common wisdom tells us, the last gasp of "traditional" family life with roots deep in the past. Rather, it was the first wholehearted effort to create a home that would fulfill virtually all its members' personal needs through an energized and expressive personal life.[36]

However, the midcentury was also an "age of anxiety."[37] The Cold War suffused contemporary living in the United States, and the American home was central to conflicting visions of a good life during a period dominated by dueling superpowers and concerns to "contain" Soviet Communism.[38] Consumer goods occupied central roles on both sides of the Cold War propaganda battles. In this way, "the commodity gap took precedence over the missile gap."[39]

In the United States, individuals were understood to have the freedom to make their own lives, in part through their access to a wealth of available resources, including affordable consumer goods and services. The "sovereign," or self-determining, choices they made among these available options marked a key distinction within US-Soviet propaganda battles: "Consumer sovereignty was the most popular Cold War wedge between east and west, one that—unlike the apocalyptic balance of nuclear terror—struck into the heart of everyday life."[40] Sociologist Don Slater argues that "the eminently modern notion of the social subject as a self-creating, self-defining individual is bound up with self-creation through consumption: it is partly through the use of goods and services that we formulate ourselves as social identities and display these identities."[41] In this sense, consumption and daily practices in a consumer culture brought the Cold War into the home.

In particular, the kitchen, a paragon of domestic comfort, family togetherness, and modern technology, "became one of the central sites of Cold War rhetoric."[42] During the infamous "kitchen debate" between US Vice President (and presidential hopeful) Richard Nixon and Soviet Premier Nikita Khrushchev in 1959, "nuclear proliferation rhetoric moved to the domestic space and to the suburban home, as the two leaders tensely debated the merits of capitalism vs. socialism in front of a worldwide television audience at the inauguration of the American National Exhibition in

Moscow."[43] Historians Ruth Oldenziel and Karin Zachmann wrote about "kitchens as technology and politics" in a book on the Cold War kitchen. They argue that after the world witnessed Nixon and Khrushchev lingering over a display of lemon yellow General Electric appliances, some researchers claimed that regardless of *Sputnik* successes and other scientific advances, "from then on, technology was to be measured in terms of consumer goods rather than space and nuclear technologies."[44] For the Soviets, investing in "technological systems" that would serve all citizens, such as buses, trains, housing programs, and childcare centers, stood against US Cold War emphasis on individual, and individually purchased, consumer goods, such as privately owned cars and suburban homes. Echoes of the related claims to lifestyle superiority can still be heard today, often connected to the same goods and services. We see then the strategic importance of focusing on certain consumer goods, and the contemporary consumer lifestyles these make possible—for example, the convenience, comfort, even glamour, of automobile ownership or the updated refrigerator—in midcentury media communications, and also why concerted efforts at communicating these messages might appear in the humble form of the LP record album cover.

A key tenet of Soviet Cold War propaganda maintained that the United States lacked a distinctive or historically developed culture of its own. Indeed, America was castigated as obsessed with trivial (and uncultured) entertainments, consumer choice, and ephemeral distractions—aspects of precisely those elements the United States engaged for Cold War cultural diplomacy and ideological defense. To counter such assertions, the United States harnessed key cultural forces of jazz, modern design, and abstract art, holding up each as a symbol of affluence, freedom, and individual expression. To be sure, modernism represented disparate movements within a variety of cultural arenas, tenuously linked together via a sense of rebellion against tradition. During the postwar era, however, "modernism took on new and surprising meanings due to the changing political and cultural environment, eventually being used in support of Western middle-class society."[45]

Modernism "illuminates both the cold war ideology and the domestic revival as two sides of the same coin: postwar Americans' intense need to feel liberated from the past and secure in the future."[46] For example, modern furniture was well-suited to a less formal era, and served to accommodate and display the new television and hi-fi sets that were becoming staples of the midcentury household.[47] As Elizabeth Armstrong, curator of the noteworthy "Birth of the Cool" exhibit at the Orange County Museum of Art, observed in 2008, "Midcentury modernist architecture and design have been appointed as backdrops for and symbols of a confident urbanity, starring in Hollywood films and fashion shoots and used by high-end advertisers and mass commercial outlets to sell everything from luxury cars, credit cards, and investment services to vodka, sneakers, and blue jeans."[48] Of course, as we shall see, modernism had been recruited for this and more since its inception. In our attempts to bring vinyl albums into a discussion about midcentury, modernist ideals, we join art historian Maud Lavin's effort to "approach design from the broader field of visual culture criticism."[49]

Cold War cultural skirmishes have been discussed in the context of art, film, furniture, jazz, magazines, books, radio, and popular exhibitions. Still, few accounts of modernism's role in Cold War cultural diplomacy, cultural imperialism, pedagogy, and propaganda mention record albums. Yet, when looking closely at midcentury vinyl LPs, an overarching sense of how the Cold War trickled down into popular-culture artifacts becomes apparent. Although some albums specifically addressed military power and advanced technology, such as *Air Power* and *X-15 and Other Sounds of Rockets, Missiles, and Jets*, the larger battle over ideological, military, and political supremacy raging between the two super powers encroached upon the design, music, and marketing of mainstream, popular albums as well. Looking back at midcentury vinyl LPs today, evidence of Cold War rhetoric abounds: Cuban music, with bright, sensual covers, released before Castro; jazz albums adorned with abstract art; and lifestyle LPs that featured attractive images of appliance-filled kitchens all appear as subtle components of the ideological struggles of the era.

NOTES ON THE BOOK

The book is divided into two main sections that demonstrate how "home" and "away" are conceptualized, envisioned, and represented in a selection of midcentury record albums. We present nearly 150 vintage album covers and discuss each one, unearthing hidden stories and unexpected insights. (All quotes without footnotes are from the specific album that is being discussed.) Each chapter is organized around a theme, such as "Modern Art and Design," "Music for Gracious Living," and "Honeymoon," derived from the records we have selected. There are instances in which our categories overlap, such as Dave Brubeck's *Countdown: Time in Outer Space*, which we put in the modern art and design category—the cover features an abstract painting by Franz Kline, rather than a rocket or space-related graphic. *Christmas in Cuba* appears in the Cuba chapter rather than "Capitol of the World," although indeed it is part of that series.

In the Home section of the book, or our side one, we discuss how the US home became an entertainment zone—a place to play music, prepare dinner, and show off one's taste for guests. In a time when stakes were high for building, selling, and embodying the modern American lifestyle, "home" records presented visions of idealized domestic settings for US consumer-citizens to bring to life in a participatory rendering of capitalist democracy.

But the more people stayed at home, the more they needed objects, artifacts, and practices that linked them to affiliated communities, or reference groups, real or imagined, *beyond* the walls, doors, and windows of home. As well, we note a related, but distinct process: in order to venture beyond familiar territory of home life and mores, popular culture knowledge, artifacts, and practices were required to usher US consumers into a broader realm.

The Away section—our side two—examines vinyl LPs from an influential era in the development of international travel and tourism for a mass US population. "Away" records—featuring music, pictures, and tourist information—helped ready US consumers to take on the world.

Thus, midcentury consumer technologies, such as vinyl LP records and hi-fi sets, helped bridge the domestic and public spheres. This process maps a course for those who sail into uncharted seas and allows newcomers to seek answers to questions of acculturation. How does one adapt to an unfamiliar environment? How does one learn a cosmopolitan culture or know which locales represent the right kind of place for a certain kind of person? Meet new friends and potential romantic partners? Have a dinner party? Decorate a home? How does one fit in? These are the puzzles that midcentury albums, focused on both home and away, help answer.

These midcentury LPs offer compelling visions from a time that brought the ideal home, continental style, and international travel more fully into mainstream US society. Our discussion includes description and analysis of each album cover.[50] In taking this peek into an analog archive, we illustrate the role of the vinyl LP in the historical context of developing contemporary consumer culture.

I   HOME

Midcentury vinyl LPs helped people imagine the place and practices of home, and how *home* could be conceptualized, enacted, and consumed. Cover photos, liner notes, and musical styles evoked an environment, an aesthetic, a *feel* for living. These records help us understand how the home became an alternative to "going out," or to a more civic, public life. These LPs revealed secrets of "gracious living" and advice for producing enticing dinners "at home" that brought the unfamiliar onto the familiar dining room table. On these records, we find recipes, ideas for arranging food, drink, and decor, and encouragement to master the manners and behaviors designed for modern, hi-fi living.

An early motivation for entertaining at home came from war agencies, supported by experts in "family economics" who encouraged US civilians to conserve resources and minimize "the strain they put on travel infrastructure," which included adhering to gasoline and tire restrictions and avoiding "needless trips."[1] "Vacationing at home" came to include many of the activities represented in the Music for Gracious Living series, such as DIY projects, gardening, and having people over for cards, buffets, and patio parties.

Liner notes and album cover art in the "home" category provide careful instructions: How should we dress for the backyard barbecue? Where would I buy a live lobster? Should we serve fruit punch or champagne if we're romancing our date *en francais*? And, of course, what music should we play to ease us through the evening?

And family? When do the cocktail parties end and gathering with mom, dad, and the kids around the organ, record player, or television begin? With notions of a "family room," "togetherness became a model concept for healthy family life, and it was broadly adopted nationwide."[2] As a couple moves from coffee time and cards, or champagne, conversation, and romance, to family time, in what ways does being at home change forever with the appearance of children? The selected LPs address an ideal audience, one that has a space for family but also desires nights on the town, on-going socializing, or even an elegant evening at home despite the presence of little ones. Indeed, the audience for these records was not expected to give up their pre-parental grasp on a glamorous life; rather, a night out, or an adult party at home, was only a babysitter away.

Certainly, record albums and their representations of US consumer lifestyles bring up issues around disposable income: How much does it cost to host a Hawaiian luau? What about those special pans I need to dish up the Italian dinner at home? Each individual household is seen as requiring the resources and props for staging performances of these idealized lifestyles: the better, one might say, to sell more stuff. Many "at home" events require the space, the equipment, not to mention the liquid resources to "have people over," all of which speaks to a level of access to consumer goods and other objects of desire.

These LP covers strategically display postwar innovations—technological, cultural, social—that continue to differentiate, in fantasy and in real lives, US consumer culture from much of the rest of the world. Take, for example, album cover images of entertaining at home, including the hosting of dinners, dance parties, or card games. These gatherings frequently feature the kitchen and the necessities the kitchen contains. Technology researchers claim, "the modern kitchen embodies the ideology of the culture to which it belongs."[3] For example, one might recall that in the nineteenth-century United States, most people had no room now associated with the kitchen concept; and crucially, only in the twentieth century did we see "the creation of a separate space with modular square appliances, a unified look, an unbroken flow of countertops and counter fronts over appliances, and standard measurements."[4] And, in the context of international exhibitions, like the infamous one in Moscow in 1959, this productive playing field garnered serious political points in the "kitchen debate."[5]

Such an emphasis on individualized single-family homes might lead to isolation for the people living within them. However, an emphasis on "entertaining at home" encouraged a sense of reciprocity, wherein each home, in turn, would welcome friends, family, and other visitors, offering multiple locations and diverse settings, that nevertheless reinforced certain key practices in accomplishing these events and upheld appropriate ideals. Just as one might design a retail space—through choice of décor, lighting, and layout, for example—to create a feeling of formality or, alternatively, informality to reflect the values of a brand, so the ideal home is the site of such choices. In this, clues can be drawn from the lessons and images provided by the vinyl album.

Cultural historian Witold Rybczynski points out that home interiors in the seventeenth century began to demonstrate *stimmung*, "a characteristic of interiors that has less to do with functionality than with the way that the room conveys the character of its owner—the way it mirrors his soul."[6] Rybczynski writes that in the West, notions of domesticity, intimacy, and privacy; austerity, efficiency, and comfort; and nostalgia and style are historically linked to home. The shifts away from public, feudal households to "the private, family home" with its increasing domestic intimacy "affected not only our physical surroundings, but our consciousness as well."[7] The LPs examined here combine visual instruction and music genres specifically marketed to reflect one's identity via an ideal home and domestic space.

Several chapters focus on various types of the home-entertaining record, including albums for dinner, dancing, and entertaining at home. Of course, LP-based familiarity with a set of musicians, or musical styles, and a glimpse of big city nightlife or continental culture might inspire a longing to get away and experience live and in person the atmospheres and sounds one has enjoyed from the haven of home. Indeed, many record albums offered an introduction to a wider world, from home décor to distant destinations, and, if this promotion was successful, could catapult listeners into the arms of appliance salespeople as well as travel agents, and the tourism industry at large.

1

BEING AT HOME

Connections between who we are and the things that surround us, and importantly how our homes communicate these relationships, open up occasions for anxiety: Is the color of my house odd? Is my armchair masculine? Should I display my vinyl albums, gun collection, or antique books where guests will see them, or would a more private space for these be better? And, how should we decorate the "rec" room? This isn't just narcissistic nonsense: recent psychological research has shown that people judge our personalities fairly accurately based on how our living rooms look.[1]

Equipping the home, decorating the home, and then, after all the preparation, entertaining at home could be seen as a life's work. Suddenly, inviting non-family members into the home becomes an expectation, just part of social life, and an interior landscape that would never be open to outside eyes comes under scrutiny. Some guidance in how to manage, and adjust for, these interlopers, from rearranging the furniture to setting the table with a "good" set of china, seems useful. *Hear How to Plan the Perfect Dinner Party* offers a spoken guide of methods, manners, and menus, pre-dating Martha Stewart by decades; and *Kodak Sound 8: Background Music for Your Personal Home Movies* provides a hint for entertaining your guests with home movies: Make the viewing experience more interesting by adding the perfect soundtrack! And, why not show off the latest hi-fi technology with LPs designed specifically for dazzling the uninitiated?

The act of playing an album that touts the cosmopolitan romance of, say, the Oak Room at the Plaza Hotel in New York City, necessarily means that you're *not* sipping drinks among the in-crowd at that legendary hotel's bar: this is a telling irony of the "being at home" genre. The LP lures you out into the larger world of cultured entertainment, and at the same time suggests bringing music into the home to accompany your dance party. So, inviting Carmen Cavallaro into your living room to play "Sukiyaki" for you and your friends, via your hi-fi stereo, is precisely what stands in the way of going out to hear the "Poet of the Piano," and dancing the night away, in the candlelit rooms of New York's Waldorf-Astoria. Yet, the albums imply that "at home" participation links the listener to this other outer world, supported by cover photos that invoke the buzz and fashionable formality of Manhattan's mood-soaked lounges or cafés in Cannes, imaginatively transferred into your home with the help of hi-fi music to further the fantasy over a French white from the family fridge or martinis from the home shaker.

There's no denying that cocktails became a core part of entertaining at home during this era, from knowing how to stock your home bar to buying the appropriate glasses for each libation. Of course, cocktails serve iconic functions: "Mixed drinks were revered symbols of business savvy and all-American know-how. The multi-martini lunch catalyzed the deals that turned America into a postwar economic super-power."[2] Cocktails signaled American—and, like the backyard barbeques, jazz, and matching appliances, became part of many midcentury evenings at home.

ALBUMS

AN EXCITING EVENING AT HOME suggests only women should be invited for a night of drinking, smoking, and music in the "rec" room. Red tones, black, and white dominate the photo, including the red vinyl of the playing LP, set off by the bold tri-color heading, "4 channels on 35 millimeter film." Under an attentive gaze, the sole male handles the sound system, fiddling with the knobs between the reel-to-reel tape recorder and the turntable. (Perhaps, these three feel the music should be turned up, defying relegation to the "background"). The sound equipment is front and center, as key elements in the night's possibilities. The curtains are drawn, the fireplace is alight, an antique hand gun hangs over the mantle, a set of encyclopedias line the corner book shelf; and the attire—perhaps echoing the aesthetic confusion of these settings—ranges from backless gowns and sundresses to black beatnik turtlenecks and something apparently from the finale of the film *White Christmas*. The gathering may lack the glamour some of these women were hoping for, but in American houses the recreational room concept suggested an informality and flexibility in furnishing and décor allowing things to be moved around depending on the desired activity, such as spontaneous dancing or opening up the ping-pong table. (There may be hope for this group yet). The "newest advances in recorded music" raise expectations for a memorable sound experience: this is not "background" music, the notes proclaim. "This is not music to 'do something else by'!"

FIGURE 1.1

International Pop Orchestra,
An Exciting Evening at Home,
Cameo C 4001;
cover design by Al Kahn
and Miller, Bodden & Rich, Inc.
@ABKCO Records.

CHANNELS 4 : ON 35 MILLIMETER FILM

THE NEWEST ADVANCEMENTS IN RECORDED MUSIC... AT NO PREMIUM COST

An Exciting Evening at Home
With The International POP Orchestra

CAMEO

C 4001

The unceremoniously scattered LPs piled in front of the RCA Orthophonic hi-fi console emphasize the central role of records in the declaration, **LET'S HAVE A DANCE PARTY!** (although an LP by folk artist John Jacob Niles seems an unusual choice). Part of RCA's Designed for Dancing series, this album provides some inspiring numbers like "Heap Big Beat," arranged and played by Buddy Morrow and his orchestra. Sadly, the blues songs sink with a sluggish white male vocalist, particularly "Beale Street Mama" (from the 1946 "race" film of the same name, directed by Spencer Williams) compared to other recordings like the swirling, racing version by Cab Calloway. No hints for beverages, or enticing your guests off the wall and onto the dance floor here, but the young woman with rolled up denim blue jeans, white cotton socks, and black moccasins appears ready for a fox trot all the same.

Distinct from the other LPs discussed here, the Hear How series from Carleton Records contains no music but features lessons of various kinds, such as *Hear How to Play Winning Bridge* (with a complete glossary of bridge terms), *Hear How to Converse in German*, *Hear How to Train Your Dog*, and even *Hear How to Achieve Sexual Harmony in Marriage*. Gaynor and Dorothy Maddox's **HEAR HOW TO PLAN THE PERFECT DINNER PARTY** guides listeners through four distinct dinner experiences: Steak Dinner ("served in a neighborly American way"); French Dinner (French men prefer feminine women; always serve good bread); Hawaiian Dinner (capped off with the impressive "Snow Mountain" dessert); and Chicken

FIGURE 1.2

Buddy Morrow and His Orchestra,
Let's Have a Dance Party!,
RCA Camden CAL 381;
photograph by David B. Hecht.

CAL 381 A High Fidelity Recording
Designed for Dancing/one of a series
RCA CAMDEN
A PRODUCT OF RADIO CORPORATION OF AMERICA
LONG PLAY 33⅓ RPM
Let's Have a Dance Party!
Buddy Morrow
and His Orchestra
Stairway to the Stars
I Can't Get Started
I Wonder Why
Heap Big Beat
Memphis Drag
Beale Street Mamma
Speak Low
Confessin' the Blues
Ain't Got Nobody
I Can't Give You Anything But Love
Rio Rita
That Old Black Magic
Photo: David B. Hecht
© RCA Printed in U. S. A.

Dinner ("don't forget the Carrots Vichy"). These represent "four deluxe dinners that can be prepared by an average good cook using ingredients found in American supermarkets" and "without extra domestic help."[3] The Maddoxes—he, a "nationally known food columnist," she, "his charming wife"—banter their way through advice on setting the table, keeping the hostess "cool," and the importance of "an uncrowded coffee table." Contemporary listeners will feel transported to a time when an aspiring hostess honed her craft, throwing backyard luaus complete with "Sesame Baked Clams" and "Chicken Momi," served on fresh pineapple shells. Did mothers and grandmothers truly spend their days carving and scooping in the kitchen, mastering radish roses and miniature potato balls to serve with "Peas Petit Pois"? The hosts describe the dinner with authority and juicy verbiage, as Gaynor encourages Dorothy to "plunk that big, fat, seasoned steak right in the frying pan."

This treasure—plucked, in the late 1980s, from St. Vincent de Paul shelves in Madison, Wisconsin—features a crisp focus photo of a dining scene, courtesy of the once ubiquitous *American Home* magazine. The black and white cover photograph exudes a glamorous formality, as three well-coiffed white couples dressed in eveningwear gather around a table for a night of gracious living. The host and hostess stand attentive, near their guests. The buffet boasts artfully arranged shiny stainless steel specialty appliances (and a matching salt and pepper set) for keeping the food warm, including an electric frying pan, and is laden with a sleek salad bowl and serving utensils, a stainless steel casserole filled with green and wax beans, and a stack of thin white china dinner plates. The lazy Susan, decorated with daisy mums, centers the table with little dishes full of accompaniments. Candles lit, a perfect dinner party is underway.

FIGURE 1.3

Gaynor and Dorothy Maddox,
Hear How to Plan the Perfect Dinner Party,
Carlton Record Corp., CHH/14;
photograph courtesy of *The American Home.*

HEAR HOW TO PLAN THE PERFECT DINNER PARTY

GAYNOR AND DOROTHY MADDOX NATIONALLY KNOWN FOOD COLUMNIST AND HIS CHARMING WIFE TELL THE SECRETS OF PREPARING FOUR GOURMET DINNERS WITH SUPREME EASE

Courtesy of The American Home © 1959 Curtis Publishing Company

CARLTON HEAR HOW SERIES CHH/14

INFORMALLY YOURS seems to invite us into a private living room concert—an evening of intimate, domestic musical engagement. The audience is romantically paired, tidily dressed, but not formally, and gathered near a black grand piano, whose partially pictured player wears a black suit and dress shoes. The marble fireplace, gold-footed fire screen, and the symmetrically placed candle sconces suggest a neoclassical formality displaced by the home piano and further disrupted by a casual Scandinavian modern style couch and chair and the lounging postures of the couples. In light of Cold War culture disputes, this cover could be read as a choreographed pictorial reproach to notions of Soviet superiority. Indeed, the blond woman in the foreground wears a blouse reminiscent of Russian constructivist patterns,[4] suggesting a communist interloper charmed in realizing that US cultural performance and accomplishment, as well as participation, simply takes diverse, less public forms.

FIGURE 1.4

Carmen Calvallaro,
Informally Yours,
Decca DL 74017.

Even when a home seems like a kind of contemporary fortress—separated from the outside world by a moat of grass and a neatly trimmed hedge—folks can still create a welcoming environment for friends and strangers alike. An upstairs window on the two-story colonial has been left open. Faint strains of melody that seem to drift out to the street are easily imagined. The painted shingle exterior, shadowed with evening light, presents an entree through a multipaned window framed by black shutters, as a warm interior glow illuminates an amiable group gathered around a piano. **SONGS FOR AN EVENING AT HOME** begins with performer Gordon Mac-Rae's "attractive wife Sheila" opening the front door and greeting the guests, as she invites us in to "A House with Love in It" for an evening of music.

FIGURE 1.5

The Van Alexander Orchestra,
Gordon MacRae,
Songs for an Evening at Home,
Capitol T 1251.

songs
for
an evening at home

GORDON MACRAE

orchestra conducted by VAN ALEXANDER

THE HOUSE WITH LOVE IN IT · SMILE · ALWAYS · THE BELLS OF ST. MARY'S · WHISPERING HOPE
IN THE GOOD OLD SUMMER TIME · LET ME CALL YOU SWEETHEART · TAKE ME OUT TO THE BALL GAME
HOME · LOVE'S OLD SWEET SONG · THREE BLIND MICE · SWEETHEART OF SIGMA CHI · TREES · A PERFECT DAY

Coffee and music together cast a spell: The charming hostess pours the beverage, while the host conjures the soundtrack, placing an album, perhaps *this* album, **COFFEE TIME**, on the turntable which is housed in a free-standing hi-fi cabinet (that to be truthful lacks a modern aesthetic). "This special mood is the coffee house mood—even if the coffee is being served at home to a group consisting only of yourself." Brand names set the stage with china, silver and lamp courtesy of renowned Danish designer Georg Jensen, and folding table and chairs courtesy of Samsonite, a company better remembered for durable luggage. Jensen's Scandinavian modern design classics help lift a simple coffee cup's level of ambition and elegance, bridging a night in with friends to a wider history of conversation and culture. As the erudite notes—written by Robert A. Simon, librettist and music critic from the earliest days of *The New Yorker*, who went on to work for J. Walter Thompson advertising agency—suggest, "The scholarly observer may inquire if there was perhaps some equivalent of this music in the early London coffee-houses. Did Oliver Goldsmith or David Garrick or Samuel Johnson leave his table long enough to put a tuppence in the musik box?" The "Jamaican Rumba," begins side two: "Obviously, the Jamaican milieu is nicely appropriate for presentations that have to do with coffee."

FIGURE 1.6

Morton Gould and His Orchestra,
Coffee Time,
RCA Victor LPM-1656.

MORTON GOULD
AND HIS ORCHESTRA
COFFEE TIME

RCA VICTOR
LPM-1656

A "New Orthophonic" High Fidelity Recording

The cover of **COCKTAIL TIME**, by the Dell Trio, offers a glimpse of a well-worn theme of so called "cocktail music" LPs—the seductive power of music and liquor. "Cocktails are shaken or stirred, rolled or muddled; they are dry or sweet, creamy or frozen. They are perfect or dirty; they are up or over. But one thing they are not is weak. There is an hour reverentially dedicated to them. Parties are named after them. Thousands of designers have created vessels to showcase them or shake them. They are truly American, a gift to the beverage culture of the world."[5] We view what looks like an intimate moment between a man, in dressy black pants and shoes, and a woman, in emerald green satin high heels, stockings, and a pale pink and green floral dress, reclining on a couch, with only the bottom half of their legs visible, the rest of their bodies obscured by a high-backed couch and see-through bamboo blind.[6] A small marble-top table hosts an ashtray with a cigarette, still burning, two mostly full cocktail glasses (a martini and a Manhattan?), and a small potted palm. Two brightly colored pillows are stacked on the floor near the table, and a globe light illuminates the scene. Clearly, the couple has moved on from drinking and smoking to more pressing matters.

Billboard's review proclaimed *Cocktail Time* "satisfactory," with a 67 out of 100 rating. The anonymous reviewer wrote: "The guitar-accordion-organ trio instrumentation is perhaps best adapted to this type of selection—standards familiar enough to be heard thru cocktail conversation. The Dell group plays them unobtrusively, chorus and verse, without trick effects. The effect is just what's intended—highly Muzak-al."[7] Thus, the music is perhaps not the point, what matters is what's happening over, or "thru" the music—conversation, and possibly more.

FIGURE 1.7

The Dell Trio,
Cocktail Time,
Harmony HL 7016;
photograph by Leombruno-Bodi.

HL 7016

COCKTAIL TIME

THE DELL TRIO

HARMONY · LP · A PRODUCT OF COLUMBIA RECORDS

COCKTAILS FOR TWO / STUMBLING / I'LL BE SEEING YOU / MOON OVER MIAMI / MOONGLOW / LAURA / CHINATOWN, MY CHINATOWN / SEPTEMBER SONG / CARAVAN / BLUE DANUBE

On **COCKTAILS AND CONVERSATION**, piano rhythms and ornamentation overtake the priority of melody on "Babalu," which is refreshing in a world of such easy easy-listening. As the liner notes say: "Our leisure lives today are all the richer because of the abundance on recordings of what we have come to call 'mood music.' And you can find the right music for almost every mood: for dreaming, for slumbering off, for remembering, for work, for studying, even for goofing off." But, the triangle and bell sound with glockenspiel and tinkling piano on "Dominique" wander off into a no-romance land of schmaltz. This is indeed "merry" piano, though whether it's "tasteful" or not is questionable. The notes conclude: "This album of the artistry of Jan August is music for quiet scintillation to accompany the gentle tinkle of the cocktail glass and thoughtful, intimate words."

In a pattern reminiscent of a tripartite flag, a strip of deep cornflower blue meets a block of off-white that merges into a sandy brown, creating graphic vertical lines set off by the man's dark suit and hair and then complemented by jewel tones of amethyst, jade, and the woman's aquamarine dress. Her red fingernails and lips and the couple's strong eyebrows provide graphic anchors along with the title words that shift from white to black as they travel across the three tonal zones. The lighting casts him into shadow, while she glows with light. They may be in conversation, or is he simply encouraging her to take another sip of that cocktail? The classic martini glass, with its characteristic conical shape, has become shorthand for drinking in a certain style, for cocktail time; and everybody needed a set whether crystal clear, art deco pink and black, or embossed with gold. Visually, martini glasses signal sophistication and possibly adventure, linked as the martini is to the character James Bond. Bachelors drank martinis, and often—in a key cross promotion—while listening to the latest hi-fi set.

FIGURE 1.8

Jan August at the Piano,
Cocktails and Conversation,
Mercury MG 20272;
photograph by Wesley Bowman.

COCKTAILS AND CONVERSATION

CUSTOM HIGH FIDELITY

Mercury RECORDS

MG 20272

featuring

JAN AUGUST

AT THE PIANO

photo by Wesley Bowman

The cartoon illustration on **WHISTLE WHILE YOU WORK** may suggest a scene from *Snow White and the Seven Dwarfs*, but the dominant blue, yellow, and pink lack the saturation of Disney's colors, giving any picture of waltzing with a broom faded appeal. Chime the liner notes, "These are songs that give the lady of the house a lift and perhaps if no one's looking, except junior in his playpen, she may even be seen waltzing about the living room, with her broom or feather duster." A sudden wind seems to have blown all the flotsam and jetsam of housework tasks into the right corner. Perhaps, inspired by the "happy songs" provided here, this housewife performs a buoyant jig, as the tools of her trade march according to her direction to their appropriate places.

FIGURE 1.9

Whistle While You Work:
Music with a Lilt to Lighten Her Housework,
Somerset P 3200.

MUSIC WITH A LILT TO LIGHTEN HER HOUSE WORK
whistle while you work

With a do-it-yourself attitude and the rise of the home improvement industry allowing everyone to participate in the yearly alterations of fashion,[8] **MUSIC TO PAINT BY**, "prepared expressly for Celanese Coatings Company," suggests that a brush and a can of paint could change a home's inner world. The liner notes move the DIY painting concept from simply keeping abreast of this year's crimson craze for entry hall walls to an entrepreneurial business savvy, probably aimed at business to business retail promotion: "color has the secret ingredient that has pulled hundreds of tunes out of the red and into the black." Staying true to theme, songs such as "Yellow Bird," "Scarlet Ribbons," and "Mood Indigo" plot a rainbow pathway of easy listening.

FIGURE 1.10

Music to Paint By,
RCA Victor PRM 208;
prepared expressly for
Celanese Coatings Company
by RCA Victor.

MUSIC TO PAINT BY

ED AMES
What Color Is A Man

SERGIO FRANCHI
Blue Moon

JOHN GARY
Yellow Bird

SKITCH HENDERSON
Mood Indigo

LENA HORNE
Polka Dots And Moonbeams

THE NORMAN LUBOFF CHOIR
Ruby

TONY MARTIN
Green Eyes

PETER NERO
Over The Rainbow

DELLA REESE
Blue Skies

JIM REEVES
Scarlet Ribbons

Linked to the *Breakfast Club* radio show begun in 1933, **MARCH AROUND THE BREAKFAST TABLE** begins with the eponymous song that seems to have inspired the family's sunrise ritual as they create a celebratory morning meal. Each member is dressed in their breakfast time best, with a red robe for Mr. Ballantine, the bandleader, and high-necked nightgowns for the gals. Family members hold iconic objects—Dad, the *New York Times*; Mom, the toaster; Sister, the milk bottle—that mark necessities for a place at the breakfast table in contemporary US culture. (Have you ever seen the confused look in the morning when you tell a guest you don't own a toaster?) The floors and walls present product placement from the Congoleum-Nairn company, credited on the back cover. The table, clothed and set in attention-grabbing sunshine yellow, provides a central focus—we're marching around it, after all—for breaking the fast of a long night with no consumption. American lifestyle designer Russel Wright created a popular and trend-setting pattern of dishware called American Modern for Ohio's Steubenville Pottery, then a similar Casual pattern for Iroquois China of New York; and the iconic shapes are easily recognizable. Though clearly echoing iconic "modern," here, the creamer and sugar bowl handles are angular and the plates slightly squared: this dish set may be from a less common Russel Wright pattern called Minion-Mandarin that came in bright yellow and was created for Paden City Pottery Company.[9]

FIGURE 1.11

Eddie Ballantine and His Band
on *Don McNeill Presents:
March around the Breakfast Table*,
Coral CRL 57291;
photograph by Jerry Tiffany,
floors and wall by Congoleum-Nairn.

Don McNeill *presents*

March Around The Breakfast Table

EDDIE BALLANTINE and His Band

THE SOUND OF

CORAL RECORDS

HIGH-FIDELITY

CRL 57291

Printed in U.S.A.

On **MUSIC TO LIVE BY**, one of the numerous high-fidelity demonstration records released in the 1950s, "every conceivable mood, emotion, and musical taste has been captured for your listening pleasure"; and the liner notes explain the Living Presence recording technique (based on a single microphone that captures "instrumental balances and dynamic range" as played) "showcased" on side B.[10] On *Music to Live By*, the people on the cover seem ready to listen. Framed by blocks of bright yellow, red, and blue, the four family members serenely tune out the wealth of promotional information, including the boldly printed suggested retail price of $1.29, "tax included," that competes for our attention. The vertical wood paneling and sea foam green accent wall seem to stretch up to a high ceiling; and the middle distance shot suggests a spacious, if cavernous, room. End tables flank the light-colored sofa over which three framed pictures are centered. A record player sits open to the left. Also in careful decorative symmetry, a framed mirror hangs between two plants positioned on the white architectural fireplace mantel. The formal hearth appears flameless and cold. The parents, seated on the sofa—the mother with feet tucked under her—smile, examining an album, as does the daughter dressed in striking pink and black as she lounges on the foreground floor. Sitting closest to the hi-fi speaker and leaning back against the furniture, the son in a pale yellow shirt buttoned to the collar perfectly matches the two throw pillows. His wistful facial expression and hand position create an unexpected femininity, suggesting that he is deeply listening, and perhaps upon hearing Tchaikovsky's "Capriccio Italien," dreaming of his ballet debut.

FIGURE 1.12

Music to Live By,
Mercury PJC-1.

Music to live by

to fit your every mood, popular, jazz and classical,
through the magic of Mercury Living Presence Sound.

POPULAR

"NIGHT CAP"
RALPH MARTERIE
MG 20128 "Salute To The Aragon"

"NIGHTINGALE"
DICK CONTINO
MG 20141 "Something For The Girls"

"MY GAL SAL"
DAVID CARROLL
MG 20121 "Waltzes With David Carroll"

JAZZ

"ALL OF ME"
DINAH WASHINGTON (MG 36065)

"SEE MINOR"
JIMMY CLEVELAND (MG 36066)

"BOULEVARD OF BROKEN DREAMS"
TERRY GIBBS (MG 36064)

CLASSICAL EXCERPTS

CAPRICCIO ITALIEN (MG 50054)

TABUH-TABUHAN (MG 50103)

SCHUMAN SYMPHONY #2 (MG 50102)

BARTOK SECOND SUITE (MG 50098)

CHADWICK SYMPHONIC SKETCHES (MG 50104)

U.S. FIELD ARTILLERY MARCH (MG 50105)

THE PERFECT BACKGROUND MUSIC FOR YOUR HOME MOVIES finds a white
nuclear family of four gathered amiably around a Chevron 8mm Kodak movie projector in a room informally set up for viewing. A small collection of LPs, a stereo, and
a hi-fi turntable are visible off to the right where presumably this record would be
playing, providing an accompanying music soundtrack for moving images of travel,
parties, and children. "Whether your films are of the Grand Canyon or the streets of
Paris or just Grandma and the children frolicking on the front lawn," the liner notes
intone, this album offers sound to enliven otherwise silent films as we experience
"the joy of showing." Music "underscores and gives a feeling of movement to what
previously was only visual."

FIGURE 1.13

The Metro Strings,
*The Perfect Background Music
for Your Home Movies*,
MGM PM-4;
photograph by Bert Owen;
8 mm projector in photograph by Kodak.

the *Perfect* BACKGROUND MUSIC
FOR YOUR HOME MOVIES
...........................THE METRO STRINGS

With twelve "orchestral moods" and thirteen "special sound effects," <u>**SOUND 8:**</u>
<u>**BACKGROUND MUSIC FOR YOUR PERSONAL MOVIES**</u> also offers the added
touch of sound to silent home movies, but not just mood music: hear we find on Side
B bands of background, homogenized sound: laughter of a large crowd; a "puppy" or
"full-grown" dog barking; 58 seconds of a motorboat starting, running and stopping;
a car starting and pulling away; and the crucial for laughs "bo-ing!" sound effect. The
cover, bright yellow and red Kodak colors, shows a Kodak Hi-Mat 8mm projector,
with automatic threading and expanded capacity.

FIGURE 1.14

Kodak,
*Sound 8 Background Music
for your Personal Movies*,
Volume 1,
Eastman Kodak Company,
C 6195.

Kodak
TRADEMARK
VOLUME 1
SOUND 8
BACKGROUND MUSIC
FOR YOUR PERSONAL MOVIES
12 orchestral moods
13 special sound effects
LONG-PLAY 33⅓ HIGH-FIDELITY RECORD

On **MUSIC TO WORK OR STUDY BY**, a young woman sits on the floor—while her mother watches over her, knitting—apparently ambivalent: should she choose the bright red apple or read her book? The room is dark, shadowy—not so great for reading—with a blue-green glow that suggests an alien ship has landed behind the mother's throne. Music designed for a particular activity suggests that anything can be commodified and harmonized with certain homogenized melodic strains: "Now that modern science has come out in favor of it, everyone agrees on the good sense of listening to music. Industry pipes it to production floors and laboratories—even where the most precise work demands absolute freedom from distraction." Factory floor work and reading in the den become equally productive. The notion of creating a "Music For" genre arose from wartime research, according to this LP: "Washington was so impressed [by a 1942 experiment] that, after a further survey to confirm the scientific report, it made phonographic equipment a high priority item for plants engaged in war work." And, this wasn't only a blue-collar issue: "In offices too, there has been a steadily rising acceptance of the 'music while you work' idea. Banks, advertising agencies, insurance companies, and publishing houses are among the employers now providing piped-in music for their white collar personnel."

MUSIC FOR READING continues the glowing green-blue background of these "Moods in Music" LPs, and also features the cursive title font and red for the words, "Moods in Music." Reading in dim light, the elegantly dressed brunette with red gauzy skirt, gold space-age belt, and alluring white translucent blouse seems utterly immersed in her hard-backed book, as she lounges legs outstretched on blue-green shag carpeting and leans back against a low satiny brown couch with braided fringe. Isolated with apparently nothing to disturb her, the visible objects—a modern lamp with fiberglass shade; a low bookcase holding some gold embossed series; a celadon ceramic scroll, perhaps a plant stand; and a red ceramic cup—become her inanimate companions made more cozy through the presence of music, and songs such as "Clair de Lune" and "Greensleeves." These LPs proposed that life needed a soundtrack, and supplied music for all occasions. Most were performed by the Melachrino Strings, led by easy listening ambassador George Melachrino.[11]

On **MUSIC FOR DINING**, a deep blue-green wall and window frame are set off by a brick red shutter, and the words, "Moods in Music" also in red. The candlewick wine glasses, candelabra, and individual salt and peppers create a formality reflected in the couple's dress and posture. They are eating with art, after all, as the modernist sculpture of the female figure dominates the right foreground and appears to be dreamily *waiting*. The echo-y room seems meant to be filled by a vinyl soundtrack, but no hi-fi equipment is visible here. "Diane (I'm in Heaven When I See You Smile)" figures as the "apértif," "and perhaps Madame would prefer that exotic cocktail of American origin, the dry martini." Songs pair with the food courses: "Too Young" while "nibbling" pâté de foie gras, "September Song" with lobster mayonnaise, "Clopin Clopant" a side dish to duckling with orange sauce; and then the "deep tones of a nine-foot grand announce the lovely strains of the "Warsaw Concerto" and overcome the discreet tinkle of silver and crystal (and perhaps a slight loosening of the belt) as the waiter presents the pastry tray." The offerings continue through brandy and "murmured whispers over the candlelight" which brings "the end of a charming dinner" and "the beginning of a brilliant evening." Steeped in notions of romance and the kindling of desire—and the role that food and alcohol, attractive and evocative atmosphere, and other consumer goods play—*Music for Dining's* vision makes room for differing situations: "Perhaps your dinner lacks a few of the courses just mentioned; perhaps it's prepared in a one-room apartment and not in the kitchen at Maxim's. Perhaps the china isn't Wedgewood and the wine hails from California. But whatever the circumstances, Melachrino's romantic music will enrich your evening beyond measure."

The back cover of **MUSIC TO HELP YOU SLEEP** features poets pondering the possibilities of a sonorous sleep, from William Shakespeare and Marcel Proust to Frederich Nietzsche and Ovid. The young woman on the cover with a prominently displayed wedding ring, sits on blue satin sheets in a sleeping beauty gown, seemingly in her home castle, and to us, her glance to the left of the frame signals more flirty-suggestive than sleep. In any case, this LP pre-dates sound machines, ambient music, and YouTube "deep sleep" channels by decades.

FIGURE 1.15

The Melachrino Orchestra
conducted by George Melachrino,
Music to Work or Study By,
RCA Victor LPM-1029.

FIGURE 1.16

The Melachrino Strings,
Music for Reading,
RCA Victor LPM 1002.

FIGURE 1.17

The Melachrino Strings and Orchestra,
Music for Dining,
RCA Victor LPM-1000.

FIGURE 1.18

The Melachrino Strings,
Music to Help You Sleep,
RCA Victor LPM-1006.

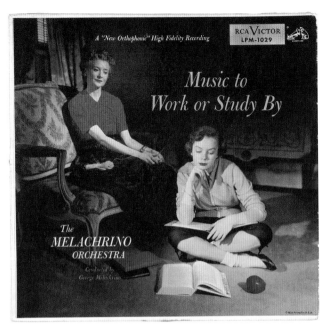

A "New Orthophonic" High Fidelity Recording

RCA VICTOR
LPM-1029

Music to Work or Study By

The
MELACHRINO
ORCHESTRA

*Conducted by
George Melachrino*

RCA VICTOR

A HIGH FIDELITY RECORDING

Moods in Music

Music for Reading

THE MELACHRINO STRINGS

LONG
33⅓
PLAY

CLAIR DE LUNE
GREENSLEEVES
FESTIVAL
DREAM OF OLWEN
MATTINATA
AMOUREUSE
WALTZ IN C-SHARP MINOR
SERENADE—Drigo
SONG OF MY LOVE
FLIRTATION WALTZ

Moods in Music

NEW
RCA VICTOR
LPM-1000
A "New Orthophonic" High Fidelity Recording

Music for Dining

THE MELACHRINO STRINGS AND ORCHESTRA

DIANE · TOO YOUNG · SEPTEMBER SONG · CLOPIN CLOPANT · DOMINO
TENDERLY · CHARMAINE · FAITHFULLY YOURS · WARSAW CONCERTO
CHANSONETTE · DARK SECRET · LEGEND OF THE GLASS MOUNTAIN

RCA VICTOR
RECORDS

Moods in Music

Music to Help You Sleep

THE
MELACHRINO
STRINGS

SOFT LIGHTS AND SWEET MUSIC
LOVE WALKED IN
SOME ENCHANTED EVENING
THIS HEART OF MINE
IT COULD HAPPEN TO YOU
PEOPLE WILL SAY WE'RE IN LOVE
THE TOUCH OF YOUR LIPS
GOODNIGHT SWEETHEART
BEAUTIFUL DREAMER
LOVE SENDS A LITTLE GIFT OF ROSES

LPM-1006

On **MUSIC FOR A RAINY NIGHT**, a young couple lounge and listen in an unusual refusal of color. No furniture either—maybe expressing that legendary moment, moving into a new apartment or house, when the only furniture is a stereo and speakers and music hovers in empty rooms; and you wonder, Should we really even bring anything else in? The notes focus on the magic power of music: "No matter how damp and dark it may be outside, music … sweet, mood-provoking melody … creates a warm, cozily romantic atmosphere inside; bringing a new sense of 'one-ness' to lovers, friends and family." The vinyl disks are tactile, scattered around the apparently unmarried young couple, as he balances his hand on one and she touches his nose with an index finger. Records and music it seems will create the foundation of this home and this relationship.

FIGURE 1.19

David Carroll and His Orchestra,
Music for a Rainy Night,
Mercury MG 20068.

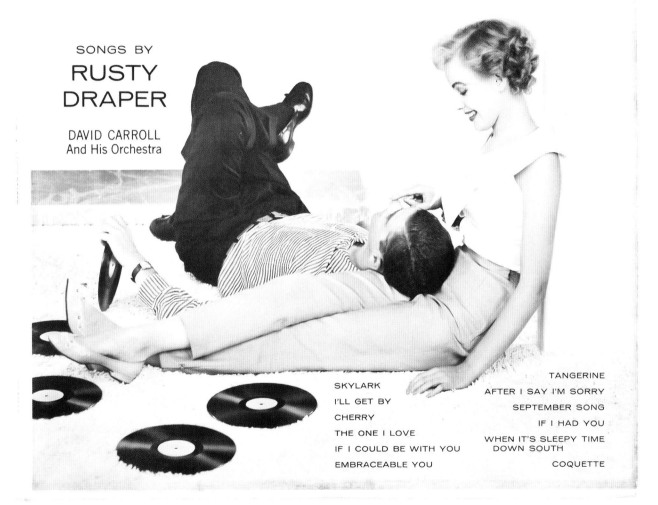

Music For A Rainy Night

SONGS BY
RUSTY
DRAPER

DAVID CARROLL
And His Orchestra

SKYLARK

I'LL GET BY

CHERRY

THE ONE I LOVE

IF I COULD BE WITH YOU

EMBRACEABLE YOU

TANGERINE

AFTER I SAY I'M SORRY

SEPTEMBER SONG

IF I HAD YOU

WHEN IT'S SLEEPY TIME
DOWN SOUTH

COQUETTE

2   MODERN ART AND DESIGN

Modern art, modernist furniture, and visions of a modern lifestyle appeared on many LP covers in the late 1950s and early 1960s. Jazz record covers, in particular, often featured abstract art, midcentury furniture, and modernist graphics, emphasizing a break with the past, and aligning design motifs with innovative sound technologies and the improvisation and arresting time signatures of jazz. It's as if the albums suggest that any aficionado of contemporary tastes will want to hear these sounds in hi-fi and also surround themselves with modern art and design, such as that displayed on these LP covers.

Whether Erroll Garner's piano pounding that morphs into a familiar melody, spattered paint on untreated canvas, or graceful chairs of molded plywood in customizable colors and stains, what might be called an improvisational aesthetics attempted to direct eyes to the consumable objects and experiences of US consumer culture. The albums selected for this chapter reveal the interplay among music, high-fidelity recording and stereo equipment, and other cultural discourses of midcentury America.

Design, music, and painting that traced their origins to American culture—for example, abstract expressionism, blues, and jazz—indicated that the United States no longer needed to refer back to the Old World for artistic direction after World War II but was positioned to take contemporary society forward with its own aesthetic values and cultural contributions.[1] A 1958 traveling exhibition organized by the Museum of Modern Art that sent about eighty mostly abstract paintings to Europe, including stops at Basel,

Berlin, Brussels, London, Milan, Paris, Stockholm, and Vienna, provides an example of the effort to shore up American cultural capital. As the *New York Times* reported at the time: "Refrigerators and other fruits of the assembly line are not the only kinds of American products prized overseas."[2]

Jazz signaled notions of contemporary sophistication, and this was emphasized when European musicians, trained and cultured in Europe, tried their hand at jazz improvisational forms. As Voice of America policy analyst Heath Bowman explained: "Jazz is useful because it keeps alive states of well-being in the young that cannot help but be associated with the West, and because it can be made to carry other propaganda freight."[3] And, from a slightly different perspective: "In midcentury hip culture, the cause of advanced art possessed something like a moral force: the progress of art stood for the progress of man."[4]

On many LP covers, midcentury modern furniture helped create visions of a contemporary US lifestyle. As art historian Lisa Phillips, writing in the context of modernist design, states: "Style in the visual arts has always been in the service of ideology."[5] Furniture design expressed cultural ideas, impacting the feeling and identity of kitchens, offices, and bachelor pads: "The world of mid-century design both mirrored the rapid changes in 1950s and '60s society and helped in making them possible, as it worked to give shape and identity to a new kind of lifestyle and a new wave of consumer products."[6] Of course, modern furniture wasn't fascinatingly modern simply because it was being created in this era; rather, modern design in many cases explored the cutting edge of new materials and manufacturing methods, as the designers Charles and Ray Eames and George Nelson prompted waves and folds in plywood and fiberglass, and Eero Saarinen worked with plastic. For example, the Eameses "used native Californian techniques, largely by-passing the European high-art, serious-culture tradition."[7] These explorations informing midcentury design gained attention and acclaim.

Modernist furniture comprised an essential component of the fabled bachelor pad. It was not your grandparents' furniture. Indeed, Playboy's conception of the bachelor pad specified the inclusion of Eames chairs, Nelson benches, Noguchi tables, and Saarinen chairs; and in 1961, they ran an influential article that treated modernist designers—including Charles Eames, George Nelson, Harry Bertoia, and Eero Saarinen—like celebrities.[8] Such furniture seems devoid of nostalgia and sentimentality: it's relatively light and easy to transport, for the man on the move. And, the Spartan, unfussy appearance of the selection of modernist-inspired LP covers exemplifies aspects of the 1950s bachelor pad, with austere, clean lines, stylish, contemporary design, and few visible indicators of family obligations. The blank studio setting of these covers reinforces a stereotypical masculine sensibility within the images. No kitchen or family room here.

With an emphasis on clean lines and surfaces and an absence of carving and other dust collecting detail and crevices, midcentury furniture in many cases connected to new realities of home, not only for the efficient bachelor pad but also to notions of the property ladder in which "moveable" wealth such as furniture, jewelry, and portable collectibles would be expected to travel with the owners to new, and often bigger or more luxurious, locations as income and financial security rose over a lifetime.

ALBUMS

TIME FOR LISTENING, from 1956, features Richard Hayman on the harmonica, playing easy-listening jazz tunes such as "The Touch" and "No Strings Attached." (Interestingly, the back cover lists the LP as *Time to Listen*, which maybe sounds too much like a schoolteacher's order). The cover readily reflects bachelor pad living: A hi-fi with three separate components occupies a modern shelving unit, signaling an enthusiast. Playing records on a sophisticated sound system provided a way to express taste, discernment, and earning power. A man in brown sport jacket, white button-down shirt, dark pants, and shoes, lies on a blue area rug, head on pillow conveniently placed on a woman's lap. His knees are up, and he is drawing on a cigarette. An ashtray is nearby, as is a record jacket and inner sleeve. LPs that were dubbed "bachelor pad music" ostensibly intended "to create a soft, luxurious mood, a theme-song for a sybarite, sultry accompaniment to sipping a martini, the soundtrack to an evening of Ritz cracker canapés and seduction."[9] For a bachelor on the path of seduction in his "bachelor pad," the hi-fi reigned supreme, and record companies eagerly offered the soundtracks.[10] The woman touches his hair and gazes down at him with interest: Clearly, the music is "working." Her coiffed hair, large earring, salmon pink top and black capris and shoes with no socks create an available but not revealing look. For better or worse, her ring suggests his bachelor days may be numbered.

FIGURE 2.1

Richard Hayman and His Orchestra,
Time for Listening,
Mercury MG 20103.

CUSTOM
HIGH
FIDELITY

Mercury
RECORDS

MG 20103

Time for Listening

with
RICHARD HAYMAN
and his orchestra

APRIL IN PORTUGAL	THE TOUCH	NO STRINGS ATTACHED
SOMERSAULT	SIMONETTA	DRIVE IN
SPANISH GYPSY DANCE	THE CUDDLE	HERNANDO'S HIDEAWAY
MR. POGO	BACK STREET	PLYMOUTH SOUND

RELAXING WITH PERRY COMO presents a light-haired woman, her head turned
with a dreamy glance. She reclines on a striking, modern chair, the blue of which
matches the album title lettering and the cover of a large book open on the floor. She
has a polka-dotted glass in her hand—no fine china for her—and a plate of strawberries nearby: the reds of the polka dots, strawberries, her nails and lips resonate,
forming a triangle. She is draped in a diaphanous pale pink chiffon negligee that
matches the shag area rug and shiny slippers. The liner notes mention the chair on
the cover (but not the model sitting in it): Bertoia chair, courtesy Knoll Associates.
The Bird Chair, designed by Harry Bertoia, appears to lend itself to music listening,
with its curves and high headrest. Handmade from steel rods that were bent to a
frame and welded together, the chairs looked good bare, upholstered, or with seat
pads.[11] Bertoia had worked with Ray and Charles Eames at the Cranbrook Academy
of Art in Michigan and went on to design several iconic chairs, as well as working as
a painter and sculptor. His chairs fill the courtyard at New York's Museum of Modern
Art, and his beautiful altarpiece graces the chapel at MIT.[12]

FIGURE 2.2

Relaxing with Perry Como,
RCA Victor LPM-1176;
photograph by David B. Hecht;
Bertoia chair courtesy of Knoll Associates.

RCA VICTOR
LPM-1176

Relaxing with Perry Como

PHOTO. DAVID B. HECHT

© RCA Printed in U.S.A.

The vividly colored cover of **LET'S LISTEN** by Harry Arnold and His Orchestra, playing the music of Cole Porter and Richard Rodgers, shows a golden haired woman in black cocktail dress and pearls, a band on her left ring finger, posed in a red Bertoia Bird chair, her feet in black high heels on the matching ottoman. (Her lipstick coordinates with the furniture.) Her arms reach up over her head and grasp the back of the chair, forming a series of angular lines that mimic its triangular shape. Her body confronts the camera straight on, but her eyes look to her right, perhaps to someone out of the frame. A console record player sits on the floor nearby, and some bright pillows and a flower vase rest on a long George Nelson platform bench. (We may have seen these same pillows and vase in the *Time for Listening* photo.) The bold yellow background sets off the model and chair, and her black dress and shoes make a visual connection with the black lines of the chair's distinctive wire frame and also with the vinyl record. Remarkably similar, the layout of both *Let's Listen* and *Relaxing with Perry Como* now represent classic "cheesecake" covers—with attractive models in varying states of dress, often unrelated to the content or performers of the record.[13] Certainly, one could read these covers as representing an independent woman enjoying music in her home; however, a number of elements tend to work against that interpretation. She remains the primary object of the consumer gaze, seemingly waiting for, or dreaming about, a man. It is a "Bird" chair, after all.

FIGURE 2.3

Harry Arnold and His Orchestra,
Let's Listen,
Mercury MG 20106.

Let's Listen

CUSTOM
HIGH
FIDELITY

Mercury
RECORDS

MG 20106

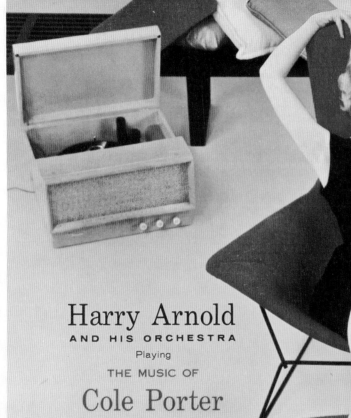

Harry Arnold
AND HIS ORCHESTRA
Playing
THE MUSIC OF
Cole Porter
AND
Richard Rodgers

MODERN JAZZ PIANOS: FOUR VIEWS features four esteemed jazz pianists, Garner, Art Tatum, Lennie Tristano, and the awesome Mary Lou Williams—represented on the cover as four Eames molded plywood chairs, painted bright yellow, red, white, and pale blue—in a sampler of piano-driven jazz standards. The cover photo shows an upright piano, its keys dirty and battered, outside on a broad expanse of asphalt. The piano, seemingly one that has had much use, contrasts with the bright newness of the chairs. The Eames chair, of course, is perhaps the most lauded midcentury design: fondly known as the potato chip chair, named by *Time* magazine as "Design of the Century," and perennially listed as a noteworthy and collectible piece of furniture. The Eames chair resonates with modernity—its organic form manufactured of plywood, based on wartime technology, simple, with no unnecessary ornamentation or details. As one commentator remarked, "No other piece of furniture has so stirred the mind and heart of the twentieth century both here and abroad."[14] George Nelson called it "a completely integrated expression of form, function, and manufacture."[15] In a statement that might also apply to the four pianists' work featured on this LP: "The Eameses' furniture seems somehow to remain always slightly apart from the space it inhabits—how its form creates space around it, how it meets the ground as if touching down. Their work sits in this world as if somehow simultaneously apart from it, as if picked out by the spotlight, as if to amplify its sensation of placed significance."[16]

FIGURE 2.4

Modern Jazz Piano: Four Views,
RCA Camden CAL 384;
photograph by Carl Fischer.

CAL 384   A High Fidelity Recording

RCA
CAMDEN
A PRODUCT OF RADIO CORPORATION OF AMERICA
LONG PLAY 33⅓ RPM

MODERN JAZZ PIANO FOUR VIEWS

MARY LOU WILLIAMS / ART TATUM / ERROLL GARNER / LENNIE TRISTANO

PHOTO BY CARL FISCHER

© RCA Printed in U.S.A.

On **THE SWINGIN'S MUTUAL!** by the George Shearing Quintet with Nancy Wilson, the chairs are credited in the liner notes: "Armchair on cover designed by: Charles Eames–Herman Miller Inc." Shearing, the blind British bandleader and jazz pianist, holds a copy of Wilson's *Something Wonderful,* her first LP for Capitol, which included one of her biggest songs, "Guess Who I Saw Today." Wilson, in turn, has a copy of *Shearing on Stage!* They are seated back to back in white Eames shell chairs, which are turned sideways to the camera. She appears to be looking over at him.

An interview with Wilson, posted on a music blog, offers a little-known fact about this iconic LP: "The photo on the cover? I believe those images were taken at separate times and then they joined the pictures together to make it seem as though we were sitting back to back. In fact, I'm sure of it. I owned an orange dress, so I didn't have to buy one for the photo shoot. But I didn't have orange shoes so I had to dye a pair."[17] At the time, showing a black woman and a white man together, as a couple, may have attracted more attention than the record company desired. In this case, showing them seated in similar positions, but not quite together, offers a disheartening resolution.[18] In any case, the cover represents an interesting image of a black woman and a white man pictured together, both as performers. The liner notes assure the listener "this album came about because of a rare thing called mutual admiration," and Shearing states: "The six vocals Nancy does on the album are even better than what I've come to expect from her." Wilson joins in the accolades: "the Quintet does six things in this album and I love them all … What else can I say? I dig him." Such covers are particularly interesting for their cross-promotional possibilities, selling music, furniture, and the modern lifestyle—including hints of racial equality—in one tidy package.

FIGURE 2.5

The George Shearing Quintet with Nancy Wilson,
The Swingin's Mutual,
Capitol ST 1524;
photograph by Maynard Frank Wolfe;
"armchair on cover designed
  by Charles Eames–Herman Miller Inc."

CAPITOL FULL DIMENSIONAL STEREO

the **GEORGE SHEARING** quintet with **NANCY WILSON**

an exciting combination—instrumentals by Shearing, vocals by Nancy...

the **swingin's mutual!**

On Ray Ellis and His Orchestra's **ELLIS IN WONDERLAND**,[19] from Columbia, Ellis sits in an Eames shell chair upholstered in red surrounded by three women in fishnet stockings and heels, dressed to represent key characters from Lewis Carroll's *Alice in Wonderland*: the White Rabbit, the Cheshire Cat, and the Mad Hatter, whose psychedelic bodysuit colors vibrate.[20] In the background, white trees—fairly obviously props—add to the cover's fantasy-like tableau. Ellis appears to be working on some music, seated at what looks like a school desk, with a rotary phone and drafting desk lamp. He holds some sheet music on his lap, and several other manuscripts are strewn about the floor. Ellis was a successful and versatile arranger, working with such artists as Sarah Vaughan, Billie Holiday, Johnny Mathis, Barbra Streisand, and, near the end of his career and at the start of hers, Emmylou Harris.

The *Ellis in Wonderland* cover has been reproduced many times and is a frequent post on album design blogs. Ellis's "creative" appearance—prominent watch, tortoise shell glasses, red vest, dark tie, white shirt with sleeves rolled up—contrasts with the *Wonderland* receptionist characters. The Eames chair, too, lends an office-like setting to the image, and provides a foil to the whimsical elements.

FIGURE 2.6

Ray Ellis and His Orchestra,
Ellis in Wonderland,
Columbia CL 993;
photograph by Hal Reiff.

ANIMALIZATION was the fourth album from the British pop group the Animals. Released in 1966, the LP produced several hits for the band, including "See See Rider," "Don't Bring Me Down," and "Inside Looking Out." The cover has the five band members sitting in white Eames shell chairs, arranged around white laminate Eames tables, as if in a school cafeteria, a classroom with its blackboard in the background, or an open-plan meeting room. Eames furniture, of course, was often used for classrooms, airports, and offices.[21] Eric Burdon in striped trousers and the other band members slump and sprawl, looking slightly bored but expectant, creating an informal, anticonformist vibe in the uniform, institutional environment.[22] We find it slightly amusing that these hit-making exemplars of the British invasion pose amid iconic American design.

FIGURE 2.7

The Animals,
Animalization,
MGM E-4384;
cover design by Acy Lehman.

BODY AND SOUL shows a model, engulfed by a white nightgown with pink satin bows, curled up in a "Womb" chair—designed by the Finnish American designer Eero Saarinen, and produced by Knoll furniture company. Florence Knoll is reported to have asked for "a chair that was like a basket full of pillows—something she could really curl up in;[23] and it makes a strong visual statement, in a living room, office, or on an album cover. The lines created by the borders of the light, but bright, pink floor, meet behind the chair in an apparent corner, where subtle blending of fuchsia and red form another line that bisects the deep marine blue curved frame, creating a triad of color centered by the model and oversized chair. (The Womb chair was reintroduced by Herman Miller in 2016.) Norman Greene and His Orchestra—the "youthful conductor," the notes state, "does his arranging work in the living room of his Brooklyn home"—play easy listening. The title song is from the 1956 film *The Eddy Duchin Story*.

FIGURE 2.8

Norman Greene and His Orchestra,
Body and Soul,
Decca DL 8377.

Body
and Soul...

Norman Greene
and his orchestra

Body And Soul
Dreaming On My Shoulder
My Foolish Heart
Holding Hands
The Touch Of Your Lips
Cheek To Cheek
I'll Close My Eyes
Georgia On My Mind
I Get Lost In His Arms
Your Sweet Smile
A Sky Blue Dove Below Me
I'm Glad There Is You

The cover of Ahmad Jamal's classic jazz album **ALL OF YOU** features Jamal, dressed in tailored brown jacket, a tie, and dark pants and shoes: the browns and blacks resonate with his hair and skin tone, as well as the chair color. Jamal sits against a neutral gray-blue background amid a few leafy branches in what looks like a studio.[24] The striking swag-legged MAA office chair, designed by George Nelson's office at Herman Miller, was produced in limited quantities when it was introduced in 1958. This iconic piece of furniture "used an innovative ball and socket design with molded fiberglass to create an office chair with an adjustable back—a highly influential design that helped to shape the evolution of the modern office chair."[25] Rare and coveted today as a design classic, the Nelson chair seats Jamal, and his music, at the center of American modernism. Jamal, who changed his name from Frederick Russell Jones when he converted to Islam in the 1950s, found success as both a jazz pianist and a club owner. *All of You* was recorded at his short-lived Chicago club, the Alhambra on South Michigan Avenue, with Jamal on piano, Israel Crosby on bass, and Vernel Fournier on drums.

FIGURE 2.9

Ahmad Jamal,
All of You,
Argo LP 691;
photograph by Don Bronstein.

AHMAD JAMAL

all of you

ARGO LP 691

On his LP **SINCERELY YOURS**, Robert Goulet leans back in a Plycraft Lounge chair, known as "Mr. Chair," designed by George Mulhauser. This lounger, one of the more successful imitations of the famous Eames Lounge chair, has become a coveted collectible.[26] Goulet turns his reclining body to the viewer, feet off the floor, knees crossed over the chair arm and stares into the camera. The chair appears to rest on sheets of shiny, reflective metallic flooring, an industrial design touch that contributes to the modern look of the cover. Goulet—"young, handsomely virile" according to the liner notes—looks comfortable in the oversize chair, which represents an icon of the masculine realms of office and bachelor den.[27]

FIGURE 2.10

Robert Goulet,
Sincerely Yours,
Columbia CL 1931;
photograph by Henry Parker.

FRANK SINATRA CONDUCTS TONE POEMS OF COLOR marks a noteworthy moment in Sinatra's career, as he assumes a conductor role, as well as beginning his productive collaboration with arranger Gordon Jenkins. Each tone poem represents a color, inspired by the poetry of one Norman Sickel, who had worked with Sinatra writing shows for radio. Several well-known composers, such as Elmer Bernstein, Andre Previn, and Alec Wilder, were recruited to write music for "a refreshing and fascinating musical presentation," that "adds a brilliant new dimension" to Sinatra's "stature."[28]

On the cover, designed by legendary designer Saul Bass, thin horizontal stripes of bright color, as if strips of cut paper that sometimes overlap to produce a new tone, suggest a different, and metaphorical, application of Bass's recognizable cut-out technique. As Bass remarked, "cover art is as important in setting the mood of a music recording as are the lyrics and music."[29] Bold graphic type in white anchors the album title, with the slightly smaller "Frank Sinatra Conducts," and finer, italicized lettering for each tone poem title: The fonts, Gothic No. 545 and Century Expanded, reinforce the contained angular qualities of the color bars.[30] A barely noticeable photo of Sinatra at work conducting floats at the top left next to the Capitol logo, interrupting the abstract design, but overlaid with color, becoming integrated. In the words of design writer Pat Kirkham, Bass "offered his own poem of color, line, and pattern."[31] This album marks one of the few Bass designed covers that was not film-related, such as his striking, characteristic work on the soundtrack LPs for *Exodus*, *West Side Story*, and *Anatomy of a Murder*.[32] *Tone Poems of Color* has become a classic of the genre, and is included in the Museum of Modern Art Architecture and Design department's collection of Bass's work.[33]

FIGURE 2.11

Frank Sinatra Conducts
Tone Poems of Color,
Capitol W 735;
design by Saul Bass.

Capitol
RECORDS

HIGH FIDELITY
RECORDING

Purple, The Schemer / Billy May

Yellow, The Laughter / Jeff Alexander

Brown, The Earthbound / Jeff Alexander

Orange, The Gay Deceiver / Nelson Riddle

White, The Young In Heart / Victor Young

Gold, The Greedy / Nelson Riddle

Gray, The Gaunt / Alec Wilder

FRANK SINATRA CONDUCTS

TONE POEMS OF COLOR

Red, The Violent / Andre Previn

Silver, The Patrician / Elmer Bernstein

Green, The Lover / Gordon Jenkins

DESIGNED BY SAUL BASS

Blue, The Dreamer / Alec Wilder

Black, The Bottomless / Victor Young

Dave Brubeck's breakthrough hit LP, *Time Out*, from 1959, offered cover art and modernist typography by designer S. Neil Fujita, who takes credit for introducing abstract art to album covers. Fujita remarked, recalling his innovative designs: "Jazz called for abstraction, a certain kind of stylization, using modern painters."[34] The cover of 1963's **TIME CHANGES** by the Dave Brubeck Quartet features a painting by the American abstract painter Sam Francis. Reminiscent of the better-known work of Jackson Pollock, Francis's cover art's drips, splashes, splotches, and spatters in bold yellow, orange, blue, and black dance across a white background. Several of Brubeck's LPs went with variations on the *Time Out* title, including *Time Further Out*, *Time Changes*, *Time In*, and *The Last Time Out*. As liner notes by Columbia producer and jazz saxophonist Teo Macero state: "The element of time in jazz and in music is a vital one, one which needs constant developing. Dave Brubeck and the quartet have probably done more in this area than any other jazz group." These LPs marked a distinctive cover style, quite apart from the black and white photography of Atlantic's and Blue Note's jazz LPs, which drew upon a rich tradition of jazz photography, Verve's figurative drawings, or Capitol's colorful photography.

FIGURE 2.12

The Dave Brubeck Quartet,
Time Changes,
Columbia CS 8927;
cover painting by Sam Francis.

The cover of **COUNTDOWN: TIME IN OUTER SPACE**, by the Dave Brubeck Quartet, includes an abstract painting incorporating thick black, orange, and white shapes, with touches of lilac and green. The painting, *Orange and Black Wall*, by Franz Kline, from 1959, is prominently identified on the cover, as from the "Collection of Mr. and Mrs. Robert C. Scull, courtesy of Sidney Janis Gallery." (Mrs. Scull—Ethel—is the subject of a famous Andy Warhol painting *Ethel Scull 36 Times*, his first commissioned fine art piece, now jointly owned by the Whitney Museum and the Metropolitan Museum of Art.) The copious liner notes on the back of the LP, written by Brubeck, with a blurb by Teo Macero, make no mention of the painting, however.

Kline, an American abstract expressionist master, become known for massive canvases with thick, bold brushstrokes of color, usually black on a white background, resembling calligraphy done by a giant's hand. As described by art historian Edward Lucie-Smith, Kline's sources of inspiration included "the techniques of graphic illustration, and … the scaffolding, girders, railways, and bridges of urban New York."[35] By incorporating Kline, a prominent member of the New York School of abstract expressionist painters, this LP joined a larger current of the Cold War that pitted Soviet realism against American expressionism, each meant to serve as an exemplar of artistic, cultural, and moral superiority.[36] In the words of art historian Serge Guilbaut, "abstract expressionism was for many the expression of freedom: the freedom to create controversial works of art, the freedom symbolized by action painting, by the unbridled expressionism of artists completely without fetters."[37] Brubeck's notes seem to echo this sensibility: he wrote that he felt "jazz must be freed from

FIGURE 2.13

The Dave Brubeck Quartet,
Countdown: Time in Outer Space,
Columbia CS 8575;
cover painting, *Orange and Black Wall*,
1959, by Franz Kline,
collection of Mr. and Mrs. Robert C. Scull,
courtesy of Sidney Janis Gallery.

STEREO
CS 8575

MONAURAL—CL 1775

COLUMBIA

COUNTDOWN
TIME IN OUTER SPACE
THE DAVE BRUBECK QUARTET

ELEVEN FOUR / WHY PHILLIS / COUNTDOWN / SOMEDAY MY PRINCE WILL COME / CASTILIAN BLUES
CASTILIAN DRUMS / FAST LIFE / WALTZ LIMP / THREE'S A CROWD / DANSE DUET / BACK TO EARTH

ORANGE AND BLACK WALL, 1959, by FRANZ KLINE, Collection of Mr. & Mrs. Robert C. Scull, Courtesy of Sidney Janis Gallery unnecessary restrictions if it were to continue to develop as an expression of a free individual."[38] The LP's title, too, obliquely refers to the space race that had heated up by its release in 1962, although Brubeck's album is not about space in the sense of space exploration of the heavens above. Rather, he makes a conceptual point that "music is concerned with time, as architecture is with space. Sound shatters time into fragments, which the musician has arranged in such patterns of periodicity that we say the music has rhythm"—and the album is dedicated to the first American in space, John Glenn.

Designed by the prolific LP design team of Moskof-Morrison, **THE GREATEST OF STAN GETZ**, on Roost Records, presents another American abstract expressionist painting, this one by Al Held. Not named, the bold and blocky geometric composition is credited to Al Held/Poindexter Gallery on the back cover. Held was known for his clean-edged, thickly painted forms, and often painted concentric boxlike shapes in his canvases. Getz was renowned for his beautiful, clean tenor saxophone sound, and certainly Held's cover art seems more "beautiful" than, say a Jackson Pollock splatter painting. In terms of its color palette and sharp lines, this cover bears some resemblance to Saul Bass's *Tone Poems of Color*, from a few years earlier, as well as Josef Albers's Homage to the Square paintings, a series of overlapping squares that provoked reflection on the interaction of the basic building blocks of color and shape. The LP includes "Dear Old Stockholm" and "Standanavian" in an apparent tribute to the Swedish jazz scene.

FIGURE 2.14

The Greatest of Stan Getz,
Roost SLP 2249;
cover painting Al Held/
Poindexter Gallery,
design by Moskof-Morrison Inc.

THE GREATEST OF STAN GETZ

ROOST

Atlantic Record's **FREE JAZZ: A COLLECTIVE IMPROVISATION**, by the Ornette Coleman Double Quartet, from 1960, was issued in an elaborate gatefold sleeve, with a cutout that reveals a detail of Jackson Pollock's painting *White Light*, from 1954. One of Pollock's last paintings, *White Light*, now in the Museum of Modern Art, displays his characteristic technique of directly applying paint, in this case, from a tube, to the canvas. Large, sans serif typography dominates the cover, which also features the swirling disk Atlantic logo. Coleman, who reinvigorated and redefined the alto saxophone, was a fan of the painter; indeed his 2015 obituary from *ArtNews* was headlined "Jazz Innovator and Jackson Pollock Lover Ornette Coleman Dies at 85."[39] On his LP *Change of the Century*, from the prior year, Coleman, an avid painter whose artwork featured on his 1973 album *The Empty Foxhole*, wrote that his saxophone playing was "something like the paintings of Jackson Pollock." Pollock, lauded in *Life* magazine, and feted by influential critics such as Clement Greenberg and Harold Rosenberg, was a key figure in the history of American painting. His work also helped lead the charge of the US government's Cold War propaganda efforts: contributing to missives about the opportunities in America's free, expressive culture. The pairing of high-art abstract expressionism with jazz signaled sympathetic links between the two, and with his use of Pollock's famous art, Coleman connects to "a national icon of artistic innovation and expressive freedom."[40]

FIGURE 2.15

The Ornette Coleman Double Quartet,
Free Jazz: A Collective Improvisation,
Atlantic 1364;
cover cutout painting,
White Light by Jackson Pollock.

FREE JAZZ
A COLLECTIVE IMPROVISATION

BY THE ORNETTE COLEMAN DOUBLE QUARTET

STEREO

ATLANTIC 1364
FULL *dynamics-frequency* SPECTRUM

We move away from jazz for the next example, to look at **MAGNIFICENT TWO-PIANO PERFORMANCES** by Leonid Hambro and Jascha Zayde on the Command label for Grand Award Records, from 1962. The LP includes two-piano compositions by nineteenth- and twentieth-century French composers Debussy, Poulenc, Franck, and Saint-Saens. The cover, designed by Charles E. Murphy, features a black and white square checkerboard juxtaposed with a variation of artist Josef Albers's series Homage to the Square in greens and blues, both surrounded by a black field. Albers, who taught at the Bauhaus before fleeing to the United States, worked at the experimental and influential Black Mountain College, which fostered interdisciplinary collaboration in the arts.

The Command label was started by musician and recording engineer Enoch Light, who hired Albers, on the advice of Murphy, to design a series of *Persuasive Percussion* albums.[41] These covers, which stood out for their simplicity and abstract form, now enjoy iconic LP cover status, exemplified by their inclusion in the Museum of Modern Art's Architecture and Design collection.[42] Like the Albers covers for the Command series LPs, this cover seems to resonate with the experimental nature of the label, and to some extent, the *Magnificent Two-Piano Performances* piano music, which, at the time, was considered "modern" and not yet in the classical canon. Command was known for extreme stereo separation, in that the sound "bounces" back and forth between speakers, so perhaps the cover can be seen as visually reflecting two distinct channels, with the black and white checkerboard on the left and the blue and green homage to the square on the right.

FIGURE 2.16

Leonid Hambro and Jascha Zayde,
Magnificent Two-Piano Performances,
Command Classics,
Grand Award Record Co. CC 11013 SD;
cover design by Charles E. Murphy.

STEREO
35 MM

Original *COMMAND* master recorded on 35 mm magnetic film

CC 11013

Command CLASSICS

MAGNIFICENT TWO-PIANO PERFORMANCES
LEONID HAMBRO AND JASCHA ZAYDE

DEBUSSY · EN BLANC ET NOIR
POULENC · SONATE
FRANCK · PRELUDE, FUGUE AND VARIATION
SAINT-SAENS · MINUET AND GAVOTTE OP. 65

DESIGNED BY CHARLES E. MURPHY

PRINTED IN U.S.A.

KENTON WITH VOICES: INTRODUCING THE MODERN MEN AND FEATURING ANN RICHARDS, from Capitol, was not a sales success. Kenton, known for bringing Latin sounds into jazz, especially bossa nova, had recently married singer Ann Richards, and this is his first album with all vocal numbers. On the cover, Kenton, slim, debonair, dressed in his trademark tailored suit and tie, cigarette in hand, leans on the wall in the midst of three abstract paintings "from the Landau Gallery," a Los Angeles gallery that showcased modern art in the 1960s.[43] The paintings are not named, but they resemble abstract expressionist works of the time, such as those by Hans Hofmann, who exhibited at the gallery. Clearly linking expressive qualities of musical and visual form, this LP cover—via less challenging jazz and vocal numbers—brings modernism into the mainstream American household.

FIGURE 2.17

Stan Kenton,
*Kenton with Voices:
Introducing the Modern Men
and Featuring Ann Richards*,
Capitol T 810;
paintings on cover from
the Landau Gallery.

KENTON WITH VOICES

INTRODUCING

THE MODERN MEN

AND FEATURING

ANN RICHARDS

3 MUSIC FOR GRACIOUS LIVING

On the album covers of the Music for Gracious Living series from Columbia Records, bright photographs from the Hedrich Blessing architectural photography studio capture evocative and pedagogically purposeful staging of the modern American home,[1] offering subtly instructive pictured scenarios to answer the uncertainties of gracious living: Which sort of centerpiece might create the right mood for an event? What's the best way to lay out silverware and salads? What type of furniture or equipment such as grill, serving table, or coffee pot, could be required, or at least desirable? Other interior design details are on display as well: pine paneling, painted color accents, full-length fabric curtains, and shelving options for knickknacks, plants, extra serving pieces, and display items.

With the home and especially the kitchen serving such an important rhetorical role in the vision of contemporary US consumer superiority, the Music for Gracious Living series follows through in featuring the tools for entertaining related to locations of food preparation and service. Three of the five albums include recipes on the back covers, as well as light-hearted, yet authoritative, advice for entertaining at home. Liner notes provide hints for hosting and successful exploration in "themed" culinary arts, including details of how to have a "buffet," a "barbecue," or a party "after the dance." "Special thought should be given the menu, of course, and music should be selected with discernment," the notes remark, as food, music, and décor claim equal importance, whether a Russel Wright platter of ham mousse and "Stormy Weather" or a summer sandwich loaf on the patio and "Embraceable You."[2]

Billboard's insightful review of the series upon its release in 1955 recognized the instructional value and stressed the visual appeal of the albums: "There rarely comes a series that invites display as does this one. The covers are full color photos of the type right out of 'Better Homes and Gardens,' each dealing with a form of modern home entertainment and avocation. On the back of each jacket is useful, easy to follow information—recipes for snacks, drinks, patio planting, dance music suggestions and remodeling hints."[3]

One of the Music for Gracious Living LPs, *Do-It-Yourself*, encapsulates many aspects of the quest to improve one's surroundings, dispensing directions for adapting the landscapes and living rooms of suburbia. Geographer Richard Harris, in his sweeping history of the home-improvement industry, helps contextualize the appearance of such an album: "it was 1952 that do-it-yourself (DIY) emerged as a distinctive market, and by 1954 it was a recognized fad."[4] Another title, *Barbecue*, offers a glimpse into the popular postwar pastime of cooking outside, inviting friends and family, and putting the men in charge of grilling. Backyard barbecues, too, can be understood within the Cold War context: "Access to and selection of 'choice' meat signaled capitalism's fruits—folk could own their own home, have leisure time to grill, and enjoy the freedom to buy the type of food they desired when they wanted it. On another level, barbecue as a practice and an idea spoke to traditional American values of individuality, ingenuity, family, community, progress, and pride."[5] In this way, barbecue embodies key American values.

Taken as a set, this series expresses how "new consumer preferences for cars, owner-occupied homes, and home modernization entailed new patterns of expenditure [and] new cultural assumptions about how families should live, how various domestic tasks should be divided between men and women, and about the very meaning of masculinity and femininity."[6] The Music for Gracious Living albums present an attractive illustration of the socializing roles LPs played at midcentury.[7]

ALBUMS

The **AFTER THE DANCE** LP provides a compelling social scenario: "When the dance is over at the club or civic center, and the music seems to have stopped too early, it isn't necessarily time to call it quits. For those who are young at heart and whose feet have caught the rhythm of the evening, a little more fun may be in perfect order. 'Let's go back to our place' can be a joyous cry in the early hours—if you're prepared." The album provides suggestions for finessing an after the dance gathering, tailored not only to couples, but also parents, bachelors, and "girl-bachelors": "If you're the hostess, you'll certainly want to have the house looking attractive—and to go on looking attractive yourself, without having to work in a hot kitchen. So fill your refrigerator early—with delicious and handsome foods to be served easily, hours after preparation. And keep the mood going with the right music—have it already selected and at hand." Late-at-night recipes include "Rye-pie" sandwiches, summer sandwich loaf, and date squares.

In the cover photo, the partiers "after the dance" sport dressy attire, the women in colorful midcalf dresses and high heel sling back shoes, amid white cabinets, countertops, and matching appliances, with splashes of sunshine yellow. Wardrobe is as important as appropriate dishware, and it seems that hosts and guests might cook and serve in a less formal after the dance mood but need not change out of their dressy clothes. An apron appears on a woman tossing a salad but also on a man with good-natured grin who forms a burger patty for the counter-top grill. Apparently, displaying finery on all fronts is encouraged even in the face of spitting grease or spattering water.

FIGURE 3.1

Peter Barclay and His Orchestra,
After the Dance,
Columbia CL 697;
photo by Hedrich Blessing.

CL 697

PHOTOGRAPH: HEDRICH-BLESSING   ® "Columbia", ℗ Marcas Reg. Printed in U.S.A.   COLUMBIA

A HIGH FIDELITY RECORDING

Lp

Music for GRACIOUS LIVING

AFTER THE DANCE

PETER BARCLAY AND HIS ORCHESTRA

Everyone appears cool, comfortable, calm, and well-dressed. The notes also guide parents in after the dance get-together training for the younger set: help "your daughter grow into a gracious hostess" making "her feel the house belongs to her for the evening"; and teach your son "the dignity of being a thoughtful host," letting him "feel his home is open to his friends, too." Although the music on *After the Dance* appears as an afterthought, the notes do recommend further albums from Columbia recording artists, such as Xavier Cugat and Harry James, for keeping the party going.

The **BUFFET** album offers extensive advice, as well as consolation for the lack of domestic help:

> One of the most gracious ways to entertain is to invite your friends to dinner. Nowadays, formal dinners are not given so often as formerly, but an attractive buffet can be just as tasteful and sometimes even more enjoyable. It's easier, too, for the hostess. And her china, her silver, and her glassware in thoughtfully designed buffet can be just as attractive as the most carefully set formal table.

The cover features the host and hostess fussing over the long buffet bar, as they dress and toss salad in a red ceramic bowl. Their taste is on display: the table is laid with heavy silverware and a distinctly nonmodern coffee pot, sugar and creamer; a wood-framed botanical print decorates the paneled back wall, hanging just above a copper chafing dish set on a small dark-wood sideboard; a blue serving platter holds

FIGURE 3.2

Peter Barclay and His Orchestra,
Buffet,
Columbia CL 694;
photo by Hedrich Blessing.

CL 694

Music for GRACIOUS LIVING

PHOTOGRAPH HEDRICH-BLESSING ® Columbia Marcas Reg Printed in U S A COLUMBIA

BUFFET

A HIGH FIDELITY
RECORDING

PETER BARCLAY AND HIS ORCHESTRA

a clove-flecked ham; and antique china dishes call attention to a country-style hutch. This couple have not (yet) gone for midcentury updating.

The *Buffet* album's recipe for ham mousse is a culinary classic. The pinkish mixture of gelatin, sugar, diced canned ham, mayonnaise, and whipping cream is chilled until firm in a six-cup ring mold and served on salad greens with extra mayo. Imagine a warm evening, the ham mousse centered on the buffet counter with "the most colorful and cool-looking linen and china," flanked by two-tone tomatoes (cut and insert slices of smoked cheese) and sweet cucumber pickle fans. On cooler evenings dishes might include hearty beef casserole (favored by men), celery scallop (bake in oven one dish of onion, tomato sauce, butter, and celery slices), or baked fruit compote (dried prunes, figs, apricots, and peach halves). Background music for conversation and eating must be carefully selected, and "symphonic works" are out: "Select instead charming light melodies, such as those played," yes, on this album. The buffet setting may lack romantic appeal, but the tunes "I Fall in Love Too Easily," "Falling in Love with Love," and "Dream Lover" provide a seamless easy-listening schmaltz.

....

A bit different from the other LPs in the Music for Gracious Living series, **DO-IT-YOURSELF** focuses on the needs of the nuclear household, and echoes the DIY movement that was sweeping the country in the postwar boom. In an era of expanding possessions with rooms built, designed, or repurposed for enjoying and showing these off, the album encourages, "Get out your tools, for here are some ideas for utilizing your house more efficiently—and for doing it yourself." The cover shows Dad and Junior with matching haircuts, in casual dungarees, button-down shirts and

FIGURE 3.3

Peter Barclay and His Orchestra,
Do-It-Yourself,
Columbia CL 698;
photo by Hedrich Blessing.

CL 698

Music for GRACIOUS LIVING

PHOTOGRAPH: HEDRICH-BLESSING   "Columbia", Marcas Reg. Printed in U.S.A   COLUMBIA

A HIGH FIDELITY RECORDING

Lp

DO-IT-YOURSELF

PETER BARCLAY AND HIS ORCHESTRA

belts, working intently on a project, with Mom, across the room, wearing a bright-red dress, matching nail polish, and slip-on platform sandals, busy sewing. A two-color linoleum floor divides the space. And, the two large visible windows with roll down blinds provide a leafy, suburban view. The notes provide specific instructions on how to modernize a porch, and build home furnishings—"easy and cheap"—such as a cabinet for your records or a "wheeled base" for the television set, allowing movement from porch to den: "You can also wheel it into the dining room when there are particular programs you're anxious not to miss at the cost of a good dinner."

One suggestion promotes the leading role of LPs in gracious living:

> In every modern home there should be a music room, devoted to the enjoyment of Columbia's superb radio, phonograph, and television equipment —to say nothing of Columbia's fabulous library of classical and popular records. If you don't know off-hand just where that separate special room might be—try your summer porch, your attic, your basement, your guest room, or the room you still call "Bob's" or "Julia's," even though by now they may be either away at school much of the year, or even married.[8]

Agreed. A room for records rates top priority.

FOURSOME's notes begin, "An important part of gracious living is certainly the joy of gracious entertaining." Sounding much like an advice column, or an article in *Better Homes and Gardens*, this LP focuses on making guests happy: "The mood of one's

FIGURE 3.4

Peter Barclay and His Orchestra,
Foursome,
Columbia CL 696;
photo by Hedrich Blessing.

CL 696

PHOTOGRAPH: HEDRICH-BLESSING ® "Columbia" ℗ Marcas Reg. Printed in U.S.A COLUMBIA

A HIGH FIDELITY
RECORDING

LP

Music for GRACIOUS LIVING

FOURSOME

PETER BARCLAY AND HIS ORCHESTRA

home—its color, warmth, and personality —is also an integral part of your guests'
enjoyment. In this collection is music especially selected for entertaining, designed
to please your guests and to create an atmosphere of charm in your home." In the
cover photograph, the game room is stylish, tidy, and colorful. A card table looks
carefully arranged, the cigarettes plentiful, the snacks in their bowls, with signs of
the evening's game underway, but where has everyone gone? Card game themed
recipes include "Lady-fare Salad," "Red Cherry Tarts: for the Queen of Hearts and
her bridge friends," along with "Pineapple Refrigerator Dessert," as well as "tricks
with mayonnaise for fruit salads."

Backyard barbecues boomed in the 1950s. Although seeming an age-old American
tradition, "having a barbecue" —friends coming over on a random weekend evening
for a kind of outdoor backyard buffet, with generous amounts of protein cooked
over flames or hot coals—was actually a fairly recent cultural phenomenon.[9] The
cover of Music for Gracious Living **BARBECUE** offers a classic tableau: men at the
grill (here, not a Weber, but a sort of white-painted brick Aga); a woman (in pearls!)
arranging the table; corn on the cob; slices of watermelon; fresh tomatoes. The coffee pot and mugs suggest less beer than one might expect.

    The notes paint a rosy picture of the tradition of cooking outdoors: "In the eve-
ning, what better living than a barbecue in your own backyard, or on your patio,
porch or terrace, surrounded by family and friends, and by music, especially selected for your out-door living? Mother's out of the kitchen, Father's in command, the

FIGURE 3.5

Peter Barclay and His Orchestra,
Barbecue,
Columbia CL 695;
photo by Hedrich Blessing.

CL 695

PHOTOGRAPH: HEDRICH BLESSING ℗ Columbia Lp Marcas Reg. Printed in U.S.A. COLUMBIA

Music for GRACIOUS LIVING

BARBECUE

PETER BARCLAY AND HIS ORCHESTRA

A HIGH FIDELITY
RECORDING

Lp

children are on a holiday at home." (There seems to be a small oddly placed stuffed dog in the left foreground.) This record includes advice for "patio planting" ("Fill your shady corners with *caladiums*"); meat ("Begin with hot dogs and burgers, then move on to skewers and steaks"); and "cool patio drinks," such as "Spiced-tea Special" and "Easy-does-it Punch"; and offers such cheerfully soothing tunes as "Summer Evening in Santa Cruz" and "Live, Laugh, Love," all played by Peter Barclay and His Orchestra. Each LP in the series includes small cartoony graphics: on *Barbecue*, a plump man in apron and chef's hat attends to grilling meat.[10]

4 LET'S HAVE A DINNER PARTY!

The Dinner Music series from RCA Victor presents "music for a dinner at home." The LPs promote turning dinners into a more cosmopolitan affair and showing an awareness of other parts of the world, less familiar ingredients, diverse cooking traditions, and aspects of global fashion. Not just any version of Italian, German, or Chinese food, these albums envisioned "fine dining" and a special kind of dinner hour: they encouraged bringing atmosphere and festiveness to the table in the form of different countries' cuisines, clothing, and an accompanying soundtrack. Indeed, a couple of the albums seem to offer a means of rapprochement with former World War II enemies via the culinary arts.

We think of these albums as precursors to television cooking and decorating shows, or YouTube videos, perhaps designed for newly housed suburbanites with few fine dining options nearby. Each album includes back-cover recipes for a full meal from appetizers through dessert, offering a guide to new culinary horizons, and, together with the cover photo, suggestions for appropriate tableware and accessories. Beyond macaroni and cheese, tuna casserole, or plain pork chops, the possibilities of an attractive foreignness, a bit more effort in the kitchen, and a curious attitude at the grocery store wrought excitement in the dining room.

As color photography, particularly as used in marketing, developed techniques for presenting each object in more compelling and attention-grabbing ways, and mass-market women's magazines featured these photos in increasing numbers, pressure for making one's home-cooked food more interesting and inventive may have supported these album cover's culinary excursions into elaborate themed presentations, such as those promoting Chinese banquets in the family dining room and golden pineapple bedecked platters for backyard luaus. The fantasy-invoking palettes brightened every-day kitchens with such offerings as orange Jell-O, purple and red Kool-Aid drinks, not to mention the brilliant green of canned peas. While midcentury advances in refrigeration and plastic wrap aided in food preparation and preservation, attempting to reproduce these saturated colors, rather than more familiar browns, creams, and pale vegetable hues, on one's suburban dinner table, surely sparked the ubiquity of artificial food coloring.

The LPs feature a few complex dishes, like baked oysters au gratin, bouillabaisse, kugelhopf, and roast duck, but most recipes attempt to capture the atmosphere without placing difficult demands on the at-home chef. These are "authentic" meals, the liner notes enthuse, but if cooking does not "delight" you, similar dishes could be purchased "at the frozen food or other prepared food departments of your nearest store." *Billboard* caught the spirit in their brief 1959 review, remarking that the series was aimed "to aid the home gourmet in the atmosphere department," with "mouth-watering" cover pho-tography and music "played in a smooth style that will please the ear as well as aid the digestion."[1] As atmospheric soundtrack, the music provides some connection to the featured region, often with a number or two sung in the country's language—only *Music for a Chinese Dinner at Home* misses out here. Orchestra conductors with country-appropriate names supply the easy-listening vibe. The covers were shot by prolific album photographer Wendy Hilty.[2] In the end, the series included only five LPs, but together, they present a window into earnest postwar strivings for cosmopolitan lifestyles.

ALBUMS

The Chianti bottle, red-checked tablecloth, antipasto salad, and aging "Mamma" create a classic cover for <u>MUSIC FOR AN ITALIAN DINNER AT HOME</u>, but the brilliant orange background, cut honeydew melon slices poised in a crystal fruit bowl, and the pink flower vase stuffed with feathers place this cover well into the realm of camp. The notes begin: "Remember the last time you and your best girl … or you and the family had dinner out at that fine Italian restaurant, the one with the atmosphere, the one that was almost like an evening in Rome, or Milano … or Venice?" The instrumentation *Italiano* may inspire visions of "a group of fine, swarthy sons of Italy" playing tableside at "the best Italian restaurant you ever dreamed of visiting," but overcooked accordion relentlessly pursues the listener through songs like "O sole mio," "Three Coins in the Fountain," and "Funiculi Funicula," performed by Romano Ledenzio and His Orchestra.[3] The minestrone, scaloppini of veal, and cannelloni recipes for the at-home chef originated in the kitchen of "Maria's Restaurant" at 141 East 52nd St. in Manhattan, supplied by chef Albert Fanfoni. Cooking hints include "Sprinkle with parmesan" and "Consider substituting olive oil for butter."

FIGURE 4.1

Romano Ledenzio and His Orchestra,
Music for an Italian Dinner at Home,
RCA Victor LPM-1938;
photo by Wendy Hilty.

On **MUSIC FOR A FRENCH DINNER AT HOME**, an elegant brunette couple in formal attire toasts to the evening ahead surrounded by the rococo splendor of gilded chairs and marble top table and a precariously large crystal candelabra. The candles are lit, the food is prepared, and the "French" bubbly is served—the bottle rests in a champagne bucket, wrapped in white napkin. The LP's logo unfortunately obscures the identity of a bust atop a marble column. The proposed night of Gallic sophistication includes "Pâté de Foie," "Beef Bourguignon," "Mousse Chocolate," and "intimate music" that moves in perfect concert with the meal from the innocent charms of "At a Little Street Café" to the waiting dessert of "Boulevard d'amour."

Much of this vision depended on notions of "fine dining" and establishments that served "continental cuisine," "an eclectic melding of French-inspired and American dishes floridly described in elaborate menus."[4] Such a dinner begins with "cocktails, an iced relish tray, and bread, continues through an appetizer of Oysters Rockefeller, Caesar Salad prepared at the table, Lobster Thermidor or Steak Diane as an entrée."[5] The menu provided on the LP's back cover offers minimal instruction for ambitious dishes, and the attempt seems more likely to breed frustration than desire. But, the notes embrace the French reputation for romance: "about the only other ingredients you need to make your French dinner at home an exquisite experience are your own attitude, soft lights and the right kind of intimacy." Pierre Felére and His Orchestra provide the musical numbers, which include French-themed selections such as "The Last Time I Saw Paris," "Midnight in Montmartre," and "La Vie en rose."

FIGURE 4.2

Pierre Felére and His Orchestra,
Music for a French Dinner at Home,
RCA Victor LPM-1937;
photo by Wendy Hilty.

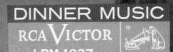

DINNER MUSIC
RCA VICTOR
LPM-1937
A "New Orthophonic" High Fidelity Recording

Music for a
FRENCH
DINNER
AT HOME
Pierre Felére
and His Orchestra

The Last Time I Saw Paris
Midnight in Montmartre
Alouette—Frère Jacques
At a Little Street Café
Boulevard d'amour
Under Paris Skies
The Petite Waltz
I Love Paris
Bistro
Valentine
La Vie en rose
The River Seine

Photo: Wendy Hilty

© RCA Printed in U.S.A.

The Living Stereo version of **MUSIC FOR A GERMAN DINNER AT HOME** features a young woman in Bavarian dress, her long blond braid coiled around her head, serving a grinning man holding a regimental beer stein. Brown bread and serving dishes of pork slices, radishes, red onion and tomato salad, and chopped sauerkraut appealingly fill the round wooden tabletop. A rustic hutch in the background holds wine glasses, ceramic platters, and a collection of steins. The gothic style typography of "German" in the title highlights the album's national affiliation, but no mention is made of the recent war. Though occasionally piano and strings break through the oom-pah-pah sound, the accordion, an aural icon of continental leisure, dominates this LP's music, performed by Franz Hermann and His Orchestra. "The Drinking Song" and "Heidelberg" are bright and lively, and "Moonlight on the Rhine" sparkly and nostalgic. All these smooth melodies help wash down the "Sauerbraten," "Bread and Apple Soup," and "Kugelhopf" offered as "outstanding and truly authentic German recipes."

FIGURE 4.3

Franz Hertzman and His Orchestra,
Music for a German Dinner at Home,
RCA Victor LSP-1935;
photo by Wendy Hilty.

LIVING STEREO

Dinner Music

RCA VICTOR

LSP-1935

"HIS MASTER'S VOICE"

Stereo-Orthophonic High Fidelity Recording

music for a **German** dinner at home

Franz Hertzman and His Orchestra

Bavarian Nights · Du, du liegst mir im Herzen
The Drinking Song · Yours Is My Heart Alone · May Wine · Blue Danube
Heidelberg · Two Hearts in ¾ Time · Dresden Doll · Moonlight on the Rhine
Auf Wiedersehen, My Dear · Serenade (from "The Student Prince")

A smiling Asian-appearing couple look ready for their feast presented on classic blue and white Chinese porcelain dishes. He sits on cushions at a low red and black lacquered table wearing a dark changshan gown with Mandarin collar, holding chopsticks and a bowl of white rice. Wearing a tight silvery *qipao*, she kneels, serving. A Chinese-style screen and lantern complete the scene against a glowing pinkish background, with bright yellow calligraphic lettering announcing, **MUSIC FOR A CHINESE DINNER AT HOME**. The liner notes proclaim, "If you'll just cook up a Chinese meal (presuming you love to cook) from the recipes we offer herewith—or pick up any number of fascinating prepared Chinese food packages at your nearest supermarket, dim the lights, and put this disc on your phonograph, we guarantee you all the enjoyment and pleasure of the unusual, that eating out at your favorite Chinese restaurant ever gave you." The recipes provided on the back cover include "Barbecued Spareribs," "Egg Foo Young," "Shrimp with Green Peas," and "Sweet and Pungent Pork." Bob Lin Wu and His Orchestra take credit for the music: "purely American tunes with a touch of the Orient about them" means pop songs with a Chinese connection, such as "On a Slow Boat to China," "Hong Kong Blues," and "Not for All of the Rice in China."

FIGURE 4.4

Bob Lin Wu and His Orchestra,
Music for a Chinese Dinner at Home,
RCA Victor LSP-1936;
photo by Wendy Hilty.

LIVING STEREO

DINNER MUSIC
RCA VICTOR
LSP-1936
Stereo-Orthophonic High Fidelity Recording

MUSIC FOR A CHINESE DINNER AT HOME

BOB LIN WU and His Orchestra · Love Is a Many-Splendored Thing
On a Slow Boat to China · Hong Kong Blues · Lantern Street · Shanghai Doll
The Emperor's Nightingale · Not for All the Rice in China · Limehouse Blues
Mountain High, Valley Low · Rickshaw · China Boy · Chinatown, My Chinatown

Photo: Wendy Hilty

© RCA Printed in U.S.A.

MUSIC FOR A BACK YARD BARBECUE might be considered the *Music for an American Dinner at Home* LP of the Dinner Music series. The cover presents two large, char-grilled steaks atop a suspiciously shiny grill, with a set of yellow sauce bowls adorned with skewers of mixed fruit and vegetables in sharp focus in the foreground. Partygoers anchor the background: Two women, in summer dresses, one blonde and retiring, the other brunette and animated, both with drinks, and a tall man, also dressed well, with sleeves rolled up, who has a hand casually on the blonde's shoulder, as he engages the brunette. The notes declare: "When a gang gathers around the barbecue of a lovely summer evening, it takes a very special kind of music to fit the mood. An intimate, yet rousing … warm, yet unrestrained type of song and performance that just hasn't been available until now." Norman Leyden, who went on to serve as musical director of *The Jackie Gleason Show*, and his orchestra supply the appropriate "intimate yet rousing" music for outdoor dining with songs such as "Hail, Hail the Gang's All Here" and "Beer Barrel Polka." Recipes for the barbecue consist of "some suggestions" for hamburgers, frankfurters, and sauces, including "Roquefort Sauce and "Scallion Sauce," as well as more sophisticated recipes for "Shish Kabob," "Skewered Shrimp," and "Broiled Lobster."

FIGURE 4.5

Norman Leyden and His Orchestra,
Music for a Back Yard Barbecue,
RCA Victor LPM-1939;
photo by Wendy Hilty.

Dinner Music
RCA VICTOR
LPM-1939
A "New Orthophonic" High Fidelity Recording

Norman Leyden and His Orchestra

Hail, Hail, the Gang's All Here—
For He's a Jolly Good Fellow
Hot Dogs and Hamburgers
The Gang That Sang Heart of My Heart
Down by the Old Mill Stream
Beer Barrel Polka
Back in Your Own Back Yard
Shine On Harvest Moon
With the Folks We Love
In the Twilight
The Doughnut Dunker
Sweet Adeline
Hi, Neighbor

MUSIC FOR A BACK YARD BARBECUE

5   MUSIC FOR HI-FI LIVING

Music for Hi-Fi Living, an ambitious series from RCA Custom, bridged the concerns of home and away. The twelve volumes of Music for Hi-Fi Living, in describing a life-style evolution from youth to maturity, offered guidance in life's lessons from a teenage dance and young romance to marriage, honeymooning, trips to the city, and destinations abroad for a sophisticated adulthood.[1] The albums clearly reveal the role in contemporary US identity of travel and seeing the broader world. This chapter reiterates core themes of the progress and development of a modern US lifecycle and sets up the second part of the book, "Away."

The Music for Hi-Fi Living LPs provided a path for an entire phase of life. Little mention was made of work, careers, or the problems of everyday life. Rather, the series emphasized "the good life"—or at least a version of it—complete with dating, parties, marriage, vacations, and more parties. Music supplied a necessary soundtrack for these visions, moving effortlessly from seduction to nuptials to married life.

The series also promoted collecting—with twelve albums to acquire, play, and organize. Collecting represents a common aspect of living with LPs, for more than most other popular media of the era, such as magazines, films, and television, the LPs had staying power; they were sought out and saved for the long haul, stacked in the hi-fi set, stored in record cabinets, and splayed across family room floors.[2] This was well before the digital age in which all manner of images, songs, and information is readily available; and apart from a few sources, such as pictures in collectible *Life* and *National Geographic* magazines, most of the images that entered the American home were ephemeral. Record album covers represented a more permanent and memorable form of graphic design, sometimes placed in frames as art. Most of our vinyl albums remain in great shape, fifty to sixty years after they were released.

Dating, marriage, and romantic travel dominate the key moments represented in the Music for Hi-Fi Living series: these albums usher us through basic cultural rituals as our couple matures into US consumer culture. In fact, two of the twelve albums in the series celebrate marriage and weddings. We don't believe that this is a concession to divorce and a second "angelic" wife (volume 9, *The Girl That I Marry*, comes after volume 4, *I Married an Angel*, in the series), but such an idea does point out an alternative, well-trodden path in contemporary culture, considering processes of reassessing, disposing, and in many cases purchasing new instances of personal and household possessions.

ALBUMS

The first LP in the series, I COULD HAVE DANCED ALL NIGHT, shows a formally dressed teenage couple—girl in chaste ball gown, boy in tuxedo and bowtie—in what appears to be the front hall or foyer of a large house, complete with curving stairway, chandelier, and hopscotch marble floor in a fantastical vision of a beautiful, or rather hi-fi, life. This album sets up the Music for Hi-Fi Living series revolving around a young couple's charmed existence and demonstrates how RCA albums might fit in to all stages of a modern lifestyle journey, providing images and music that mirror central stops on the way. In a hi-fi life, with a sophisticated soundtrack, the vinyl LP accompanies all the major signposts.

FIGURE 5.1

Hill Bowen and His Orchestra,
I Could Have Danced All Night,
RCA RAL 1001;
photo Howard Graff.

VOL. 1 FOR HI-FI LIVING

I Could Have Danced All Night • If I Loved You • On the Street Where You Live • The Best Things In Life Are Free
All the Things You Are • Button Up Your Overcoat • I Love Paris • Getting To Know You • I've Grown
Accustomed To Her Face • I've Told Ev'ry Little Star • I've Got You Under My Skin • Buckle Down, Winsocki

HILL BOWEN AND HIS ORCHESTRA

RAL 1001

LONG PLAY 33⅓ RPM

RCA CUSTOM
A PRODUCT... ...RPORATION OF AMERICA

A "NEW ORTHOPHONIC" HIGH FIDELITY RECORDING

I Could
Have Danced
All Night

PHOTO: HOWARD GRAFF

Volume 2, **HANDS ACROSS THE TABLE**, offers a G-rated vision of budding romance, as a smiling young woman tenderly takes her paramour's hand *across the table*, over coffee and cigarettes. His face is blurred, but hers radiates happiness and the promise of a relationship, at the very least. So this is music for romance and perhaps seduction. With Tony Osborne and his orchestra performing "safe" songs such as "I Surrender Dear," "Take Me in Your Arms," and "I'm Getting Sentimental over You," *Hands Across the Table* offers sentimental sounds for dating and desire, and a reminder of the close intertwined aspects of music and romance.

FIGURE 5.2

Tony Osborne and His Orchestra,
Hands Across the Table,
RCA RAL 1002;
photo by Bob Ritta.

VOL. **2** FOR HI-FI LIVING

Hands Across the Table · Girl of My Dreams · I've Got the World on a String · I Surrender, Dear
Serenade in the Night · Stars Fell on Alabama · Belle of the Ball · Take Me in Your Arms
I Can't Give You Anything But Love · That's My Desire · Sweet Lorraine · I'm Getting Sentimental Over You

TONY OSBORNE AND HIS ORCHESTRA

LONG PLAY 33⅓ RPM   RAL 1002

 CUSTOM

A PRODUCT OF RADIO CORPORATION OF AMERICA

A "NEW ORTHOPHONIC" HIGH FIDELITY RECORDING

Hands
Across
the
Table

What romance could claim to be modern without a Hollywood trip to celebrate big screen depictions of love-addled couples living out their lives, singing, dancing, and solving mysteries? On the cover of volume 3, **HITS FROM HOLLYWOOD**, the cars' motion and brilliant colors—yellow, blue, and glowing red—provide foreground interest as the crowd of people are funneled into the narrow opening for the party. Participation extends the possibility of membership, and our young couple may take heart that in their own little town similar events, such as dress-up dances at local country clubs, might be planned, organized, and attended, bringing the buzz and glamour of this more consequential world home.

FIGURE 5.3

Ronnie Ogden and His Orchestra,
Hits from Hollywood,
RCA RAL 1003;
photograph by Gene Lester.

VOL. 3 — FOR HI-FI LIVING

I Feel a Song Comin' On · Love is a Many-Splendored Thing · All I Do is Dream of You
Sweet and Lovely · Laura · Be My Love · It's a Most Unusual Day · Three Coins in the Fountain
Ramona · High Noon · I'm in the Mood for Love · Over the Rainbow

RONNIE OGDEN AND HIS ORCHESTRA

RAL 1003

LONG PLAY 33⅓ RPM

RCA CUSTOM

A PRODUCT OF RADIO CORPORATION OF AMERICA

A "NEW ORTHOPHONIC" HIGH FIDELITY RECORDING

HITS FROM HOLLYWOOD

GALA HOLLYWOOD PREMIERE TONIGHT

Photo: GENE LESTER

© RCA Printed in U.S.A.

Perched on a column that serves as a pedestal, the beatific bride is mostly unadorned in her bountiful pale pink dress, drop earrings, and angel wings. She looks tempted by the tiny bouquet of flowers held up by the beaming man in dark suit and bow tie. I MARRIED AN ANGEL supplies swoony favorites "Taking a Chance on Love," "I'll Never Be the Same," and "Blue Moon." She must come down sometime, and what will happen then?

FIGURE 5.4

Hill Bowen and His Orchestra,
I Married an Angel,
RCA RAL 1004;
photo by Murray Laden.

VOL. **4** FOR HI-FI LIVING

I Married An Angel · Lovely Lady · Taking A Chance on Love · Song of Love
I'll Never Be the Same · Doll Dance · I Love You · More Than You Know
That Old Feeling · Once In a While · Blue Moon · Down Among the Sheltering Palms

HILL BOWEN AND HIS ORCHESTRA

LONG PLAY 33⅓ RPM

RAL 1004

 CUSTOM
A PRODUCT OF RADIO CORPORATION OF AMERICA

A "NEW ORTHOPHONIC" HIGH FIDELITY RECORDING

I
Married
an
Angel

Photo: MURRAY LADEN

RCA Printed in U.S.A

The fifth Music for Hi-Fi Living album, **LOVE ON BROADWAY**, from Hill Bowen and His Orchestra, features a couple in New York, heading to a show, with the bright lights of the theater district behind them. The LP contains a sampling of hit Broadway tunes, such as "Smoke Gets in Your Eyes," from 1933's *Roberta*, "Some Enchanted Evening," the huge hit from *South Pacific*, which opened in 1949, and "September Song," from 1938's *Knickerbocker Holiday*, as well as the 1950 film *September Affair*. Broadway, of course, was and is a popular destination for visitors to New York from all over the world, and its inclusion in the Hi-Fi Living series underscores its importance for a modern lifestyle.

Volume 6, **LATIN HOLIDAY**, from Don Amoré and His Orchestra, offers a selection of Latin-inspired numbers, building on the growing interest in the rhumba, merengue, and mambo. Released in 1957, just before the Cuban revolution and subsequent blockade, the album provides an appealing vision—water skiers, framed by a blue sky and a metropolitan harbor. The album title is brightly spelled out in alternating yellow and red block letters. Not expressly a "honeymoon" record, *Latin Holiday* nevertheless lends itself to promoting that much anticipated consumer trip, a getaway from family and friends to mark the couple's new beginning.

Small yellow daffodils from a dinner table centerpiece at a party out of town, a show attended during a girls' weekend away, a bottle of Mumm's bubbly: **THESE FOOLISH THINGS** presents mementos that lead our thoughts back to the beloved; and with another glass of wine and a cigarette at hand, the telephone connects us as the evening winds down. With "Love (Your Spell Is Everywhere)," "Yearning," and "Oh, How I Miss You Tonight" playing in the background, bold yellow and pink pair with white against a pale turquoise background, embracing a whimsical yet urgent aesthetic for desire.

Volume 8, **A LAZY AFTERNOON**, with music by Malcolm Lockyer and His Orchestra, shows a young couple on a sunlit coast, lounging rather precariously along the rocky shore. They are alone. The man, turned away from the camera, gazes on his companion, perched upon a red blanket with white edges, arranged in a way that, from a distance, resembles Salvador Dalí's famous "Mae West Lips" sofa.[3] The eye certainly seems meant to focus on her, framed by the bright, almost erotic red—we don't see his face, and he sits on a carelessly bunched up non-descript striped towel or cotton blanket. She gazes intently at him, as she leans back and stretches out. Dreams seem to be a key topic for RCA's idea of lazy afternoons— the music includes "You Stepped out of a Dream," "Jeannine (I Dream of Lilac Time)," and "I'll See You in My Dreams." Perhaps the lull of the waves provides a ready rhythm for fantasy.

FIGURE 5.5

Hill Bowen and His Orchestra,
Love on Broadway,
RCA RAL 1005;
photo by David B. Hecht.

FIGURE 5.6

Don Amoré and His Orchestra,
Latin Holiday,
RCA RAL 1006;
photo by Ormond Gigli.

FIGURE 5.7

Jack Say and His Orchestra,
These Foolish Things,
RCA RAL 1007;
photo by Alan Fontaine.

FIGURE 5.8

Malcolm Lockyer and His Orchestra,
A Lazy Afternoon,
RCA RAL 1008;
photo by Renault/Strosahl.

VOL. 5 FOR HI-FI LIVING

LONG PLAY 33⅓ RPM   RAL 1005

RCA CUSTOM

A PRODUCT OF RADIO CORPORATION OF AMERICA

They Didn't Believe Me · My Ship · Wunderbar · Make Believe · Smoke Gets in Your Eyes
June is Bustin' Out All Over · Love Walked In · Some Enchanted Evening · The Night Was Made for Love
Orchids in the Moonlight · September Song · Falling in Love with Love

HILL BOWEN AND HIS ORCHESTRA

A "NEW ORTHOPHONIC" HIGH FIDELITY RECORDING

LOVE ON BROADWAY

VOL. 6 FOR HI-FI LIVING

LONG PLAY 33⅓ RPM   RAL 1006

RCA CUSTOM

A PRODUCT OF RADIO CORPORATION OF AMERICA

Amor · Cuanto Le Gusta · Lisbon Antigua · Brazil · Frenesi · Tico-Tico · Perfidia
El Cumbanchero · Sweet and Gentle · Besame Mucho · Adios · Green Eyes

DON AMORE AND HIS ORCHESTRA

A "NEW ORTHOPHONIC" HIGH FIDELITY RECORDING

LATIN HOLIDAY

VOL. 7 FOR HI-FI LIVING

LONG PLAY 33⅓ RPM   RAL 1007

RCA CUSTOM

A PRODUCT OF RADIO CORPORATION OF AMERICA

Love (Your Spell is Everywhere) · Yearning · Oh, How I Miss You Tonight · Music, Maestro, Please!
When You Wish Upon a Star · San Antonio Rose · These Foolish Things · Wabash Moon · When They Ask
About You · Lullaby of the Leaves · I'd Climb the Highest Mountain · With a Smile and a Song

JACK SAY AND HIS ORCHESTRA

A "NEW ORTHOPHONIC" HIGH FIDELITY RECORDING

These Foolish Things

VOL. 8 FOR HI-FI LIVING

LONG PLAY 33⅓ RPM   RAL 1008

RCA CUSTOM

A PRODUCT OF RADIO CORPORATION OF AMERICA

Deep Purple · You Stepped out of a Dream · In a Little Spanish Town · Don't Blame Me · Tune on My Hands
The Wedding of the Painted Doll · Let Me Love You To-night · I'm Always Chasing Rainbows
Jeannine (I Dream of Lilac Time) · At Sundown · I'll See You in My Dreams · Good Night Sweetheart

MALCOLM LOCKYER AND HIS ORCHESTRA

A "NEW ORTHOPHONIC" HIGH FIDELITY RECORDING

a lazy afternoon

THE GIRL THAT I MARRY features an out-of-focus branch of cherry blossoms over-laid with pink lettering against a pale pink background as an emotionally unreadable bride stands in profile, eyes turned down, seemingly unaware of the viewer. Perhaps more real, if still ethereal, than the angel on the pedestal, in this fantasy vision of traditional (nineteenth-century) attire, a young woman in a white wedding dress with satin bow shows off the now familiar pearls and gloves and a flower bouquet. Attached to a delicate decorated cap, a long lace veil flows down her back. The music of Irving Berlin proposes the perfect soundtrack to "Say It with Music."

FIGURE 5.9

Jack Say and His Orchestra,
The Girl That I Marry,
RCA RAL 1009;
photo by Murray Laden.

VOL. **9** FOR HI-FI LIVING

THE MUSIC OF IRVING BERLIN: Soft Lights and Sweet Music · Remember · Cheek to Cheek
How Deep is the Ocean · Say it Isn't So · Blue Skies · Say it With Music · Always · Lady of the Evening
The Girl That I Marry · A Pretty Girl is Like a Melody · All by Myself

JACK SAY AND HIS ORCHESTRA

LONG PLAY 33⅓ RPM

RAL 1009

RCA CUSTOM
A PRODUCT OF RADIO CORPORATION OF AMERICA

A "NEW ORTHOPHONIC" HIGH FIDELITY RECORDING

THE GIRL
THAT I
MARRY

Photo: MURRAY LADEN

© RCA Printed in U.S.A.

VERY HI-FI ORGAN, volume 10 in the series, features a close-up of an elaborate organ console, with several rows of keyboards, and dozens of stops. One side is blurred, lending some visual action to what might be a rather staid photographic subject. The central subject of the cover, however, is a young woman standing in front of the massive organ, her arms wide, smiling, looking off to her right. She is wearing pearls and a dotted pink cocktail dress drawn in by a form-fitting white belt. It does not look like her Sunday church dress, lest we think the album includes religious music for the organ. *Very Hi-Fi Organ* joins a veritable genre of midcentury LPs that showcase organ music, often dressed up with "cheesecake" covers of women sprawled out over the keys, replete with tenuous innuendos to "organs," "mighty sounds," and "power." (These include one of the first midcentury LPs in our collection, *Organ Moods*, by Jerry Thomas from 1961, on the Strand label.) Could the woman on this cover be Jocelyn McNeil, who is credited as the organ player? It seems that the music was actually recorded by organist George Wright, who enjoyed a prolific career, including a stint as the organist and composer for the long-running soap opera *General Hospital*. Mr. Wright, "a flamboyant performer who developed an easy rapport with his audiences,"[4] apparently recorded under several pseudonyms, including Jocelyn McNeil. So, although it may appear to the casual observer that the cover includes a picture of the recording artist, indeed this female model serves as "eye candy." In any case, the music within, mostly versions of standards such as "Stormy Weather" and "Star Dust," offers less gender intrigue and more of the usual "flamboyant" organ fare.

FIGURE 5.10

Jocelyn McNeil,
Very Hi-Fi Organ,
RCA RAL 1010;
photo by Irving Elkin
"at Radio City Music Hall."

VOL. **10** FOR HI-FI LIVING

Who's Sorry Now? · Sophisticated Lady · Pavanne · Star Dust · The Creole Love Call · Home
Blue Mirage · Jealous · I Got Rhythm · Emaline · Stormy Weather · The Dream of Olwen

JOCELYN McNEIL AT THE PIPE ORGAN

RAL 1010

LONG PLAY 33⅓ RPM

 CUSTOM

A PRODUCT OF RADIO CORPORATION OF AMERICA

A "NEW ORTHOPHONIC" HIGH FIDELITY RECORDING

VERY HI-FI ORGAN

photo: Irving Elkin at Radio City Music Hall

RCA Printed in U.S.A.

Nearing the end of this hi-fi journey, on **A TRIP TO ROMANCE**, the shiny Pullman car reflects the colorful signal lights and the oranges and pinks of our heroine's coat and flowers. The train car's open door welcomes in the touring couple, formally dressed from white gloves to necktie, luggage in hand. With a bon voyage bouquet, they smile and wave, acknowledging an audience of well-wishers that apparently have accompanied them to the train station. In this vision, others cheer on our lives' adventures, witnessing and confirming our consumption choices. Perhaps a change of scenery can refuel a relationship turned dreary, but moving beyond the comforts of home can be challenging as well, and songs such as "Love Me or Leave Me," "I Had the Craziest Dream," and "A Little Bit Independent" suggest some ambivalence and renegotiation of boundaries.

FIGURE 5.11

Tony Osborne and His Orchestra,
A Trip to Romance,
RCA RAL 1011;
photo by Howard Graff.

VOL. **11** FOR HI-FI LIVING

The Moon Was Yellow · The More I See You · Romance · You'll Never Know
Serenade in Blue · Holiday for Strings · Fools Rush In · Love Me or Leave Me · Our Waltz
Little White Lies · I Had the Craziest Dream · A Little Bit Independent

TONY OSBORNE AND HIS ORCHESTRA

LONG PLAY 33⅓ RPM

RAL 1011

 CUSTOM

A PRODUCT OF RADIO CORPORATION OF AMERICA

A "NEW ORTHOPHONIC" HIGH FIDELITY RECORDING

A
Trip
To
Romance

PULL

Photo: HOWARD GRAFF

The final volume in Music for Hi-Fi Living, **WE'RE HAVING A PARTY**, with more music by Malcolm Lockyer and His Orchestra, has an eye-catching photograph of the eponymous party, shot from overhead. Even adult parties imply celebratory decorations and dress. More to the point, they require music. Through colored crepe paper streamers and Japanese-style paper lantern lights, we peer down to see a smiling young woman surrounded by several men. She wears a light blouse, or perhaps a dress, while they all wear dark somber suits or sweaters. We glimpse her face, while the men remain more anonymous. She pops out of the frame, positioned dead center of the album cover. Upon inspection, the men seem awfully close, almost as if they are closing in on her. Perhaps this cover reveals more about parties and gender politics than is immediately apparent.

FIGURE 5.12

Malcolm Lockyer and His Orchestra,
We're Having a Party,
RCA RAL 1012;
photo by Ben Rose.

VOL.12 FOR HI-FI LIVING

I've Found a New Baby · Heartaches · (I Love You) For Sentimental Reasons · Under Paris Skies
Everybody Loves My Baby · Undecided · Little Girl · Tu Sais (You Know) · I'll Never Smile Again · The Petite
Waltz · Baby Won't You Please Come Home · Now is the Hour

MALCOLM LOCKYER AND HIS ORCHESTRA

RAL 1012

LONG PLAY 33⅓ RPM

 CUSTOM

A PRODUCT OF RADIO CORPORATION OF AMERICA

A "NEW ORTHOPHONIC" HIGH FIDELITY RECORDING

We're
having
a party

© RCA Printed in U.S.A.

Photo: Ben Rose

II AWAY

Many record companies' midcentury vinyl albums reflected the desire to travel and experience other countries and cultures, along with the rapidly expanding ability to join the jet age. In this section, we focus on records of faraway places: big cities and exotic islands, the ancestral homelands, and the varied sights, sounds and flavors of the globe. Just as "home" record albums guided postwar consumers in decorating a rec room or hosting a dinner party, "away" albums, focused on the world beyond home, and helped ready US consumers to take on the world. The accompanying LPs might offer music from the destination; less distinctive destination-themed music; or sounds of the destination, for example, recorded in streets and cafés, at festivals, or capturing well-known highlights of a destination, like the bells of Big Ben or trains in Tokyo. These travel albums acted like tourist brochures—a stop in Salzburg serves up elegant waltzes and crisp white wine; the steel drum beach party on Jamaican sands captures the rum-soaked limbo and ocean breezes.

"Away" albums typically encouraged stylish voyages and many celebrated air travel as new levels of consumer choice were mapped onto the globe. These travel record covers are iconic, often featuring the great cultural and architectural sites that are part of any respectable world tour—Cairo's pyramids, Rome's Colosseum, Cuba's Havana Hilton—preferably with photogenic females offering trays of honeyed pastries or seductively serving plates of pasta or bottles of rum. On the Asian front, legendary geishas bow in full regalia and sailboats ply the waters along the Kowloon peninsula. As the stars of Hawaii and Alaska were making their way onto the flag and into the consciousness of US mainlanders, these far-flung locations also found representation through album covers, liner notes, and the music itself.

Travel albums abound with informative, even instructional, liner notes, beautiful Kodachrome cover photos, and international itineraries that include continental Europe, the British Isles, Asia, Africa, and the Caribbean. Often released by airlines or travel companies, many feature destination-tinged easy listening. In some cases, travel albums were created to align with another promotional event, such as the launch of a new cruise-line itinerary or airline route.[1] Verve and *Esquire* magazine paired to create a Sound Tour series of LPs. At Capitol, *Holiday* magazine had agreed to allow relevant text from back issues to be included in album liner notes.[2]

These records nourished the modern travel industry, opening up American eyes, ears, and wallets to faraway lands. They were also part of a post–World War II push to reintegrate Europe with the United States. The Hollywood film industry began shipping hundreds of films into European markets after the war's end and the repeal of the fascist monopoly law. In turn, the recording industry, concentrating on the American market, brought global culture to the homeland. At the same time that the Marshall plan was rebuilding Europe, travel records introduced millions of Americans to continental charms.[3] Thanks to regular international jet service and high fidelity stereo, everyone might tell the Tower of London from the Eiffel Tower and the Eternal City from the Forbidden City.

During the 1950s and 1960s, a "new mode of consumption was emerging, based on the idea of leaving home and work in search of new experiences, pleasures, and leisure."[4] Travel suspends some of the rules and habits that govern behavior, and substitutes different norms and customs, in particular those that are appropriate to being in the company of strangers. Traveling can lead to new and exciting forms of play, inquisitiveness, and gregariousness that home or work lacks. And, the call to leave home entails some guidance. Profiles of top destinations in newspapers, magazines, and travel albums offered to help: "By transforming multifaceted nations, regions, and cities into vacationlands, destination profiles acted as a type of geographic pedagogy."[5] The arts, leisure, and tourism industries all played important roles in the cultural transformation of places into consumption sites.

As anthropologist Orvar Löfgren points out, vacationing and travel require certain skills, an odd paradox of working at leisure: "vacationlands may appear like territories of freedom, freedom from work, worries, rules, and regulations. But behind this carefree façade there are many unwritten rules … and into each new vacationscape we bring expectations and anticipations as well as stable routines and habits."[6] Records came to the rescue, as it was particularly common for LP liner notes focused on faraway places, to become opportunities to teach consumers these and other kinds of lessons.

The series put out by Capitol Records called Capitol of the World included recordings from such far flung locations as Finland, Australia, and Lebanon. Holiday Abroad albums sponsored by Sabena Airlines featured painted cover images of the same youthful couple (sporting a tiny Sabena flight bag) engaged in an iconic touring moment. Vox Records distributed the Cook's Tour series in collaboration with Cook's Travel Service that included a stop in Cuba. In 1958, to celebrate the tenth anniversary of the long-playing record, Columbia introduced its Adventures in Sound series, which sought out interesting sites and captured musical performances from around the globe. (We've spotted a few recent re-releases of this classic series.) This genre prefigured "world music" by decades. Here we explore more closely several voyages in vinyl.

6

AIRLINES

Often sponsored by the airlines and travel magazines, vinyl albums in the "away" genre embraced and encouraged the rise of air travel in midcentury America. Not surprisingly, travel-themed album covers often featured airplanes as striking visual elements emblazoned with eye-catching logos, as the airlines' own promotional graphics entered the picture. With the design of a plane's interior space crucial to enticing customers, and airline personnel's needs to communicate aspects of an airline's brand, over the decades the airlines turned to fashion designers and artists for assistance. For example, Braniff International Airways brought in famed Italian fashion designer Emilio Pucci to revamp stewardess uniforms; industrial and interior designer Alexander Girard to create new color schemes;[1] and, later, artist Alexander Calder to "paint a jet."[2]

The "jet set" still suggests the group that moves faster, and with more glamour, than the average person; and these albums embody jet-age affluence, confidence, and optimism that typified US consumer identity in the postwar economy. The mix of cutting-edge technology, style engineering, and romantic imaginings represented airline travel as an aspirational, but attainable, fantasy. Indeed, airlines provided a growing segment of the US population with access to faraway places once available only to those with vast stretches of leisure time and vaster fortunes—particularly after Pan Am launched its passenger jet New York–London route in 1958.

That same year, RCA Victor released their Holiday Abroad LPs, "recorded in Europe by leading continental orchestras" and featuring "musical trips to cities serviced by Sabena, Belgian World Airlines." RCA invited dealers "all aboard for high-flying profits," and promised ads in *Holiday*, the *New York Times*, and the *New Yorker* to promote the series, as well as a "national disk-jockey promotion and contest, featuring 18 overseas trips as prizes."[3] Each title showcased a different orchestra, with watercolors by Pittsburgh-born African American artist Mozelle Thompson, who designed dozens of covers for RCA, as well as Broadway posters and children's books.[4]

ALBUMS

EUROPEAN HOLIDAY with Mitch Miller and His Orchestra offers a glimpse into the cross-promotional agenda of "travel" records. The bright, full-color photograph shows a Scandinavian Airline System (SAS) Royal Viking jet, with the coats of arms of Denmark, Norway, and Sweden emblazoned on the fuselage, waiting on airport tarmac while a group of well-dressed travelers climb aboard, the last chatting with the pilot. As they walk on a red carpet toward the plane, they pass an SAS sign that advertises "Extra City Trips to," a roster of European routes—Scandinavia to Rome, Venice to Nice, and Geneva to Madrid. Miller, chief of Columbia's Artists and Repertoire at the time, the "bearded wonder of the record business," would enjoy great success with a succession of Sing Along with Mitch LPs, tied in with his television show of the same name. On the cover of the 10″ LP, he's directing a multicultural band, with musicians dressed in traditional and ceremonial "European" regalia, including an English beefeater on trombone, a Flamenco guitarist, and a German (or Swiss?) tuba player. In the foreground, a couple sits in their own living room, as if receiving a private concert from Miller and company (compliments of this LP), and planning their journey. Scandinavian modern table and chair, numerous tourist brochures, and a portable record player surround them. A "sophisticated" ensemble—bowl of fruit, cup of espresso, and small bull sculpture seem to stand in for the little luxuries that await them on their European holiday. The notes tell an amusing story of "two young travellers" on their extensive trip to Europe, including stops at Loch Lomond, London, Paris, the Alps, Rome, and, of course, Scandinavia.

FIGURE 6.1

Mitch Miller and His Orchestra,
European Holiday,
Columbia CL 2586.

CL 2586

EUROPEAN HOLIDAY

SAS

MITCH MILLER AND HIS ORCHESTRA

JILL COREY, JERRY VALE, and the MICHAEL STEWART CHORUS

Side one opens with a song "Flyin' Up to Europe," and continues with spoken words interspersed with Broadway-style numbers, including one about a helpful travel agent, "Dealer in Dreams," sung by Jerry Vale. The LP's songs and conversational interludes earnestly explain the process of buying an SAS ticket and answer the couple's spoken concerns and questions. Jill Corey sings "Trip of Your Dreams," and we hear boarding announcements and the steward's listing of the cocktails and gourmet food available in flight. Once in Europe, the amusingly accented guides greet the couple, encourage yodeling in Switzerland, and mention the modern design of Scandinavia. The couple can't help but sing of their deepened love for each other on "Entre Nous" and recommend the trip to their family upon their return to the United States. On side two, Miller conducts a set of French songs, including "Autumn Leaves," a "sadly romantic song that only the French can write." The packaging included a copious four-page insert, "Voilà! ... vous êtes en Europe! ... (There you go! ... you are in Europe!)," with brief notes about how to travel to Europe, what to see, and how to get a passport, along with information about customs, provided by the Travel Counselling Service of SAS. In addition, the insert lists other Columbia LPs, including *French for Travel*, *Dinner at Maxim's*, and *April in Paris*.

A MUSICAL TRIP 'ROUND THE WORLD, 'ROUND THE CLOCK VIA PAN AMERICAN was released in the unusual 16⅔ rpm format, which the Vox label extolled as "an opportunity to give the music lover more for his money," as the slower speed meant longer records. The format, used primarily for early versions of audio books for the blind, never caught on for mainstream releases.[5] Described on the liner notes as

FIGURE 6.2

*A Musical Trip 'Round the World,
'Round the Clock via Pan American*,
Vox Records VSL 4.

'ROUND THE WORLD

'ROUND THE CLOCK

a

musical

trip

X 16 RPM
-4
VOX

VIA PAN AMERICAN
WORLD'S MOST EXPERIENCED AIRLINE

"the first classical record to contain up to two hours of music," the LP offers an international selection of tunes, from Austria's "Deutschmeister March," to Cuba's "Bayame La Jaula." The notes dwell on the issue of speed: "as the speed of transportation speeds up, the speed of recordings slow down," and suggest that it would be "fun to take a nice slow trip lasting the time honored eighty days … on a lively, luxurious *Pan-American Clipper*." The LP, "a musical Baedeker," closes with some numbers from the United States. After returning home, the listener can "turn on your Hi-Fi set and enjoy a few American favorites before falling off to sleep."

....

The tail of a blue, gold and silver plane from Panagra Airways—a cooperation between Pan Am and Grace Shipping that flew the West coast of South America—forms the backdrop to a uniformed captain and a color coordinated passenger as they start down an aircraft stairway, perhaps, to love. Notes on **FLIGHT TO ROMANCE** linger over the exotic flight path view: the Colombian plains, the jungle areas of El Chaco, the Amazon, and "as though presiding over all this mysterious greatness, the lofty Aconcagua, highest peak of the Andean range." This inspired co-branding of South American airline, Venezuelan musician Aldemaro Romero, and musical numbers "characteristic" of Chile, Bolivia, and Ecuador offers an enticement to a rarely featured part of the globe (at least on US record industry releases).

FIGURE 6.3

Aldemaro Romero and His Salon Orchestra,
Flight to Romance,
RCA Victor LPM-1209;
photo by Hal Rieff.

The warmer climes produced many travel record classics linked to tourist transportation, including **A VISIT TO HAWAII**, "recorded in Hawaii." On the back cover, a Matson Line cruise ship plies the Pacific. On the front cover, "natives" dressed in bright yellow, green, and red "traditional" garb greet, with kisses and leis, a tour group posed in front of a Pan Am jet: the arriving men have one arm around their wives and the other around a barefoot hula girl. Each "stop" on the Hawaiian tour coincides with a song, in workable, if uninspired renditions. The first stop, the Shell Bar at the Hawaiian Village, "site of TV's *Hawaiian Eye*," is paired with the song, "Hiilawe"; the next stop, "the world famous Royal Hawaiian Hotel where Charles Kaipo is featured in the Monarch Room" features "Kalua"; later, for sitting on Waikiki Beach, there's "Little Brown Gal"; the evening luau includes the "Hawaiian Wedding Song"; and a sad farewell inspires the wavering strains of "Aloha Oe." This record echoes hundreds of similar albums, featuring "native girls" promoting packaged paradise.

FIGURE 6.4

A Visit to Hawaii,
Mahalo M-4007;
photo courtesy Pan American.

A VISIT TO Hawaii

PAN AM

M-4007

 LP MAHALO
RECORDED IN HAWAII

Back on the mainland, IT'S ALASKA—originally conceived as a "Broadway-type musical production" that offered a visit to Alaska as "a simulated tour through song, dance, and film"—presents a little-known genre, records of the forty-ninth state. Hawaii sparked thousands of albums, while the *other* new state seemed to lack the right blend of warm weather, near-nudity, sensual fauna, and tropical intrigue to fire the imagination of the record industry. *It's Alaska* is an exception: with a flaming fuchsia cover, furry husky dog, native crafts, and a come hither girl with bare legs in fur jacket and mukluks draped over a grizzly bear rug.

The songs speak directly to a destination and travel experience as imagined by the creative team at Alaska Airlines who worked to promote tourism to Alaska, drawing at least initially upon notions of Alaska as wilderness, the gold rush state, and suggesting a "Gay '90s" atmosphere of saloons and honky-tonk piano. "Come on up to Alaska, USA" has a show tune spirit, and welcomes the northbound passenger with the whine of airplane engines. Strains of the "Walrus skin drum" and an "Eskimo whale hunting" chant remind the modern adventurer that cultural and geographical wilds await. The instructional nature of this LP continues with "Call the Milkman," a waltzy number that provides help in finalizing the to-do list before departure: "don't forget to stop the paper!"

The hearty souls of the final frontier gather at the "Golden Nugget Saloon." Clinky-piano nostalgia accompanies the tale of "Nel" as she moves from San Francisco to Seattle and just keeps going north. Signaling the make-a-new-start and do-it-yourself vision of Alaska, Nel moves into the saloon and becomes the town madam. An earnest, mellow-dramatic voice-over tells the listener of how the "very

FIGURE 6.5

Elizabeth Firestone Willis,
It's Alaska,
featuring Harry Simeone Chorale,
RCA Custom ALS 0656.

IT'S ALASKA

FEATURING
HARRY SIMEONE CHORALE
MUSIC COMPOSED BY
ELIZABETH FIRESTONE WILLIS

last American frontier" brimming with "pioneer spirit" and the occasional drumming and chanting of anonymous natives, was sold to America "for cash" by exploring Russians who built the "towns of yesteryear." Musician and philanthropist Elizabeth Firestone Willis, who at the time was the wife of the president of Alaska Airlines, composed the music. She was a Firestone Tire and Rubber Company heiress creating an interesting cross-promotion of rubber tires and airline travel. (Her sister, Martha Firestone, married William Clay Ford, grandson of Henry Ford). Alas, *It's Alaska* appears to be one of the only recordings of her compositions.

Mozelle Thompson's illustration for the cover of **HOLIDAY ABROAD IN DUBLIN** pictures a touring redhead with blond beau in tie and boating blazer peddling on a bicycle built for two—umbrella and tiny Sabena bag in tow—gliding alongside the River Liffey across from the Four Courts at Inns Quay, with the arches of O'Donovan Rossa Bridge in the background. The Dublin locals watch, momentarily intrigued. As for the music, occasionally a simple flute melody leads for a few bars before being interrupted by syrupy strings and sentimental accordion; and the all-purpose European symphonic sound overtakes the single burst of serious fiddling in "Irish Washerwoman." "Kerry Dance" almost survives with Celtic dignity intact against less successful renderings of "Rose of Tralee," "Londonderry Air," and a winds-only version of "Wearing of the Green." A few paragraphs from *Richard Joseph's Jet Guide to Europe* draw upon shared music to bridge any distance between the United States and Ireland and provide a wee introduction to traveling the country: "You'll

FIGURE 6.6

Reg Owen and His Orchestra,
Holiday Abroad in Dublin,
RCA Victor LPM-1597;
cover illustration by Mozelle Thompson.

HOLIDAY ABROAD° in **DUBLIN**
REG OWEN and His Orchestra

RCA VICTOR
LPM-1597
A "New Orthophonic" High Fidelity Recording

DUBLIN
LONDON
PARIS
VIENNA
LISBON
ROME

INSPIRED BY **SABENA** BELGIAN *World* AIRLINES "HOLIDAY ABROAD"

mogelle thompson

®RCA Printed in U.S.A.

hear these melodies all over Ireland; at the Shelbourne or the Gresham Bar during the famed Royal Dublin Horse Show in August, in country pubs from County Cork to Donegal, and in thousands of Irish homes when the welcome mat is out every year for the *An Tostal*, or 'Ireland at Home' celebration in late spring when Ireland becomes the land of *Cead Mile Failte*—a hundred thousand welcomes."

....

Our redhead in pink ball gown and white gloves, stood on a horse-drawn carriage near the Colosseum, throws open her arms to the eternal city, as her beau with Sabena bag and cast off umbrella attempts to capture a photo as they continue their **HOLIDAY ABROAD IN ROME**. The carriage driver looks on and two dark-haired *ragazzi* stand by, one staring directly at the viewer, creating some good-natured uncertainty about the free-spirited foreigner's behavior. Sam Boal, a contributor to *Holiday* magazine writes: "Let us, for these purposes, consider the sounds of Rome. They are manifold. Yet, perhaps above all else, there is the sound of the *fontane*—the incredible, endlessly bubbling, restlessly sparkling fountains." The standard instrumentals of strings, accordion, and occasional electric guitar on numbers like "Chella lla!," "O Sole Mio," and "Funiculi Funicula" tend to be more driving than sparkling, more energetic than romantic.

FIGURE 6.7

Carlo Savina and His Orchestra,
Holiday Abroad in Rome,
RCA Victor LPM-1595;
cover illustration by Mozelle Thompson.

HOLIDAY ABROAD* in ROME

CARLO SAVINA and His Orchestra

RCA VICTOR
LPM-1595
A "New Orthophonic" High Fidelity Recording

INSPIRED BY **SABENA** BELGIAN *World* AIRLINES "HOLIDAY ABROAD"

mozelle thompson

© RCA Printed in U.S.A.

The now familiar couple continue their travels with **HOLIDAY ABROAD IN PARIS**, as the young woman in yellow ball gown, white gloves, and red shoes gazes dreamily over her drink as her beau negotiates with a flower seller who has approached their outdoor café table. The blue Sabena bag sits unattended near her feet. The red, yellow, and green awning above them provides swaths of bright color; and a lightly sketched in Eiffel Tower emerges from behind a poster covered kiosk and leafy green branches. In the liner notes, Richard Gehman, a writer and biographer of some renown in the 1950s and 1960s, as well as an early contributing editor at *Playboy*, writes of Paris: "The first time I saw Paris, I saw her all at once from the cockpit of an aircraft. … For the first week, I lived a strange life—walking everywhere, exploring, then rushing back to my hotel to put it all down before I forgot it. Then I did not know that it is not necessary to write about Paris: one simply lives there, and the memories become part of one's personality." He continues, "in the evenings I went to the clubs, where there was more music—gypsy music sometimes, jazz other times and always the lilting French pop tunes that somehow seem more danceable than those we hear in the States." He turns his attention to the songs, "This music of Pierre Sommers' orchestra has captured the feeling of Paris beautifully. All I need to do is close my eyes and listen—and again I am in Les Halles, or the cafés, or the nightclubs. This is truly music for one who treasures recollections of a first, or second or, for that matter, sixteenth visit to Paris." There is an attractive leisureliness of strings on "La Vie en rose," but it would be difficult to distinguish the sounds of "Sous le ciel de Paris" from something on the companion *Holiday in Rome* LP.

FIGURE 6.8

Pierre Sommers and His Orchestra,
Holiday Abroad in Paris,
RCA Victor LPM-1600;
cover illustration by Mozelle Thompson.

HOLIDAY ABROAD in PARIS

PIERRE SOMMERS and His Orchestra

RCA VICTOR LPM-1600

A "New Orthophonic" High Fidelity Recording

INSPIRED BY SABENA BELGIAN *World* AIRLINES "HOLIDAY ABROAD"

© RCA Printed in U.S.A.

On **HOLIDAY ABROAD IN LONDON**, the Tower Bridge looms in moody greys over the Thames as men in bowler hats stroll along the river. The now familiar young couple endeavor to find their destination—he wrangling an immense red map with camera and Sabena bag hanging from his arm, and she attempting with white gloved hand to point out their goal. Presenting what might suggest the comings and goings of an American at home abroad, the notes, again by Richard Gehman, offer a list of favorite London experiences. He writes: "I love to stand around in a pub like the White Bear and watch the dim light reflected in the burnished woodwork. … I love the demonstrations and mass meetings in Trafalgar Square. … I love to go into Grafton Street and spend a long time with Mr. Dingle of F. Tautz deciding what material he will use for my next suit. … I love to ride on the top deck of the double-decker buses. … I love the book shops and the newsstands." This is not the London of a novice tourist, planning a visit from the travel magazine's "destination profile" and ticking off key sights: this is aspirational London, where you pop in to see your tailor when in town, drop in on your local pub, and stroll through your favorite back streets. Experiencing the wonders of cities in faraway places may take time, the LP seems to suggest, but such familiarity is open to all of us: We just need to return again and again.

FIGURE 6.9

Reg Owen and His Orchestra,
Holiday Abroad in London,
RCA Victor LPM-1599;
cover illustration by Mozelle Thompson.

George Wright takes a **FLIGHT TO TOKYO**, and his "5 manual" Wurlitzer theater pipe organ in a golden shipping case—oddly echoing kabuki aesthetics—has flown along with him. He's accompanied as well "by a Japanese cutie to act as his guide." Bright orange and yellow Japanese characters boldly overwrite the cover photo, which is dominated by the blue and white Pan Am jet; and a man, apparently Mr. Wright, in a rumpled beige trench coat stands next to a young woman in a red kimono. "Just twenty-two flying hours are between the U.S.A. west coast and Tokyo, dreamland of most American tourists," the notes proclaim; but whether Tokyo was a true 1958 US tourist "dreamland" or not, this album provided an "imaginative musical excursion" enabled by the multi-pedaled, stopped, and keyed Wurlitzer with which "George has invented new Oriental sounds of Tokyo with a few other startling ear ticklers thrown in just for fun." Most songs have some charming Japanese connection, such as, "Poor Butterfly," "Rickety Rickshaw Man," and "Kyoto Beguine," although "Nagasaki" might provide less than pleasant reflections. Authenticity is not the point here; however, the engineering and recording process receive detailed description, and "the final pressings are of pure virgin vinyl." Filling much of the back cover, in tiny print, are the "specifications of a Special 5 Manual Wurlitzer Pipe Organ originally installed 1931 in the 4,000 seat Paradise Theater, Chicago," along with a small pen and ink drawing of a human figure who wears a kimono and *geta* sandals, and—holding a *koinobori*, or carp windsock—leans against a photo of the complex-looking instrument.

FIGURE 6.10

George Wright,
Flight to Tokyo,
High Fidelity Recordings R 717.

GEORGE WRIGHT

RECORD
HIGH FIDELITY RECORDINGS, INC.

N90948

東京
ジョージライ

FLIGHT TO *TOKYO

JAZZ IMPRESSIONS OF EURASIA finds Dave Brubeck hefting several bright blue Pan Am tote bags with the help of two women in traditional saris, one of whom has placed a jeweled turban on the jazz master's head. They are all in front of a Pan Am jet, bags brimming with souvenirs—textiles, brass pitchers, and what looks like a small statue of Saraswati, the Hindu goddess of knowledge, arts, and music. The liner notes inform us that Brubeck did indeed tour through Eurasia, including Turkey, Iran, Iraq, India, Pakistan, Afghanistan, and Ceylon, in 1958, and Brubeck's huge hit, "Take Five," was famously influenced by Turkish folk music. Brubeck's tour was part of a US State Department sponsored cultural program that promoted jazz as an American art form, sending such greats as Count Basie, Dizzy Gillespie, Duke Ellington, and Louis Armstrong on international tours. The US state department tour made Brubeck "a spokesperson for values that, for him, were heartfelt—most importantly, the love of jazz, the love of liberty, and the belief that the two were intertwined."[6] As recounted on a current State Department website: "Through the power of jazz, these artists were able to transcend national boundaries, build bridges and tell a larger story about freedom in America."[7] As for the music, Brubeck explains, "these sketches of Eurasia have been developed from random musical phrases I jotted down in my notebook as we chugged across the fields of Europe, or skimmed across the deserts of Asia, or walked in the winding alleyways of an ancient bazaar." He fondly recalls his experience in India, playing with Indian musicians: "we all felt that given a few more days, we would either be playing Indian music, or they would be playing jazz." Brubeck, who had released *Jazz Impressions of the U.S.A.* prior to *Jazz Impressions of Eurasia*, went on to record the well-received *Jazz Impressions of Japan* and *Jazz Impressions of New York* in 1964.

FIGURE 6.11

The Dave Brubeck Quartet,
Jazz Impressions of Eurasia,
Columbia CS 8058;
photo by Bob Willoughby;
models courtesy of Government of India
Tourist Office, San Francisco.

CS 8058

STEREO FIDELITY

COLUMBIA
GUARANTEED HIGH FIDELITY

lp

Jazz Impressions of Eurasia
THE DAVE BRUBECK QUARTET

MODELS COURTESY OF GOVERNMENT OF INDIA TOURIST OFFICE, SAN FRANCISCO

PHOTOGRAPH: BOB WILLOUGHBY

Ramsey Lewis holds a tall straw hat and a model-size Pan American jet on the cover of his GOIN' LATIN LP. Dressed in black suit, tie, and his trademark glasses, and flanked by the album title in decorated typography, he poses in front of a "Jet 'Round South America" Pan Am Panagra travel poster that features an authentic-looking gaucho. Released shortly after Lewis's breakthrough hits "The In Crowd," "Hang On Sloopy," and "Wade in the Water," *Goin' Latin* features jazz stylings of contemporary hits like "Summer Samba," "One, Two, Three," and "Cast Your Fate to the Winds" and "original compositions with a soulful south of the border beat." Cleveland Eaton on bass and Maurice White on drums join Lewis on piano. Although the Latin aspect of the album remains rather downplayed, the selections sparkle with arrangements by Richard Evans and demonstrate Lewis's crossover appeal.

FIGURE 6.12

Ramsey Lewis,
Goin' Latin,
Cadet LPS 790.

JET 'ROUND South America

GOIN' LATIN

RAMSEY LEWIS

ARRANGED AND CONDUCTED BY RICHARD EVANS

CADET RECORDS

CAST YOUR FATE TO THE WINDS • SPANISH GREASE • ONE, TWO, THREE

I'LL WAIT FOR YOU • BLUE BONGO • FUNCTION AT THE JUNCTION

DOWN BY THE RIVERSIDE • SUMMER SAMBA • HEY, MRS. JONES

LARA'S THEME • FREE AGAIN

PAN AM

PAN AMERICAN

PAN AM

7

HONEYMOON

Honeymoons provide a key motivation for travel. Moving beyond the borders of home, newly married couples set out on a trip immediately following their wedding. These "honeymoon" albums create a sense of romance in the ruins of Rome, the cafés of Paris, and the palm lined beaches of Hawaii. They also narrate a consumption ritual that carries the couple into adulthood and imbues them with the air of the sophisticated traveler.

Though stretching back to earlier eras in the form of various rituals and customs, the honeymoon took its modern form, including the "wedding trip" for the just-married couple alone, in the 1860s and 1870s. This private excursion evolved earlier for more affluent couples, who also were more likely to take their honeymoon abroad.[1] Honeymoon packages, honeymoon resorts, and honeymoon getaways urged newlyweds away from previous eras' visits with family and friends, as a convention emerged that stressed "the importance of the honeymoon as a transitional event where the couple was expected to engage in intimate disclosure and develop a sense of mutual fulfillment."[2] Honeymoon travel afforded a chance to learn and experience new things together and to create memories and dreams to be shared in the future. In some cases, all-inclusive honeymoon resorts provided for everything, freeing the couple to focus on themselves and their new relationship.[3]

Often in tropical environments like Hawaii there was a chance to take on the carefree "aloha spirit" and tap into the inner native "other," if only for the honeymoon.

Stereotypically pale, restrained mainlanders could gain access—in a safe, controlled way—to desirable, "primitive," and "exotic" traits. Many honeymoon album covers illustrate this theme, as the new bride adopts the "local" look, posing in the palms, native cloth tied around her hips, flower behind her ear, left hand prominently displaying her wedding band: "She becomes 'Hawaiian' easily, for this transformation translates into exotic native guilt-free sexuality and a sensual playfulness for her and her new husband. Let's take off our clothes! Let's frolic in the waterfall! What a great place for a honeymoon!"[4]

From the beach walks in Hawaii, to the urbane pleasures of New York City and the fairytale castles of Europe, the honeymoon got people out of the house and into motion, whether by car, train, or plane, to experiment with the wider world. Many American couples hold strong beliefs about the magical properties of a honeymoon, and nurture "the expectation that at some point in their marriage they will have that highly desirable experience and that it will meet the many dreams and fantasies they share regarding intimacy, the exotic, and the romantic."[5] These LPs reflect honeymoon dreams and fantasies, at the same time they promote air travel to European, tropical, and cosmopolitan destinations.

ALBUMS

On <u>**HONEYMOON IN SOUTH AMERICA**</u>, against a purple background, the outlines of two maracas form discrete frames for long shot portraits. One presents a light-skinned couple standing face to face beneath the palms on a hotel-lined white-sand beach. In the other, a "native" pair in straw hats appears on a less developed oceanfront that is backed by a muddy canal. (Film developed for photographing white skin often fails to capture dark-skinned features, and here facial details are utterly absent.[6]) A man kneels down on one knee while another person, whose sex is indiscernible despite an apparently feminine leg bend, plays a small guitar. Although potentially the scene of a romantic song, or a marriage proposal, the music on the album seems an unlikely serenade for this couple's honeymoon. "Turn on your phonograph and say adios to your troubles—we're going on a honeymoon in South America" explain the notes. Tangos, sambas, and cha-chas "make the old young again, and the young warm and excited," explaining the connection to honeymoon moods.

FIGURE 7.1

The Rio Carnival Orchestra,
Honeymoon in South America,
Stereo-Fidelity SF 1900;
cover art by Joe Krush.

HONEYMOON in SOUTH AMERICA

THE RIO CARNIVAL ORCHESTRA

On the cover of **HONEYMOON IN MEXICO**, one of the first albums in the Capitol of the World series, cocktails, a camera, and three serenading mariachi musicians foster a feeling of leisure and foreignness around a couple lingering at an outdoor café table. The gray-green tinted photo, courtesy of the Mexican Government Tourist Bureau, along with white, red, and black lettering, does little to evoke the "bouquet of the multicolored begonias" or a romantic atmosphere of old Mexico; it does however provide contrasting skin tones between the newlyweds and the guitar-playing "natives." The woman, pale, but with dark lips, her blond hair pulled back, displays a prominent wedding ring and a wide smile. "Countless thousands of hand-holding honeymooners" walk a well-trodden tourist path through Mexico City to the strains of songs such as "Las Mañanitas": "at convenient Chapultepec Park and Castle, amid the fountains and flowers of Alameda Park, in the far-famed and lovely floating gardens of Suburban Xochimilco and farther out at the inspiring Temple of Quetzalcoatl." Although "Las Mañanitas" is often sung for birthdays, waking a loved one who has yet to greet the day—"the birds are singing, the moon is down"—the song touches a romantic note, reminiscent of "The Nightingale" in *The Decameron*. Musician Pepe Villa's "records are popular with Mexicans in all parts of the country," claim the liner notes, but now Capitol of the World "makes it possible for the distinctive flavor of music played by his orchestra, El Mariachi Mexico, to be enjoyed north of the border as well." Although recognizing that the packaging leans toward "Northern buyers," a reviewer for *Billboard* assumes that interest in this music will be greatest in areas of the country where "the population is closer to the culture of this music."[7] Side one contains only instrumentals; but side two features vocals. One can almost imagine putting together the Mexican fiesta equivalent of a tiki party.

FIGURE 7.2

Pepe Villa and El Mariachi Mexico,
Honeymoon in Mexico,
Capitol T 10001.

HIGH FIDELITY

RECORDED IN MEXICO CITY

Honeymoon in Mexico

Pepe Villa and El Mariachi Mexico

"The rare beauty that Gauguin found in painting Tahiti is now discernible to the ear," gushes the notes for **SOUTH SEAS HONEYMOON**. The cover features a silver and blue Pan American Airways Clipper Ocean Rover framed by palm fronds, and the friendly pilot leans out and waves from the cockpit window. From a time when formal travel attire helped keep class visible at 35,000 feet, both members of the wedded white couple wear suits, he with a black tie, she with heels, white gloves and small hat. The transition to carefree sensual newlywed native has begun, however, as flower leis bedeck the new bride in a blaze of orange that emphasizes her jacket's puritanical tone. Tanned skin, barefoot natives in bright cloth hold out more blossoms to the newly married husband, welcoming him to paradise. The music "in all its authentic and blatantly sexy glory" features a host of Tahitian singers and instruments recorded in the presence of a dozen native dancers assembled to insure "the proper, most authentic Polynesian tempos—and enthusiasm." And although the era is over "when a man could ship off to Papeete and spend the rest of his days as a beachcomber, surrounded by beauteous, mauve-skin maidens," this LP, a souvenir of a fantasy abroad, communicates the violet sand beaches and greenest coconut trees of French Oceania, offering musically "an atmosphere immensely conducive to romance." The sound is typical easy listening, with vague auditory references to the tropical locale.

FIGURE 7.3

Voices of the Atolls/Zizou Bar Trio,
South Seas Honeymoon,
Capitol T 10080.

Red heels and a red flower lei mark the spot she cast off the excess trappings of a **HONEYMOON IN HAWAII** to feel the sand between her toes, as he guides her toward a new horizon. Following their footprints down the beach, we glimpse the couple, almost out of sight, as they embrace. They are alone together, in nature, in the tropics—key honeymoon ingredients. The notes inform us that the featured musicians, the Hilo Hawaiians, toured Europe in 1956, proving music's "international bond," especially "while entertaining a packed auditorium of escapees from Iron Curtain countries such as Hungary, Czechoslovakia, Poland, Bulgaria, and Russia." The band performs a number of the LP's songs in the Hawaiian language.

FIGURE 7.4

Hilo Hawaiians,
Honeymoon in Hawaii,
Concert-Disc Records M-1046.

HONEYMOON in HAWAII

HAWAIIAN WEDDING SONG

HAWAII CALLS

HAOLE HULA

ENCHANTED ISLES

NANI WAIALEALE

and many others

HILO HAWAIIANS

M-1046 **CONCERT-DISC** *Balanced Acoustic*

Near the attractions of the Arc de Triomphe, which appears in the distance, a young couple outlined with a white heart stroll by Fouquets, the iconic brasserie with red-awning at 99 Avenue des Champs-Elysées on the cover photograph of **HONEYMOON IN PARIS**. These stars of new love seem to be a main attraction for the newspaper reading, drink sipping patrons in the typically French street-facing wicker café chairs. This intersection with Avenue George V was the former location of the Trans World Airlines office (now a Louis Vuitton store), and one can just make out the airline's signs with a French and US flag flying on either side of the palatial entrance. One hopes that the honeymoon couple flew TWA. "Come join us as we take a night walk along the Seine or linger over a bottle of *vin ordinaire* in a Montmartre café, The Paris Theatre Orchestra is taking a trip to a *Honeymoon in Paris*." Songs such as "Sur Le Pont De Paris," "Champs Elysee Café" and "Pavement Pigalle" create musical maps of this "city for people in love."

FIGURE 7.5

The Paris Theatre Orchestra,
Honeymoon in Paris,
Stereo-Fidelity SF 2500;
cover art by Joe Krush.

HONEYMOON in PARIS

the Paris Theatre Orchestra

All song titles are in *Italiano* on Capitol of the World's **HONEYMOON IN ROME**, with words and phrases such as *ascoltate* and *buon divertimento* sprinkled into the liner notes. Rome is romantic, the notes say, Romans love love, and the entire population is either passionately in love or seeking love. Rome, which provides "a rich physical setting for love," talks love; and in an amusing comparison, Detroit, it is said, with a similar number of possible lovers, "talks automobiles." Courtesy of Pan American World Airways, the cover photo focuses on a romantic couple seated at a simple café in an improbable location next to the Coliseum tended by a waiter dressed in white jacket and black bow tie. Although the two men at a background table reflect less romance, the couple appears lost in their honeymoon experience, together in a famous, foreign locale, enjoying new culinary, historical, and interpersonal encounters.

FIGURE 7.6

Renato Carosone,
His Piano and Quartetto,
Honeymoon in Rome,
Capitol T 10031;
photo courtesy of Pan Am
World Airways.

RECORDED IN ITALY
Capitol RECORDS
HIGH FIDELITY
Honeymoon in Rome
RENATO CAROSONE his piano and quartetto

"No place is more romantic, more leisurely pleasant, than Lisbon," we are told, and the conclusion of World War II marked an opening for misty-eyed lovers and other visitors to answer the city's call. **HONEYMOON IN PORTUGAL**, from Capitol of the World, presents authentic music from the Trio Odemira and Carlos Ramos and includes tunes capturing "the lights of the city dancing in the warm, fragrant, nocturnal air," as well as *fados*, "a sort of blues in which the lyrics are frequently improvised on the spot." Iconic guitars and emotional harmony seem to captivate and isolate the couple, utterly alone and enjoying the view near a crenelated castle with striped pointed towers shot in Kodachrome between Lisbon and the town of Estoril. The fairy tale–like setting resonates with visions of a magical honeymoon.

FIGURE 7.7

Carlos Ramos and Trio Odemira,
Honeymoon in Portugal,
Capitol T 10145;
photo by Red Burns.

Honeymoon in

PORTUGAL

RECORDED IN LISBON

Fados and Cançãos featuring
Carlos Ramos and Trio Odemira

'CAPITOL' OF THE WORLD HIGH FIDELITY

HONEYMOON IN MANHATTAN allows us to observe a new bride and groom in the amorous heart of New York. He, in muted gray suit and red tie, and she, in a pale blue and white tea dress with bonnet and matching wrist length gloves, cuddle close in a Central Park carriage for two as they squint into the alluring light from above, surrendering to the wonder and size of the City. Aside from their carriage driver, the couple is completely alone, despite being in the middle of Manhattan.[8] Skyscrapers and city streets frame Frederick Law Olmsted's pastoral landscape where an urban-rural aesthetic ignites romance. Capturing the halcyon honeymoon days, "In this album we depict the many moods and places in Manhattan; from love in the handsome carriage in Central Park to the wonderful glow of curtain time at a hit musical. From the teeming tenements to a gay brisk morning of window shopping." In this vision of a New York City honeymoon, poverty and playtime seem to serve equally as beckoning backdrops to newlywed travelers in much the same way as global tourists have been accused of exoticizing foreign cultures, selectively absorbing and appropriating custom and costume even while ignoring a socially conscious "bigger" picture. Here, in the US cultural capital, securely stateside, songs such as "Slaughter on 10th Avenue," "Street Scene," and "Curtain Time" suggest ways of life, fantasies and fates, accessible to the eyes and understandings of even the casual visitor, inviting them in, but also providing a packaged version to be carried back and replayed in the familiar setting of home.

FIGURE 7.8

The New World Theatre Orchestra,
Honeymoon in Manhattan,
Stereo-Fidelity Records SF 3000;
photo by Frank Zimmerman;
cover art by Joe Krush.

THE NEW WORLD THEATRE ORCHESTRA

honeymoon
in
manhattan

8   NEW YORK CITY

New York City represents the height of US cosmopolitanism and sophistication, the place to go for the best museums, biggest retailers, finest restaurants, and latest Broadway shows. Midcentury albums showcase New York as an important travel destination, for theater, dining, and romance. They tell consumers what to do, where to go, and how to experience a metropolis. For example, carrying over from the previous chapter, *Honeymoon in Manhattan* provides a seductive soundtrack for the "first time Mr. & Mrs." as they encounter the city.

On LP or radio, CD or YouTube, the music of Broadway beckons to young people—dancing and singing in summer camp shows or obscure community theater productions in high school auditoriums—whether or not they have visited New York City. So many dancers, so many choruses, so many extras to fill the stage, there must be room for one more. New York City promises the possibility of participation, to authentically be *of* the city, to feel like a creative member of a community of culture makers, not only by joining musical productions, but walking in the footsteps of Allen Ginsberg and Patti Smith at St Mark's Church in the East Village, expanding food horizons at an Indian restaurant on Sixth Street between 1st and 2nd Avenue, or embodying a fantasized insider's bearing at the latest exhibit at the Museum of Modern Art or a pop-up gallery in Brooklyn. These possibilities manifest the promise of consumer culture and the familiarity acquired through consumption: participants consume aspects of the city and the city becomes part of them.

New York City offers opportunity in the midst of disconnection, as one leaves not only small town thinking and cultural mores but also home, family, and familiarity behind. Notions of setting off to New York City on one's own to pursue dreams, follow ambitions, exploit talent, and meet like-minded people to share the journey tread now-familiar waters. Leaving behind the confines of hometown friends and connections, new arrivals are unanchored from their roots, unmoored from the limits, but also benefits, of familial affiliations, customs, and aspirations.

ALBUMS

The cover photo for **HOLIDAY IN MANHATTAN** transports us to Rockefeller Center, where flags of many nations luff in the breeze as people loiter, taking in the energy of the multilevel plaza. Fountainside, where formally attired waiters attend well-dressed diners joining the buzz under the café's green and white umbrellas, we feel the "closeness … of the romantic pleasures and the smoldering excitement that comes to all couples who have spent a Holiday in Manhattan." Warmth, friendliness, and other people enhance this holiday, even as "thanks to the advent of high fidelity techniques … still glamorous sounds are relived for you right in your own home."

FIGURE 8.1

Holiday in Manhattan,
Waldorf Music Hall Inc.
MHK 33-1215.

Holiday in MANHATTAN

LONG PLAYING 33-1/3 R.P.M.
MHK 33-1215

KING SIZE

FDR

FULL DYNAMIC RANGE
NEW HIGH FIDELITY

PIANO SOLOS
with Rhythm Accompaniment

MANHATTAN
SERENADE

OUT OF NOWHERE

WHERE OR WHEN

DANCING ON THE
CEILING

IT HAD TO BE YOU

HAUNTING MELODY

TEA FOR TWO

BEWITCHED

MANHATTAN

LIEBESTRAUM

MILLION DOLLAR
BABY

LOVER'S LAMENT

WALDORF MUSIC HALL Inc.

HOLIDAY IN NEW YORK features Grand Award albums' distinctive alternating black and white border, the four sides of which form a frame for the image pertaining to each album's central, evocative theme or location. Here, a pen and ink drawing, *Fifth Avenue at the Plaza*, is rendered in the style of the era's advertising illustration. The green, gold, black and gray watercolor details enliven a multiperspective, impressionistic collage of legs, ankles, and feet clad in white high heels that emerge from flowing red hemlines and partially obscure a couple leaning on a bar. To the left, an imposing column from the Plaza's grand porch looms above a tiny horse and carriage, the driver with black top hat. On the right, wrought iron benches set in an intimate park complete the atmospheric picture. Song titles, such as "Manhattan," "Cocktails for Two," and "Blue Room" announce a sampling of "New York's smartest café music."

"On your holiday in New York no more delightful place for cocktails can be found than the Plaza on Fifth Avenue." And, so begins the plan for your evening, including dinner at the St. Regis. Traditions dating back to the early nineteen hundreds celebrate a ritual of drinks, dinner, show, drinks, and wrap New York holiday travelers in an attractive, comforting, circle of closeness to cultured historical heritage, as well as fame and wealth. Mentioned on the night's agenda are legendary locales, such as, the Hoffman House, Delmonico's "old stand," the Hotel Astor, and Rector's—where one might rub shoulders in drinking and eating with Florenz Ziegfeld of the Follies (highlighted in the hit 1968 movie, *Funny Girl*, with Barbra Streisand and Omar Sharif) or the Floradora Girls from the Casino Theater.

A third of *Holiday in New York*'s liner notes are dedicated to the bio and career of artist Tracy Sugarman.

FIGURE 8.2

Holiday in New York,
Grand Award GA 33-317;
design by Tracy Sugarman.

Holiday In New York

A NEW HIGH FIDELITY RECORDING OF NEW YORK'S SMARTEST CAFE MUSIC!

15 delightful arrangements including

Manhattan, Cocktails for Two, Body and Soul, Blue Room, Tea for Two, Lover, Fascinatin' Rhythm, Don't Blame Me, Where or When, plus 6 other enchanting songs

Featuring Rod Gregory at the piano, Frank Carrol on bass, Bob Rosten on drums

Grand Award — *World's Greatest Music*

Grand Award — *World's Greatest Art*

Tracy Sugarman

FIFTH AVENUE AT THE PLAZA

by TRACY SUGARMAN

courtesy THE GRAND AWARD COLLECTION

LONG PLAYING RECORD

33-317 · 33⅓ R.P.M.

Revealing the process behind the cover art:

This young artist brings to record covers a creative talent rarely utilized in this field. Unlike most artists, he did not receive specific instructions to produce a particular type of cover, but was merely told the subject of the record album, and from there his wonderful creative ability took over to produce the imaginative cover you see. His use of strong blacks and bold splashes of color combine to give a feeling of youth and vitality to his work and an exciting sense of movement and direction.

....

The cover of Norrie Paramor's **NEW YORK IMPRESSIONS** reveals a typical downtown New York street scene, with well-dressed pedestrians in the foreground, crossing a busy Manhattan street; women with skirts flowing, men in sober dark suits and ties, many with hats. A lone policeman stands on the street's centerline to guide them. A porter wields his way across the street, wheeling a wardrobe cart among the traffic. In background, a haze of cars, taxis, and trucks and busses seems a bit ominous, as the shot telescopes the street into a packed segment of the city.

The rather unglamorous scene resembles the street photography movement in serious photography circles, exemplified by Helen Levitt's unblinking portraits of New York and Robert Frank's meditation on everyday American life, and often linked to improvisation in jazz.[1] Just as Frank, a Swiss immigrant, captured an outsider's perspective in his American photographs, the liner notes indicate that Paramor, who

FIGURE 8.3

Norrie Paramor and
His Strings and Orchestra,
New York Impressions,
Capitol T 10063.

new york
impressions

NORRIE PARAMOR, his strings and orchestra

hailed from England, succeeded in conveying New York in sound: "No music has ever described the mad Manhattan scene better than Paramor's 'New York Impressions.'" As Paramor writes in the notes: "Perhaps I enjoy New York more than most men. For I am an Englishman, a musician, and my chances to enjoy it are few. I offer 'New York Impressions' in long-playing album form, a labor of love and devotion. Some fifty musicians and singers assisted me in producing this collection of twelve melodic portraits—modern listening music which, I hope, weaves the moods and tempo of the world's most exciting metropolis into more than forty minutes of pleasure."

On **MANTOVANI MANHATTAN**, from 1963, we see a black and white shot looking down on a group of midtown buildings, including the Woolworth building, clustered together in a familiar city scene. The cover seems contemporary—its bold modernist font hovers above a simple image of buildings with a blank background, with only the song titles interrupting the visual field. Mantovani, the prolific and successful conductor, known for his easy-listening "cascading strings" sounds, was the first artist to sell over a million stereo LPs in the United States.[2] The liner notes mimic celebrated New York ambition: "Reaching for the New York he has grown to love and admire on all his touring concerts, Mantovani has put together his musical memories of that grand city to create the most magnificent musical portrait ever attempted on LP." The album includes New York linked tunes like George M. Cohan's "Give My Regards to Broadway," and Leonard Bernstein's "West Side Story (Maria/Somewhere)" as well as classics such as "Take the 'A' Train," and "Autumn in New York."

FIGURE 8.4

Mantovani and His Orchestra,
Mantovani Manhattan,
London PS 328.

STEREO PS 328

FULL FREQUENCY RANGE RECORDING

MANTOVANI MANHATTAN
AND HIS ORCHESTRA

SLAUGHTER ON TENTH AVENUE
WEST SIDE STORY (Maria/Somewhere)
HARLEM NOCTURNE
AUTUMN IN NEW YORK
TAKE THE "A" TRAIN
GIVE MY REGARDS TO BROADWAY
MANHATTAN SERENADE
BELLE OF NEW YORK
MANHATTAN LULLABY
THE BOWERY
TENEMENT SYMPHONY

Clearly, **MANHATTAN TIME** is the hour of adoration, when the sun sinks out of sight, highlighting in dusky blue a skyline, somehow familiar, outside a city apartment's room with a view where a well-coiffed woman wearing ornate, sparkling jewelry rests her unadorned left hand along the loveseat's back and accepts her faceless male companion's caress. A single girl in the city on a classic "bachelor pad" album cover. The plump cherry in her cocktail glass glows with the same fuchsia as her lips and nails, while "the Quintet sets up a light, swinging rhythm that never loses its pulse, and then goes on to trace delightful variations around old favorites and new conceits alike."

FIGURE 8.5

Art Van Damme Quintet,
Manhattan Time,
Columbia CL 801;
photo by Bottwyn-Sommer Studio.

JUMPIN' AT THE LEFT BANK: EXCITING NEW VOCAL STYLINGS BY THE JOHN LASALLE QUARTET features a front cover photograph by Lee Friedlander, whose early work often focused on New York street life and musicians. Friedlander's photographs adorn dozens of albums, including John Coltrane's *Giant Steps*, Ray Charles's *The Genius of Ray Charles*, on Atlantic and Dakota Stanton's *Time to Swing* on Capitol.[3] The *Jumpin' at the Left Bank* LP refers not to the Left Bank in Paris, but the Left Bank club in New York's West Village, owned by Dick Kollmar, a fairly famous actor, radio personality, and Broadway producer in his day. Kollmar and his wife, journalist and television star Dorothy Kilgallen, were well known for their radio show *Breakfast with Dorothy and Dick*.[4] The quartet was formed to capitalize on the burgeoning boom in folk music. Lyrics to "Welcome to the Left Bank," a short tune that opens the album, compare the East and West sides of New York, suggesting that the East Side doesn't have "Kilgallen and Kollmar."

FIGURE 8.6

The John LaSalle Quartet,
Jumpin' at the Left Bank,
Capitol T 1176;
photo by Lee Friedlander.

Jumpin' at the Left Bank

exciting
new vocal
stylings
by

THE
JOHN
LASALLE
QUARTET

Many of the albums in this section propose travel to New York as a kind of short-term, cultural enrichment program. **MANHATTAN TOWER** presents a vision of those who make the move to NYC, in the form of a basic boy (Steven) falls for girl (Julie) plotline with narrative-carrying songs. The cover places the hero high above the city, in midtown, presumably in the eponymous tower, looking past the Chrysler Building, the Tudor City sign just visible, down 42nd Street to the East River, blurred red lights of traffic zooming through the streets. They meet at Billy's Bar and Grill, take a "pre-dawn ride in Central Park," stroll through Greenwich Village, then entertain the tower's varied inhabitants at a party. But Steven catches a westbound train "back" home, perhaps because Julie is a city girl with too many choices and opportunities to slip from romance to marriage, despite his proposals. Composed by Gordon Jenkins, a prolific and successful arranger, *Manhattan Tower* was originally released on 78 rpm discs from Decca in 1946. Jenkins greatly expanded and rerecorded the piece for a new Capitol version a decade later, to tell "a much broader panorama of New York."

FIGURE 8.7

Gordon Jenkins,
Complete Manhattan Tower,
Capitol T 766.

GORDON JENKINS

complete **MANHATTAN TOWER**

newly recorded in
HIGH FIDELITY

The album **A FRENCHMAN IN NEW YORK / AN AMERICAN IN PARIS** pairs musical numbers and provides an opportunity to imagine a continental visitor experiencing New York City. The liner notes mythologize the city: "New York has been the subject of an eternal quest. Sentimentalized, brutalized, commercialized, the city somehow manages to elude the reporters and yield itself to the poets." Photographed in Rockefeller Center's lower plaza café, the Frenchman—topped with a black beret, *Le Figaro* newspaper and cigarette in hand—has finished his cocktail, eschewing the red cherry, and pauses, looking up, as if sensing the presence of the woman behind him as she strolls by sculptor Paul Manship's iconic *Prometheus* fountain. She seems to have sparked a different kind of fire. With movements such as "Horse and Carriage in Central Park" and "Times Square," the notes remark that the LP represents "a New York transfigured by a master's sense of wonder." Although composer Darius Milhaud's specially commissioned *Frenchman in New York* has its moments, it was not destined to match George Gershwin's beloved *American in Paris.*

FIGURE 8.8

Arthur Fiedler and the Boston Pops,
A Frenchman in New York /
An American in Paris,
RCA Victor LSC-2702.

LSC-2702 **STEREO**

Milhaud A FRENCHMAN IN NEW YORK
COMMISSIONED BY RCA VICTOR · RECORDING PREMIÈRE
Gershwin AN AMERICAN IN PARIS
BOSTON POPS / ARTHUR FIEDLER

RCA VICTOR
RED SEAL
DYNAGROOVE
RECORDING

CHRISTMAS HOLIDAYS AT RADIO CITY MUSIC HALL celebrates one of New York City's iconic winter season destinations, along with Rockefeller Center's ice rink and department store Christmas displays. The album cover photo's saturated color exhibit the hallmarks of Kodak's long-running "Colorama" marketing campaign, for which it was produced.[5] These enormous panorama photographs, actually 35-millimeter transparencies, appeared in Grand Central Terminal for decades, often featuring vivid reds, seem especially apt for capturing the long line of high kicking Rockettes dressed as Santa's sexy helpers on the LP's gatefold sleeve. The album contains a multipage, color booklet, much like a *Playbill* souvenir filled with backstage shots and detailed information on the Christmas show, and lingers on massive sets and the Rockettes' spectacular choreography of synchronized movement.

FIGURE 8.9

*Christmas Holidays
at Radio City Music Hall*,
RCA Victor LOP-1010.

RCA VICTOR
LOP-1010
A "New Orthophonic" High Fidelity Recording

CHRISTMAS HOLIDAYS AT
RADIO CITY MUSIC HALL

"To spend Christmas time in New York is a never-to-be forgotten experience," chime the liner notes on **CHRISTMAS IN NEW YORK**, and as with many things the city manages to find itself right at the center of the holiday. "A star rose in the Bethlehem sky, and a host of angels related the glad tidings. New Yorkers are reminded of that historic night twenty centuries ago as the magnificent voice of Mario Lanza is heard in "The First Noël." "The Little Drummer Boy" follows the observation that "A familiar sight in many New York churches is the Christmas crèche, a tiny replica of the stable at Bethlehem." The liner notes present a compact guide to spending Christmas in New York and attempt clever, or idyllic, connections to the songs: "Gotham is a gourmet's delight! New York City restaurants are famous for their holiday fare. Perhaps talented Henry Mancini has these culinary treats in mind as he interprets "The Christmas Song" which contains a musical description of "Chestnuts Roasting on an Open Fire."

The LP was issued as a "Special Collector's Edition" from RCA in 1967, and gathered a greatest hits from other RCA Christmas releases, including Vic Damone belting out "Santa Claus Is Coming to Town" and Marian Anderson's beautifully peaceful "Silent Night." "In New York City children and adults alike look for snow to crown the beauty of the yuletide season" —hence, the inclusion of "White Christmas." Rockefeller Center graces the cover with a snowy, hazy, almost blizzarding, scene of shoppers in front of the "mammoth Christmas tree." Rockefeller Center acts a bit like a town square for the United States, particularly with the numerous television shows produced nearby; and the annual lighting of the Christmas tree has become a media tradition. Christmas records, of course, remain popular, and almost every pop star ends up releasing their own version of the Christmas canon.[6]

FIGURE 8.10

Christmas in New York,
Special Collector's Edition,
RCA Victor PRS-257;
photograph by David Attie.

STEREO

CHRISTMAS
in
New York

Ed Ames
What Child Is This

Marian Anderson
Silent Night

Sir Thomas Beecham/
Royal Philharmonic Orchestra
Handel: Hallelujah Chorus

Vic Damone
Santa Claus Is Coming to Town

Arthur Fiedler/Boston Pops Orchestra
Rudolph the Red-Nosed Reindeer

Morton Gould and His Orchestra
The Little Drummer Boy

Mario Lanza
The First Noël

Norman Luboff Choir
White Christmas

Henry Mancini, His Orchestra and Chorus
The Christmas Song

Jan Peerce *O Little Town of Bethlehem*
O Holy Night

Robert Shaw Chorale
Joy to the World
It Came Upon a Midnight Clear

Kate Smith
Silver Bells

SPECIAL COLLECTOR'S EDITION

"HIS MASTER'S VOICE"
RCA VICTOR

CHRISTMAS IN NEW YORK, VOLUME 2, released the year after the first volume,
states that New York City "is a giant melting pot in which eight million inhabitants
try to find a common denominator. With such an endless variety of cultures and customs, being in New York at Christmastime is like taking a holiday tour around the
world." Thus, the back cover paid tribute—if weak—to the city's diverse areas and
the resident populations' Christmas traditions and the contribution of these to an
understanding of Christmastime in New York: German immigrants and the Christmas tree; Dutch settlers and Saint Nicholas; Scandinavians and their love of snow;
Puerto Ricans and other Spanish speakers' festive singing and dancing; Chinese and
"succulent Oriental dishes"; "Romanian, Hungarian, and Russian restaurants"; "Armenian, Syrian, and Turkish eating places"; Greeks and a coin in a loaf of bread; Italians,
butcher shops and fried eel; the Irish and religious devotion. Peter Stuyvesant named
a part of town after the Dutch city of Haarlem: "Today, the Negro peoples who dwell
in this crowded, busy area have brought to it a rich heritage of spirituals and folk
music," and this commentary leads to Harry Belafonte singing, "A Star in the East."
Indeed, each bit of ethnic commentary leads tenuously to one of the LP's songs. English colonists get credit for mince pie and plum pudding, and harkening back to that

FIGURE 8.11

Christmas in New York,
Special Collector's Edition,
Volume 2,
RCA PRS-270.

STEREO

CHRISTMAS
in New York
Volume 2

ED AMES
Let It Snow! Let It Snow! Let It Snow!

HARRY BELAFONTE
A Star in the East

LANA CANTRELL
I'll Be Home for Christmas

VIC DAMONE
Deck the Halls

ARTHUR FIEDLER/
BOSTON POPS
Sleigh Ride

MORTON GOULD
and His Orchestra
Good King Wenceslas

AL HIRT
Here Comes Santa Claus

THE NORMAN
LUBOFF CHOIR
Medley: Hark! The Herald Angels Sing;
God Rest Ye Merry, Gentlemen; The First Noël

HENRY MANCINI
and His Orchestra
O Little Town of Bethlehem

PETER NERO
Medley: Jingle Bells; Winter Wonderland

LEONTYNE PRICE/
Choir of Men and Boys,
of St. Thomas Episcopal Church
Ave Maria (Schubert)

THE ROBERT SHAW
CHORALE
Medley: O Come, All Ye Faithful;
Angels We Have Heard on High

RCA

SPECIAL COLLECTOR'S EDITION

mysteriously large ship, "Even the Mayflower carried among its cargo holly and laurel to decorate the Christmas tables." Vic Damone's rendition of "Deck the Halls" follows.

The front cover eschews diversity, turning back to the fountain in front of the Plaza and Fifth Avenue near Central Park. An impressionistic painted effect creates accents of snow and Christmas lights, and an odd prominence of fuchsia. Clutching wrapped packages, and dressed in mother-daughter matching red coats, the central pair seem to have exited the FAO Schwartz toy store paradise; and the little girl waves back, perhaps, to the life size toy soldier standing guard outside the door, or to her father lagging behind.

9

CUBA

For those who grew up after the 1950s, it can be difficult to believe that Cuba played such a huge role in the postwar US imagination for glamorous, cultured, and well-heeled travel. However, Cuba served as a popular destination for tourists and honeymooners for decades before the Castro revolution. Billed as a nearby playground and convenient for weekend getaways, Cuba seemed colorful and glamorous, yet familiar with pastimes of cocktail hour, dancing, and gambling. Cuba attracted US travelers who came to "enjoy the exotic charms of a distinctive old Spanish colonial city, and later, to experience the excitement of gambling casinos."[1] Cuba inspired an entire genre of LPs, some sponsored by Hilton Hotels and Cook's Tours, many others driven by the Latin dance crazes of the era. Often, Cuban albums lingered on the "colorful" aspects of Cuban heritage: "Afro-Cuban culture, embodying elements of music, dance, and religion, became essential to both nationalistic and touristic image builders. Tourism promoters exalted sensual and mystical qualities of Afro-Cubans … and foreigners saw Cuba as an erotic, exotic island devoted to their pleasure and entertainment."[2] For Americans, such romantic visions vanished after Cuba's communist revolution in 1959. No cigars. No rum. No Havana Hilton honeymoon. Cuba became off-limits for United States tourists, and Cuban albums all but disappeared, replaced by "Latin" "Caribbean" and, later, "Miami Sound" recordings. Opening a window on a very different era of US-Cuba relations, these albums provide a fascinating glimpse of the former tourist hotspot, largely closed to the US for decades.[3]

A succession of Latin dance fads emanated from or circulated through Cuba on their way to the United States, including the rhumba, conga, mambo, samba, merengue, and cha-cha. In the 1950s, "From fashionable supper clubs in midtown Manhattan to the Los Angeles Coliseum, from Harlem to *el barrio*, from nightclubs in Seattle to summer resorts in upstate New York, Cuban rhythms were in vogue; the obligatory fare for virtually all orchestras, dance troupes, and singers in cabarets, nightclubs, and ballrooms, highbrow and lowbrow alike, in big cities and small towns."[4] LPs from both Cuban and American musicians packaged Cuban music as an essential part of Latin dance, and helped spur interest in travel to the nearby island:

> Starting with the rhumba and the Cuban bandleaders who made it famous— from Xavier Cugat to Desi Arnaz—Cuban music and dance inevitably led to a desire to visit the genre's musical source, Havana. Combined with low-cost sea travel and air travel after World War II, Havana suddenly became the "exotic" destination of choice for hundreds of thousands of Americans excited to see the land of Babalu.[5]

Arnaz's success helped drive the Cuban music boom of the 1950s, and he counted as the world's most famous Cuban for many years before Fidel Castro assumed the title.[6]

The Havana Hilton had been open for only a few months before becoming engulfed in the Cuban revolution, and the hotel's fate provides a vivid symbol of the sudden change in the Cuban phenomenon under Castro. Architect Welton Becket—known for his modernist buildings such as the Capitol Records Building in Los Angeles, the Polynesian resort at Walt Disney World, and the Xerox Tower in Rochester, New York— designed the Havana Hilton.[7] The hotel, showcased on the 1958 LP *Dancing at the Habana Hilton*, was a major project for the imperiled Batista government:

> Built in a strikingly prominent location at the top of La Rampa, a street sloping up from the sea in the downtown district of Vedado, the project was funded through the pension plan of the Cuban Catering Workers' Union, to be run by Hilton Hotels International, and designed by the Los Angeles firm of Welton Becket & Associates along with a Cuban firm, Arroyo and Menéndez.[8]

When complete, an advertisement for the new hotel noted that the thirty-story building had 630 "lavishly appointed rooms and suites," a casino, a Trader Vic's restaurant, and a terrace bar. Becket and Conrad Hilton attended the opening in March 1958, hosting "officials, celebrities and journalists, many flown in from the US."[9] The party did not last long.

Once rebel forces reached the capital, they quickly commandeered the luxury hotel for their provisional headquarters:

> "Latin America's tallest, largest hotel" was the Habana Hilton's slogan when it opened in Cuba's capital in 1958. Eight months later, Fidel Castro and his revolutionaries marched into this unapologetic icon of capitalism to begin their socialist rule of Cuba. Soon, the hotel was nationalised and renamed Habana Libre (Free Havana); throughout its existence, Habana Libre has charted the turbulent relationship between Cuba and the US.[10]

After a fifty-year standoff, diplomatic relations between the United States and Cuba were formally restored in July 2015.[11] Direct flights from New York to Havana are available; travelers can book accommodations through Airbnb.[12] Cuban rum will once again be available to US consumers.[13] In March 2015, a descendent of the man who built the Havana Hilton posed for a selfie with Fidel Castro's son: "America's historic rapprochement with Cuba was given a celebrity seal of approval at the weekend when the heiress Paris Hilton visited the hotel her great-grandfather opened in Havana the year before the communist revolution."[14] It seems that once again, entertainment, politics, and commerce animate US-Cuba relations. Taking a closer look at a set of typical and evocative 1950s Cuba LPs, we witness Spanish heritage and Latin rhythms that anchored a crucial site of the Cold War close to home.

ALBUMS

CHRISTMAS IN CUBA is one of several "Christmas in" albums from the Capitol of the World series. Debuting in 1956 with *Christmas in England*, *Christmas in Germany*, *Christmas in Holland*, *Christmas in Mexico*, and *Christmas in Sweden*, these holiday albums closely conformed to the contours of American immigration patterns. Cuba was part of the second round of releases, which included Australia, Austria, Brazil, Poland, and Portugal. All were recorded "on location," and they were promoted as a collectible set.[15] *Christmas in Cuba* features Cuban folk singer Fernando Albuerne performing "cherished Cuban Christmas music" with a pop feel. A Cuban Christmas, we are told, represents a very different holiday than the snowy white Christmas of Bing Crosby: "The golden, warming sun beams down through the azure December skies to provide amazing contrast to the traditional conception of sleigh bells, snowdrifts and log fires."

The cover photograph depicts a young woman, piously dressed in a black veil, posed near a set of crèche figures of the three wise men, one who has taken off his crown in worship, holding their gifts for the newborn Christ. This image represents the deep Catholic heritage of the isle in ways that dozens of rhumba and cha-cha LPs do not. The notes appear in both English and Spanish, perhaps in a nod to the album's overseas interest, and the growing Spanish-speaking population in the United States; nevertheless, the appearance of dual language liner notes on a major label is noteworthy.

FIGURE 9.1

Fernando Albuerne
and Coro de Madrigalistas,
Christmas in Cuba,
Capitol T 10165;
photo by Adrian Associates, Inc.

'CAPITOL' OF THE WORLD

RECORDED IN HAVANA

CHRISTMAS IN CUBA

Fernando Albuerne • Coro de Madrigalistas

"Mississippi-Mambo" might not be the first song that would come to mind on an album titled **HOLIDAY IN HAVANA** by Noro Morales and His Orchestra, but here we have "dance music that's as modern as the Sputnik and accepted at the Debs Ball … The College Prom … The Country Club … and your own living room or den." Numbers like "For Me and My Gal" and "Who's Sorry Now" brim with rhythm, bringing together the established and the exotic from the close, yet rum-fueled distant coast of Cuba. Bright pink and orange half-circles evoke an island party atmosphere and the light brown skinned brunette, shoeless in fishnet stockings and bright lipstick, her fingers poised over a tall conga drum, brings out the cha-cha of "smart dine-and-dance spots," like those listed in the *New Yorker*, that appeal with familiar tunes set to a Latin beat. "Play it and find out how much fun there is for yourself and friends," the liner notes advise, informing how the album might supply the entertainment for an evening at home—"even the youngsters have to admit that these latin tempos have something that can make them turn away from 'rock and roll.'" The album includes details about its "spectra-sonic sound," and provides meticulous information about the recording process, including microphones, mastering, and pressing specifics—the label's "controlled production" that "assures you of receiving a perfect record every time you choose a Design LP."

FIGURE 9.2

Noro Morales and His Orchestra,
Holiday in Havana,
Design Records,
DLP 86.

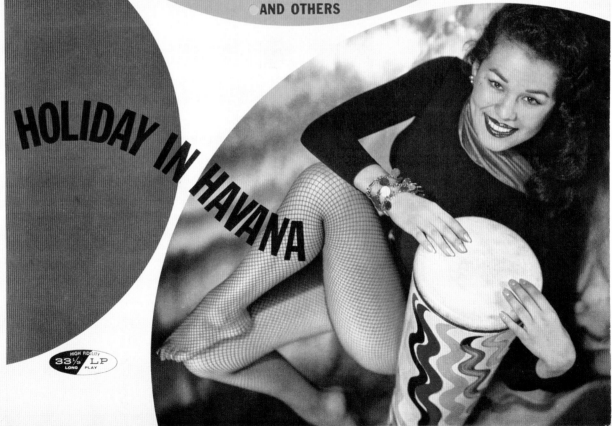

DLP 86

NORO MORALES

and his orchestra

- MISSISSIPPI-MAMBO
- FOR ME AND MY GAL CHA-CHA
- I CAN'T GIVE YOU ANYTHING BUT LOVE CHA-CHA
- I'M GETTING SENTIMENTAL OVER YOU CHA-CHA
- DARK EYES-MAMBO
- AND OTHERS

DESIGN
RECORDS
Full Spectrum Sound

HOLIDAY IN HAVANA

HIGH FIDELITY
33⅓ LP
LONG PLAY

On the cover of **HAVANA ... 2 A.M.: FOR DANCING AND LISTENING** from José Madeira and His Orchestra, a young woman, dressed casually in black with a jaunty straw hat, sits barefoot, a bit out of focus, behind an acoustic guitar, an opened—let's call it rum—bottle, and a cocktail glass. Not dressed, as so many Cuban LP covers' girls are, in bright colors, fishnet stockings, or tight-fitting dresses, she might be a model in a sketching class, eager to get on with her day ... or night. The liner notes stress the late hour of the LP title: "This album brings you (in Hi-Fidelity) the pulsating beat of Havana as it thunders through the night." The text touts the music's transformative abilities: "When you flick on your phonograph, you are transported to Havana during its most fascinating hours" and gives a nod to the creolization of the locale: "Havana is a city with a unique magnetism one feels in its music—a music with a tantalizing rhythm derived from its African and Spanish ancestry." In Havana, we are told, "music and dance come as naturally as eating and sleeping. Music is an integral part of every Cuban's daily life and rhythm is an inborn characteristic." Side one offers a set of "authentic cha cha music," while side two presents flamenco, the "Spanish atmosphere of Havana." Most of the tunes, including "Rosita Amorsita" and "Variaciones Por Rosa y Alegrias" are listed in Spanish. The LP offers the "Ultimate in High Fidelity" to "give you the finest possible true reproduction of sound on Hi-Fidelity equipment, as well as equipment of standard quality."

FIGURE 9.3

José Madeira and His
Orchestra/Carlos Montoya,
Havana ... 2 A.M.,
Master Seal,
MSLP 5003

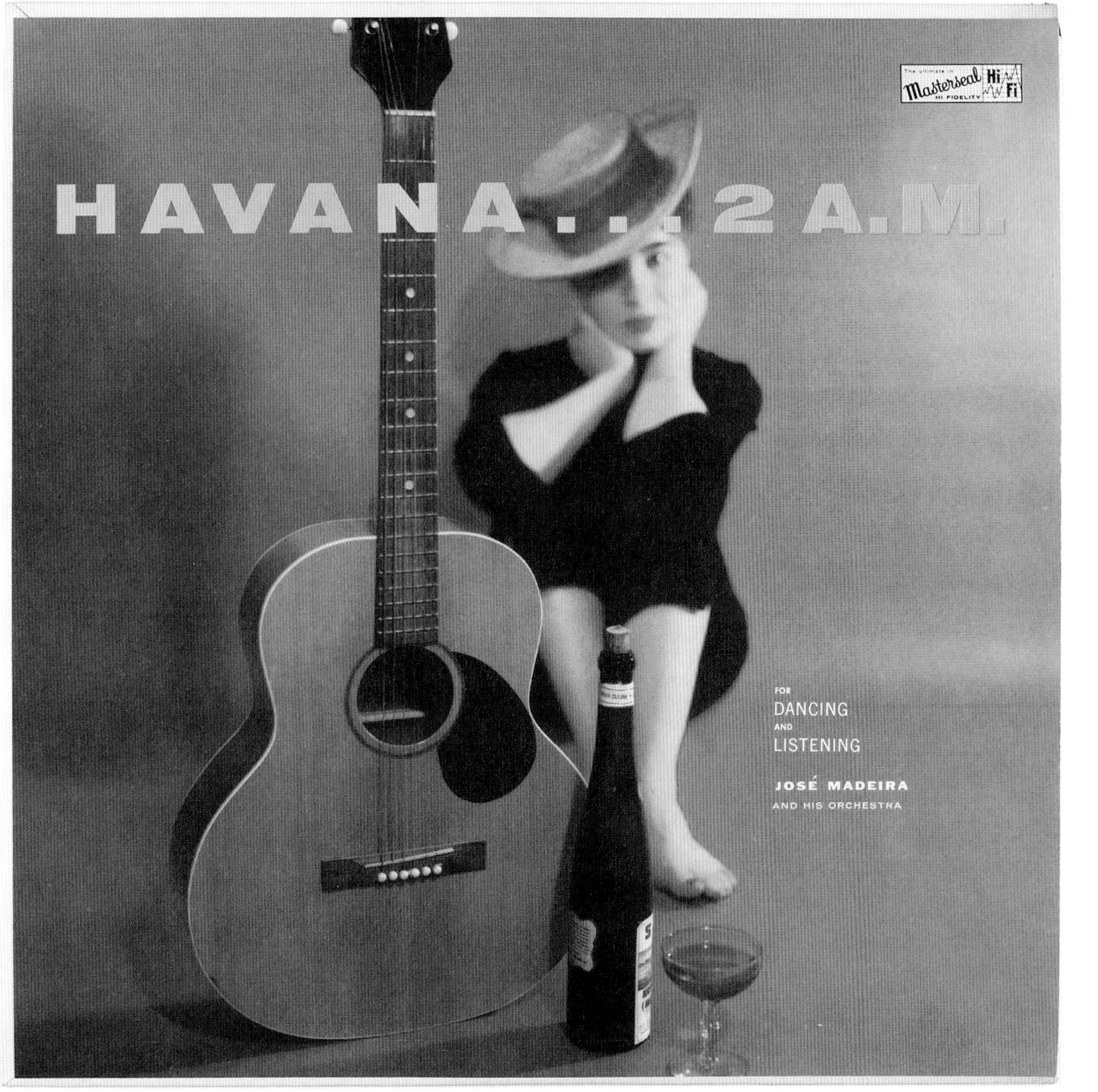
The ultimate in Masterseal HI FIDELITY Hi Fi
HAVANA . . . 2 A.M.
FOR DANCING AND LISTENING
JOSÉ MADEIRA
AND HIS ORCHESTRA

DINNER IN HAVANA with Rene Touzet and His Orchestra is part of RCA Victor's "Dinner In" series, which included such LPs as *Dinner in Buenos Aires, Dinner in Caracas, Dinner in Mexico City*, and *Dinner in Rio*. Like many Cuban LPs aimed at an American audience, the liner notes credit Christopher Columbus with discovering Cuba, and provide a brief history of the colonial period, before turning to effusive descriptions of fabled Havana hotspots like the Tropicana, the Montmartre, and Sans Souci. The notes go on to describe Touzet, a Cuban musician who moved to the United States in the 1940s, as "a tall handsome fellow, with a delightful sense of humor," who "is responsible to a sizeable degree for the popularity of Cuban music in this country." To reinforce the "dinner" theme, the LP's back cover also includes a simple recipe for "ground meat creole style (*picadillo a la criolla*)."

FIGURE 9.4

Rene Touzet and His Orchestra,
Dinner in Havana,
RCA Victor LPM-1016;
photo by Mitchell Bliss.

A "NEW ORTHOPHONIC" HIGH FIDELITY RECORDING

RCA VICTOR
LPM-1016

DINNER IN HAVANA

RENE TOUZET AND HIS ORCHESTRA

© RCA PRINTED IN U.S.A.

PHOTO: MITCHELL BLISS

HAVANA IN HI-FI, from Richard Hayman and His Orchestra in "Custom High Fidelity," forms part of the Wacker series of LPs from Mercury Records, named after their longtime address in Chicago. A harmonica virtuoso and pops conductor, Hayman started out with Borrah Minevitch and His Harmonica Rascals, and was an artist and repertoire chief at Mercury in the 1950s. The cover, a classic in the genre, shows a woman intensely playing a conga drum balanced on her hip, and attached to a strap around her shoulder. A set of bongos and a maraca seem to float in the air, and a well-used conga drum sits beside her. She is barefoot, wearing a brightly colored, traditional ruffled skirt, reminiscent of a *bata cubana*, or rhumba dress, worn by dancers, performers, and carnival celebrators. Unusually for this type of image, the model is not wearing stockings here—she appears focused on playing her drum. "Cuban" music receives a full orchestra treatment, and the arrangements reveal Hayman's experience as a film arranger. The LP gestures only slightly toward a Latin sound, as strings dominate tunes "My Hopeful Heart" by Cuban composer Ernesto Lecuona, and "Del Prado," interspersed with percussion and marimba.[16] The liner notes focus on the music, with short entries about each piece, and also provide copious details about how the album was recorded, who served as engineer, which microphones were involved, and what machine was used to tape the sessions (an Ampex 300). The LP was recorded at Capitol Studios in New York, not Havana.

FIGURE 9.5

Richard Hayman and His Orchestra,
Havana in Hi-Fi,
Mercury MG 20296.

Mercury RECORDS

HAVANA
IN
HI-FI

RICHARD HAYMAN
AND HIS ORCHESTRA

HIGH *Custom* FIDELITY

MERCURY MG 20296 • RICHARD HAYMAN AND HIS ORCHESTRA • HAVANA IN HI-FI

"Of all the island paradises in the Caribbean, no place spells the word fun more than Havana," assure the liner notes of **GOT A DATE WITH YOU IN HAVANA: CHA-CHA-CHAS**. The album addresses a frequent traveler: "On your next Caribbean trip be sure to include this fabulous fun filled island on your itinerary." Three "top cha-cha orchestras" contribute to the LP, including those led by Hermanos Aviles and Enrique Aviles, both part of a long-established musical family from eastern Cuba.[17] The cover apparently offers the "date" of the title, lips and eyes half-closed, head tilted back a bit, red nails on bosom, wrapped in a turquoise off-the-shoulder gown, with a come-hither look. It appears as if the background lake scene was rear projected, along with a disembodied palm frond, to make it seem that she indeed was in Havana for the date. In a possible hi-fi in-joke, the LP's "High-Fidelity" designation seems strategically placed right over her right breast.

FIGURE 9.6

Hermanos Aviles Orchestra/
Enrique Aviles and Orchestra/
AAMCO Cubano Orchestra,
*Got a Date with You in Havana:
Cha-Cha-Chas*,
AAMCO ALP 305.

GOT A
DATE
WITH
YOU IN
HAVANA

CHA-CHA-CHAS

RECORDED IN HAVANA

High-Fidelity

AAMCO
FULL FREQUENCY SOUND

ALP
305

A DIVISION OF ALISON ENTERPRISES INC.

The cover of **DANCING AT THE HABANA HILTON** with Mark Monte and the Continentals presents an illustration of the high-rise Havana Hilton hotel, including such details as the elaborate outdoor pool complex, terrace bar, and an outdoor mural by celebrated Cuban artist Amelia Peláez. Certainly, no hint of the coming Communist takeover hovers over the scene. The cover art, which resembles an architect's rendering, is by Seymour Leichman, who taught at the Art Students League and the Pratt Institute in New York, and went on to write and illustrate the best-selling children's book *The Boy Who Could Sing Pictures*. Aside from providing a concise history of Cuba from 1492 to 1902, the notes describe the hotel in great detail: "Towering over Havana and overlooking its famous harbor and historic Morro Castle is the exciting new Habana Hilton, a magnificent 30 story hotel and the largest and tallest building in Latin America." Built following a pro-development push by the Batista regime, the Habana Hilton's restaurants and bars included "the exotic Trader Vic's Restaurant" (renamed *Polinesio* when the hotel was nationalized in 1960, and open for business today with the original Trader Vic's tiki décor intact).[18] The tunes on the LP, medleys of "Fast Rhumba," "Cha-Cha-Cha," and "Mambo," take the listener through a typical, lively set of Latin dance classics.

FIGURE 9.7

Mark Monte and the Continentals,
Dancing at the Habana Hilton,
Jubilee JGM 1072;
cover design by Si Leichman.

1072 jubilee

dancing at the habana hilton

WITH MARK MONTE AND THE CONTINENTALS

habana hilton

On **COOK'S TOUR OF CUBA** from Vox Records, we meet a pasty white family on a sandal-clad visit to the island. In a Kodachrome shot, courtesy of Pan American World Airways, looking across Havana Harbor to Morro Castle (El Morro) in Havana Harbor, the daughter snaps candid photos as the dad, in a white Panama hat and Kodak red sweater, points at a decrepit seaside fortress. Cook's refers to Thomas Cook & Son's travel company, a pioneering provider of tours and travel information. Founded in the nineteenth century, Cook's Travel Service also produced a series of Cook's Travellers Handbooks beginning in 1840, which continues today.[19] Cook's teamed with Vox Records to produce a series of "Cook's Tour" LPs in the late 1950s, including *Cook's Tour of the Caribbean* and *Cook's Tour of Latin America;* and Cook's promoted the albums in its travel office and on its cruises.[20] *Cook's Tour of Cuba* showcases a dance band Latino sound with some great horns, expressive bass, and occasional vocal choruses on songs such as "Mambo En Espana," "Barcellona Mambo," and "Carnaval Andaluz." The European continent-based song titles point back to a pre-Castro colonial era.

FIGURE 9.8

Don Marino Barreto Jr. and
His Cuban Orchestra,
Cook's Tour of Cuba,
Vox VX25020;
Kodachrome by courtesy
of Pan American World Airways.

COOK'S
TOUR of CUBA

DON MARINO BARRETO JR. AND HIS CUBAN ORCHESTRA

VOX
VX25020

Reductions By Courtesy of Pan-American World Airways

On the cover of **HAVANA HOLIDAY**, several couples, silhouetted by a waning sunset, dance outside on a palm tree lined terrace overlooking a harbor. *Havana Holiday* invites us to "Thrill to the world's finest true high fidelity! You must hear it to believe it!" with Tito Rivera and His Cuban Orchestra with special appearances by Yo Yo Gonzales and Jose Morales. The LP, from Tops Records, which started out buying and selling used records in Los Angeles in the late 1940s, lists a different title—*Echoes of Havana*—on the back cover. The notes emphasize Rivera's association with the Cuban *conjunto* (a percussive, trumpet-fired African-influenced style band), which played an important role in development of salsa.[21] (Bandleader Tito Rivera's son, Paquito D'Rivera, is a successful, Grammy-winning jazz saxophonist.) *Havana Holiday* includes cha-cha and mambo dance favorites, as well as the huge Cuban hit "Peanut Vendor." Despite Tops's reputation as a discount label that often recorded past-their-prime musicians, the album sounds good, with explosive congas providing a highly danceable beat.[22]

FIGURE 9.9

Tito Rivera and His Cuban Orchestra,
featuring Yo Yo Gonzales
and Jose Morales,
*Havana Holiday: Cha-Cha and
Mambo Dance Favorites*,
Tops L 1637.

10

HAWAII

Pineapples, Pearl Harbor, and statehood in 1959, fueled mainland awareness of the Hawaiian Islands. And airlines, travel agencies, the Kodak Film Company, and the US government's support of the long-running *Hawaii Calls* radio show worked to develop visions of paradise for the would-be traveler. On LP covers, "the lure of the islands" was frequently represented by a Hawaiian woman barely dressed, posed on waterfalls, brown skin decorated with flowers, and pleasingly embodying Hawaii's qualities as a sensual resort paradise.[1] Fewer covers feature Hawaiian men, though when pictured they are typically dressed in theatrical "traditional" garb, usually half-naked.

The iconic hula dancer became a stock image and common trope of native sensuality repeated in sheet music graphics, Hollywood movies, television, and of course record albums. Writing in 1950, anthropologist Philippa Pollenz observed: "while the religion, the traditions, the government and the economy of ancient Hawaii has disappeared, and while the Hawaiian himself has mingled with other races, *hula*, the dance of Hawaii, is still flourishing."[2] "Hula girls" appear in hundreds of images; and most Hawaiian records feature at least one song about a caricatured and sexualized hula dance. In one frequently recorded song, listeners are teasingly instructed to keep their eyes on the dancers' hands during a hula performance, and not be distracted by "the lovely hula hips."[3] The Hula girl and her musical accompaniment have for decades formed the foundation of a strongly appealing and attractive Hawaiian identity, helping make Hawaii instantly recognizable the world over.

As part of a cross-promotional package, Hawaiian albums were often distributed by travel agencies. Deluxe packaging for these albums might include five or six blank, or lined, pages that could be filled with personal reminiscences, or snapshots of the laughing Hula girls, the white sand, and the lush island paradise. Other features included color photos of key sights and tourist-attraction maps for each island, as well as the vinyl LP of songs and sounds, including waves on the beach at Waikiki and exotic birdcalls.[4] These inspirational visual and aural images presented the Hawaiian experience, whether one eventually traveled to Hawaii or found satisfaction simply sitting in the living room with the LP and a record player.[5]

Indeed, many tourist-marketing campaigns not only relied on a visual representation of Hawaii but also characterized a Hawaiian sound. The marketing of Hawaiian popular music aided in Hawaii's transformation from a so-called primitive paradise into the fiftieth state and provided a soothing soundtrack for South Pacific holidays, backyard luau parties, and Hawaiian dinners at home.[6] Of course, what became known worldwide as Hawaiian music was often familiar easy listening, injected with slide guitar, and created mostly by white mainland songwriters with little or no connection to the islands.[7]

Nevertheless, the marriage of stereo technology and "authentic" music was a potent force in the audio branding of Hawaiian paradise. By capturing the tropical sounds of Hawaii on the latest hi-fi advanced recording equipment, the recording industry offered up Hawaiian music as part of the latest achievement of modern technology, promoting paradise as a sound as well as a place to visit.[8]

ALBUMS

The bright reds, yellows, and blues of **HAWAIIAN HOLIDAY**'s cover capture a calm sea, colorful flower leis, and the golden sun-reflecting hair of three young white women bidding aloha to the "mystic tropical isles." They stand aboard the Matson Line's SS *Lurline*, a ship that sailed from San Francisco to Honolulu, and went on to provide first-class only service between Hawaii and the US mainland in the late '50s and early '60s. If you took the cruise from California to the new state in the Pacific, there's a good chance you sailed the *Lurline*. The LP's notes enthuse:

> Hawaii has a special attraction for, and something to offer to, everyone—radiant young couples, enjoying blissful, all-too-brief honeymoon evenings under a bright moon—elders in their golden years, soaking up the golden sunshine—adventuresome youths and thrill-seeking misses admiring each other on the warm beach by day and seeking each other out on the dance floor by night—all ages plunging into the festive spirit of a luau, gingerly sampling the strange native dishes and swaying along with the flexible hula dancers.

Airline competition picked up in the '60s, however, and the romantic boat deck vision of Hawaii appearing on the ocean horizon vanished for most travelers.

FIGURE 10.1

George Wyle Orchestra and Chorus,
Hawaiian Holiday,
Imperial Records LP 9109;
photo courtesy of Matson Line.

HAWAIIAN HOLIDAY

IMPERIAL HIGH FIDELITY

LP 9109

George Wyle
Orchestra and Chorus

S.S. LURLINE
HONOLULU

Photo
Matson Lines

DANNY KUAANA PRESENTS HOLIDAY IN HAWAII, from Capitol, features a photograph "posed by the Hawaiian dancer, Leialoha," who was a performer on the *Harry Owens Hawaiian* television show for CBS in Los Angeles in the 1950s. Photographed by Paul Garrison, a pioneer of glamour photography techniques, the composite cover image resembles a film still, superimposing the Hollywood mythos over an island imaginary.[9] Danny Kuaana and his band "are all native islanders" assure the liner notes, but "Nationality and geography seem to play little part in the appeal of true Hawaiian music." The sensuous and atmospheric cover takes advantage of color photography's apparent realism—red highlights accentuate flowers, lips, and hands and contribute to the overall feel. *Holiday in Hawaii* joins a wider representational convention of linking Hawaii with hula, and hula with sensual dance. As cultural historian Adria Imada claims: "Hula and Hawai'i have become nearly synonymous in the global cultural imaginary … Hawai'i has been personified through the figure of the female dancer. … More than any other cultural or ethnographic artifact, the gendered hula dancer—or as she is known more familiarly in Americana, the 'hula girl'—has come to represent Hawai'i."[10]

FIGURE 10.2

Danny Kuaana,
Holiday in Hawaii,
Capitol T 169;
photo by Paul Garrison,
posed by the Hawaiian dancer Leialoha.

CAPITOL RECORDS
HIGH FIDELITY
RECORDING
DANNY KUAANA presents
holiday in hawaii
Mauna Kea · Lovely Hula Hands · Noho Paipai · Ke Kali Nei Au · Hilo Hattie · E Kuu Lei My Darling · Kilima Waltz · He U i · Kohala March · King's Serenade · Hawaiian War Chant · He Manao No'u Ia
Capitol
REG. U.S. PAT. OFF.
RECORDS

On **DESTINATION HONOLULU**, the pink Royal Hawaiian Hotel with lit beachfront terrace looks out over sand and sea at Waikiki. A small crescent of beach paradise curves along the cove of low-rise buildings, jutting piers, and sparse palm trees, but ugly modern buildings seem to be encroaching even here. Still, on this LP, the role of Sam Kailuha and the Islanders—"authentic interpreters of Hawaiian music"—is to "leave the listener with a feeling of being right in the idle of Waikiki Beach." Once there, the would-be traveler is assured, the Hawaiians won't seem unusual, their customs and culture marketed as "generally similar to the United States." Should being away from home, whether for honeymoon, wedding anniversary, or singles get-away, create anxiety, our liner notes tell us: "Communications, currency, tobacco, motion pictures and various other little luxuries are similar to the mainland." The only thing "exotic" here is the "jumble of apothecary, jade and food shops." Nevertheless, with songs like "Maunaloa Minnie," "Hawaiian Wedding Song," and "My Kilgueo Sweetheart," there are still hopes for going native. Along with an airline luggage tag graphic— and the blue and white logo above an announcement that Hawaii is a destination "along the routes of Pan Am"—on the front, and a Pan American jet pictured on the back, the album offers "You can take a Pan Am jet Clipper from the West Coast and be there in less than five hours."

FIGURE 10.3

Sam Kailuha and the Islanders,
Destination Honolulu,
Cavalier Records C-55006.

STEREO

(S) C-55006

DESTINATION **Honolulu**

SAM KAILUHA & THE ISLANDERS

ON THE BEACH AT WAIKIKI
SONG OF THE ISLANDS
HAWAIIAN WEDDING SONG
MY WAIKIKI LANI
MY KIHAULO SWEETHEART
AGA
IN HAWAII
MAUNA LOA MINNIE
SUMMER IN HAWAII
NANI WAIMEA

Cavalier RECORDS

RECORDED IN HAWAII

PRINTED IN U.S.A.

PAN AM

ALONG THE ROUTES OF PAN AM

YOUR MUSICAL TRIP AROUND THE ISLAND OF HAWAII WITH THE "HILO KALIMAS," from London International, features a stretched white Chrysler sedan, with four doors on each side, ready to depart on an island tour. The car, from Tradewind Tours, sits in front of a long low building with a grass roof. One woman, clearly a tourist, runs toward it, eager not to miss her tour, as a few others wait patiently. Everyone seems to be wearing a lei. The back of the LP offers an illustrated map of Hawaii, "the big island," courtesy of the Hawaiian Visitors Bureau. The map fits in a myriad of information for the listener, complete with entertaining historical notes, drawings that denote major lava flows on the island, and cartoonish figures of the "natives" that tourists might see in their dream journey around the island. This LP provides a selection of popular Hawaiian tunes as well as a memento of a Hawaiian vacation, or just an album of a future journey. *Your Musical Trip around the Island of Hawaii* received an "International Special Merit" from *Billboard* upon its release in 1966 (seven years after Hawaii became the fiftieth state): "since the market for Hawaiian music continues to flourish, this package of island music should do quite well."[11]

FIGURE 10.4

Hilo Kalimas,
*Your Musical Trip around
the Island of Hawaii*,
London International SW-99398;
photo by Camera Hawaii,
courtesy of Inter-Island Trade-Wind Tours;
cover design by Grace S. Hashimoto.

your musical trip

AROUND THE ISLAND of HAWAII

with the "Hilo Kalimas"

SW-99398 **STEREO**

LONDON
INTERNATIONAL
RECORDED IN
HAWAI'I

Identified as "ideal background music for your Hula Show films," HAWAIIAN MUSIC FROM THE KODAK HULA SHOW from Waikiki Records represents a noteworthy cross-branding effort, promoting photographic film, movie film, tourism, and vinyl LPs in one package. Fritz Herman, Kodak's Marketing Director in Hawaii, "saw a need to give visitors a complete picture of the islands which they were not otherwise able to photograph … hula dancers and Polynesian entertainment." The Kodak Hula Show began in 1937, two years after the introduction of Kodachrome, which brought color film to the masses, and ran for over 60 years.[12] Film was sold near the show, which provided many photo opportunities, as it was staged outdoors expressly for tourists to photograph, and the performers wore brilliant green "grass" skirts, yellow leis, and red flowers—perfect Kodak colors. The album's notes also included "pointers for picture-taking," as "Hawaii is a photographer's paradise, with a wealth of natural subjects": "If you're looking for natives, you'll find gracious hula girls, Polynesian fishermen sun-drying their nets and bright-eyed children from a dozen races." As a spectacular site, the Kodak Hula Show has garnered attention from scholars; however, few mention the eponymous LPs that tend to endure long after tourist slides and photographs disappear or fade away.[13]

FIGURE 10.5

Hawaiian Music from the Kodak Hula Show, Waikiki Records 302.

HIGH-FIDELITY STEREO 302

Hawaiian Music from the

Kodak HULA SHOW

Kodak Hula Show Record Produced by Waikiki Records Company in Honolulu, Hawaii

Jerry Byrd and His Orchestra's **ON THE SHORES OF WAIKIKI**, from 1960 features
Danny Kuaana and his group of Hawaiian musicians. Byrd, an accomplished steel
guitar player, recorded with country stars such as Patsy Cline, Ernest Tubb, and
Hank Williams, released several "Hawaiian" albums in the 1950s that showcased his
guitar playing, and later moved to Hawaii to participate in the steel guitar revival.
The selections from this LP sound a bit frenetic, as if Byrd is determined to show off
his chops. The cover's requisite beach photograph, framed by palm trees, is slightly
unusual in that it does not include a hula dancer, lei, or sun-kissed tourist.

FIGURE 10.6

Jerry Byrd and His Orchestra,
On the Shores of Waikiki,
Mercury MG 20230.

Liner notes on **ENCHANTMENT FROM HAWAII** offer a bit of history; and for the armchair traveler-historian, in the case of the Hawaiian Islands, this often means enlightening details: "Originally a kingdom, they were annexed to the United States in 1898, became a territory in 1900, and, ultimately, entered the union as the 50th state." *Annexed*? Ah, but the "enchantment"! Tropical drinks in carved pineapples; banana leaves and flowers covering the low beach front table; a beaming white woman who seems to have cast off her swimsuit cover sat among the apparently native women as she considers her new husband's rapt attention to the hula dancers: This is a classic Hawaiian record cover shot.[14] An album of songs "played in the authentic island style" and with "native percussion" reveals similar melody, instrumentation, and arrangements as other so-called Hawaiian LPs, although the numbers here may be more fraught with marimba. "Minoi Minoi E," a Samoan song, begins with what sound like wood blocks—no *'ili'ili* or *kala'au* here.

FIGURE 10.7

Hawaiian Islanders,
Enchantment from Hawaii,
Cameo C-1035;
photo courtesy of Pan American Airways.
@ABKCO Records.

Enchantment
from
HAWAII
BY THE
HAWAIIAN ISLANDERS

SWEET LEILANI
VAHINE ANAMITE
MOON OF MANAKOORA
SWEET SOMEONE
MINOI MINOI E
MAPUANA
NANI WAIMEA
EBB TIDE
SEA BREEZE
BEACH AT WAIKIKI
MARURU A VAU
MAKAHA

PHOTO COURTESY OF PAN AMERICAN AIRWAYS

CAMEO

C-1035

HUKILAU HULAS, from Gene Norman Presents, provides basic instruction for at-home hulas. (Norman, producer and jazz impresario, founded the jazz label GNP Crescendo.) The front of the LP, in vivid color, accentuated by bright yellow typography, shows a group of four hula dancers performing outside, for what is undoubtedly a tourist show. The back cover states: "The lovely music of Hawaii makes you want to do MORE than just listen!" The notes, combined with a set of useful drawings of "interpretive motions," attempt to guide the student through the entire "Hukilau" song, with step-by-step notation of each hula motion:

Remember these four points:
1. The feet keep time and generally move in short steps.
2. The hips accentuate the rhythm of the music.
3. The fingers, hands and arms interpret the words.
4. The face and eyes express the mood.

Hula instruction records were popular gifts for tourists to bring back to the mainland, along with Hawaiian shirts, macadamia nuts, and fresh pineapples.[15] The album spawned a second volume, *Hukilau Hulas, Vol. 2*: both are available on CD and MP3 formats.

FIGURE 10.8

Hukilau Hulas,
GNP Crescendo.

FIGURE 10.9

Hukilau Hulas,
GNP Crescendo, back cover.

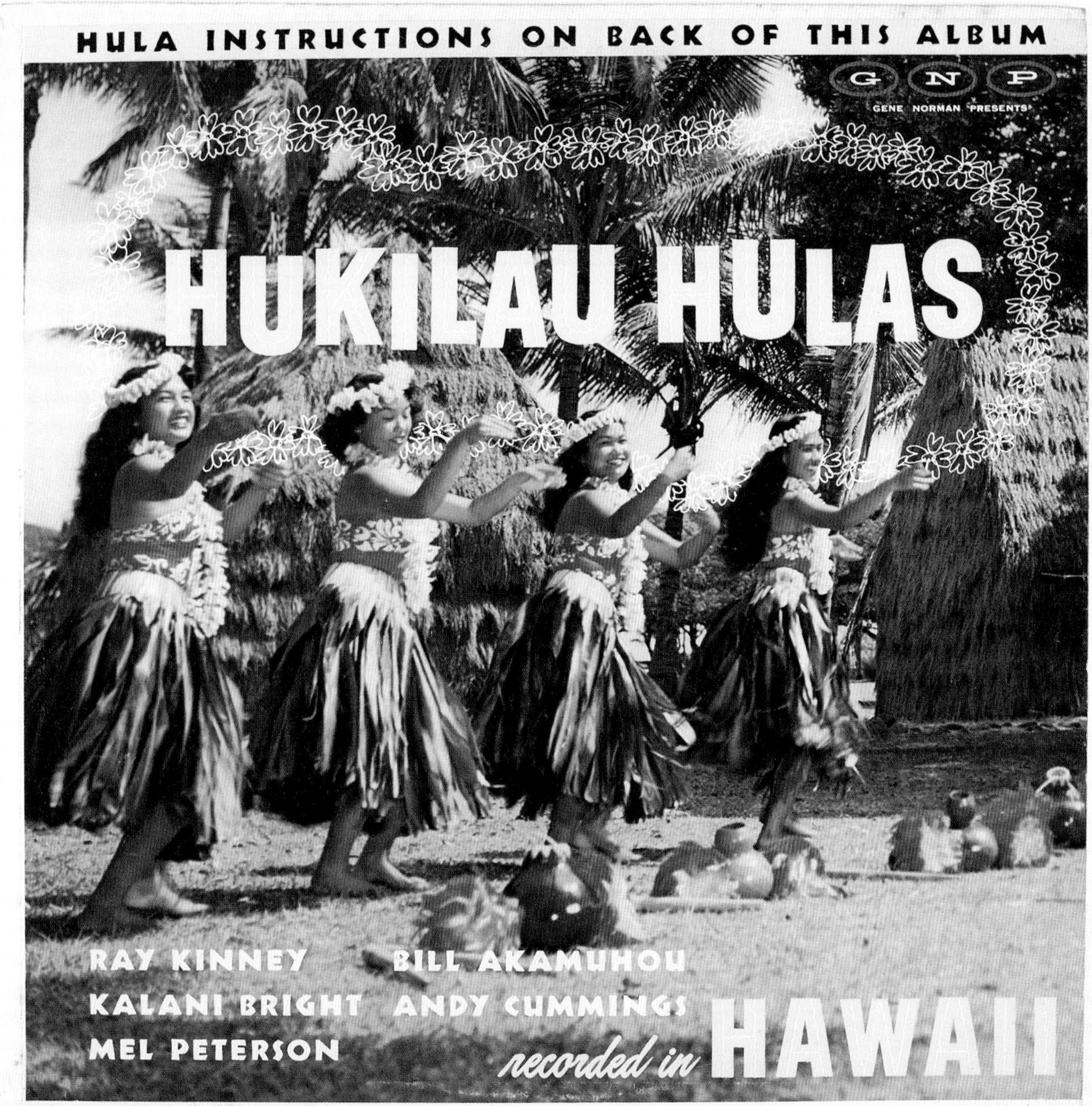
HULA INSTRUCTIONS ON BACK OF THIS ALBUM
GNP
GENE NORMAN PRESENTS
HUKILAU HULAS
RAY KINNEY
BILL AKAMUHOU
KALANI BRIGHT
ANDY CUMMINGS
MEL PETERSON
recorded in HAWAII

HUKILAU HULAS

GNP
GENE NORMAN PRESENTS

THE lovely music of Hawaii makes you want to do MORE than just listen! It's an invitation to try your hand (and the rest of you) at the art of fluent motion—THE HULA—interpretive dancing at its most basic level. THE HULA gives you the opportunity to express physically the meaning of the words of the song in gracefully abstract motions of the body ...anybody can do it and do it well, whether "malihini" (stranger) or "kamaaina" (old timer).

HERE ARE SOME BASIC INSTRUCTIONS...HAVE FUN!

The secret of a successful hula is the coordination of the hands, the graceful swaying of the hips and the movement of the feet in one lovely fluid motion.

REMEMBER THESE FOUR POINTS:
1. The feet keep time and generally move in short steps.
2. The hips accentuate the rhythm of the music.
3. The fingers, hands and arms interpret the words.
4. The face and eyes express the mood.

THE VAMP

This is the basic step and is used to mark time. First, raise the arms level with the chest. Extend hands gracefully, holding fingers together.

— THE VAMP — — SOME BASIC INTERPRETIVE MOTIONS —

RIGHT VAMP Moving arms slowly to right, take short step to right then slide left foot up beside right. Repeat. Shift weight gracefully to left as arms move gradually left.

LEFT VAMP Short step to left. Right slides up beside. Repeat. Keep knees bent slightly at all times.

SPEAK OR SING Bring hands to mouth then move gracefully outward.

ALOHA Cup hands toward you. Then extend arms, gracefully while opening hands.

MOON OR SUN Raise arms high overhead in a circle, palms upward, fingertips touching.

MOUNTAINS OR HILLS Arms raised sideways, palms outward. One hand is peak, other is slope.

LOVE OR CUDDLE Arms crossed over chest. Head tilted slightly.

GRASS SHACK OR HOUSE Hands form roof-top.

PAU (The End) This is used to mark the end of all hula dances. Point right foot forward extending arms forward over toes, hands together. Bow head, bend forward from the waist.

*HUKILAU A fishing festival in which everyone in the village takes part. Men, women, children ...all help to pull in the fish nets. Afterward there is a big LUAU (feast) with singing and dancing.

1. OH WE'RE GOING... Walk forward, swaying, hands on hips.

2. TO A HUKILAU... Vamp right, using hands and arms as though pulling fish net.

3. HUKI HUKI HUKI HUKI HUKILAU... Pull four more times (as in #2), continue sliding four more steps to right.

4. EVERYBODY... Sway hips wide, extending arms out to audience.

5. LOVES... Cross arms on chest. A HUKILAU... Repeat #2.

6 WHERE THE LAULAU Sway left, cupping hands upward.

7. IS THE KAU KAU Sway right. Point two fingers toward mouth as if eating.

8. AT THE BIG LUAU Sway left. Move both hands to mouth, smiling broadly.

9. WE THROW OUR NETS OUT INTO THE SEA... Raise both arms high over head. Then seem to throw net far out in front.

10. AND ALL THE AMA AMAS COME SWIMMING... Place right hand over left, palms down. Wiggle thumbs. Move hands outward and side to side as fish (ama) swimming.

11. TO ME Point hands to yourself. OH WE'RE GOING TO A HUKILAU... HUKI, HUKI, HUKI, HUKILAU (Repeat #1 to #3)

12. WHAT A BEAUTIFUL DAY... Sway right and left, raising arms slowly outward and upward toward sun.

13. FOR FISHING THE OLD HAWAIIAN WAY Sway right and left. Raise right arm as if to throw spear.

14. AND THE HUKILAU NETS ARE SWISHING... Sway right and left. Hands sway side to side gracefully, palms forward (like swishing net).

15. DOWN IN OLD LAIE BAY Arms make circle in front to represent bay.

16. OH WE'RE GOING TO A HUKILAU. A HUKI, HUKI, HUKI, HUKILAU (Repeat #1 to #3) PAU (end)

SIDE 1			
TITLE	ARTIST	COMPOSERS	TIME
1. THE HUKILAU SONG	MEL PETERSON	J. Owens	2:28
2. MY LITTLE GRASS SHACK IN KEALAKEKUA, HAWAII	KALANI BRIGHT	Noble — Cogswell — Harrison	2:46
3. THE COCKEYED MAYOR OF KAUNAKAKAI	ANDY CUMMINGS	Anderson — Stillman	2:37
4. BLUE LEI	BILL AKAMUHOU	Beamer — Anderson	2:16
5. E NAUGHTY MAI NEI	MEL PETERSON	Peterson	2:10
6. LOVELY HULA HANDS	RAY KINNEY	Anderson	2:44

SIDE 2			
TITLE	ARTIST	COMPOSERS	TIME
1. A SONG OF OLD HAWAII	MEL PETERSON	Beecher-Noble	2:16
2. HAPA HEOLE HULA GIRL	ANDY CUMMINGS	Cunha	2:40
3. (If You Wanna) DANCE THE HULA	KALANI BRIGHT	Tavares	2:00
4. HAWAIIAN HOSPITALITY	RAY KINNEY	Kinney — H. Owens	2:15
5. LITTLE BROWN GAL	BILL AKAMUHOU	Wood — McDiarmid — Noble	2:01
6. ACROSS THE SEA	RAY KINNEY	Kaai — Kinney — Noble	3:34

11

SOUND TOUR

In 1962, Verve and *Esquire* magazine teamed up to produce a series of four Sound Tour LPs, each packaged in elaborate fold-out sleeves, with color photographs, and extensive notes that intimated insider information. The unusual cover design opened out from the center, much like an altarpiece, to reveal the attached Sound Tour booklet, written by *Esquire*'s travel editor, Richard Joseph, and cleverly illustrated by Tracy Sugarman—who designed many album covers for the Grand Award label. The LP slipped in from the top, instead of the side, of the heavy cardboard package. Around the same time, a sampler album, more plainly packaged as a single LP titled *Sound Tour: Impressions in Sound of an American on Tour*, was sent to radio stations to promote the series. *Esquire* ran extensive cross promotion of the set in its June 1962 issue, and retailers were provided gold stickers with the *Esquire* logo for the covers.[1]

Formed around the "impressions in sound of an American on tour," France, Spain, Italy and the United States's newest resort, Hawaii, came to life to seduce bachelors in search of passion in every port. The set brings together several themes: the attentive listener, the cosmopolitan traveler, and the discerning gourmand. And, the sampler's liner notes promised:

> Sound Tour was created to present, in music and the printed word, as nearly perfect and satisfying a tour of an exciting foreign country as possible. The only

tickets needed for the trip are a phonograph and an easy chair, and suddenly you are munching delicacies at a Luau or pitching a coin into the Fontana di Trevi or ordering wine in a café in Seville or riding a bicycle in Brittany.

Certainly, the effort that went into the liner notes hints at a knowledgeable and worldly *Esquire* consumer:

> The senses are called into play to savor the countries as the sophisticated traveler does … he seeks out the little restaurant or cafe that a Frenchman or an Italian would prize. The man-about-the-world gets off the beaten track where he can feast his eyes and ears and, of course, his stomach. He will take alternate routes so that his trip between cities will be different and filled with the adventure of encountering the unexpected.

These titles subtly suggest a solo, male traveler, open to "discover" new territory.

The Sound Tour liner notes heralded the vinyl LPs as "the new and exciting concept in recording. It wraps into one neat package of superb sound a host of keen impressions of a country certain to start pleasant trains of memory or begin the whetting of an appetite that will be satisfied only by a trip abroad." And, a *Billboard* reviewer noted: "Verve Records has combined production and exploitation talents to create a distinctive set of four albums, keyed to reach travel bugs and sound fanciers."[2] They provide quite a vision of the well-traveled, cosmopolitan-yearning, midcentury man absorbing the delights of France, Italy, Spain, and Hawaii and experiencing the power of his hi-fi sound system.

Each album's liner notes included elaborate descriptions of how the music was recorded, with charts of which microphones recorded which instruments—accordion, Telefunken U47; saxophone, RCA 44B ribbon mike—a photograph of the studio's twelve-channel master control board used for the LPs, extensive credits for the album's personnel, including engineer, the engineering technician, and "sound pictures." Although the set comprises selections on France, Italy, Spain, and Hawaii, they often refer to the "countries" featured on the LPs: "Here is the *feel* of a country. Through the skilled blending of music, sound, and the written word, the Sound Tour traveler can know the sparkling Mediterranean, the grey-green Seine, the rich smells of food in a Neapolitan market place, the sweet smell of blossoms in a Hawaiian flower grove." The notes highlight how memories flow from the LPs, lasting longer than any actual tour: "memories which this musical tour will bring back to you again and again for as long as you care to remember."

Esquire, founded in 1933 as a men's magazine, featured "a slick, sophisticated style and drawings of scantily clad young women."[3] A key goal in the early days of the magazine, according to historian Kenon Breazeale, was to "fabricate" a certain type of male consumer, one that was "in the market" for status.[4] The magazine, which "testified to the greater glories of being a hip epicurean and serves as a detailed guide to get you there,"[5] had a long history of promoting jazz. Their yearly jazz "poll" evolved into a celebrated series of *Esquire* Jazz Concerts, which included the first jazz concert at the Metropolitan Opera House, as well as several acclaimed *Esquire Jazz Concert* albums. *Esquire* had also collaborated with RCA on the 1956 LP *The Esquire Album of Music for the Continental Host*. *Esquire* remains popular today, publishing over 25 international editions, and has stayed focused on men, or at least a particular vision of men, with features such as their annual "Sexiest Woman Alive" awards and their regular "The Women We Love of Instagram" section.

The other member of the Sound Tour team, Verve Records, founded in 1956, helped bring jazz to a world audience. The label produced many classic jazz records in the 1950s and 1960s, including those by Ella Fitzgerald, Stan Getz, and Oscar Peterson. Verve's founder, Norman Granz, also organized the legendary "Jazz at the Philharmonic" concerts that traveled throughout the United States beginning in the 1940s, which attracted considerable attention and helped put jazz on the cultural map.[6]

The Sound Tour records featured music by Kenyon Hopkins, a well-known jazz arranger and composer of such film scores as *12 Angry Men*, *The Hustler*, and *Downhill Racer*. He assembled an experienced team of jazz musicians, including trumpeter Doc Severinsen, who was just on the verge of becoming the bandleader for Johnny Carson's long run on the *Tonight Show*. Creed Taylor, highly respected for his work at Verve, produced them.

The ingredients were in place for a set of sophisticated records; and one might expect sophisticated, unusual music, hidden itineraries, and erudite commentary from a co-branding collaboration of *Esquire*, Verve, and Kenyon Hopkins. Generally, however, the LPs tend to reproduce standard tourist locale motifs, along with middling musical selections. Unlike many other travel-related LPs, the Sound Tour albums eschewed "local" musicians and performers, with less "authentic" and more uniform results. Although the notes provide a concise, dense introduction to each destination, the music tends to homogenize, as if all these cultures might be expressed through American-style jazz; and instrumentals carry the day, so no foreign language appears, except for snippets of conversation in the LP's "sound pictures." The LPs do include ambient sounds such as a ship's whistle and birdcalls, and these added touches open an interesting possibility for their use as background music for home movies of an overseas tour.

ALBUMS

The cover of **SOUND TOUR: HAWAII** offers a classic Hawaiian sunset, bright orange-yellow sun, a few clouds, framed by palm tree silhouettes. The only Sound Tour series LP featuring a US destination, it lists "traditional" Hawaiian tunes such as "Song of the Islands" and a gently swinging "Hawaiian War Chant," but the songs only hint at the stereotypical sound of "island music." The guidebook writer explains: "Kenyon Hopkins has wisely decided to bring you a mainlander's musical impression of the islands, saving for your visit to Hawaii the pleasure of hearing the old tunes in their proper native setting." We hear a boat whistle, complements of the Matson Line, the major ocean carrier into Hawaii, which continues its service today. Bongos appear on "Outer Island" to close out side one. With a nod to Hawaiian music personalities such as Martin Denny and Arthur Lyman, a few birdcalls are included, but generally, the music resembles mellow, easy-listening jazz more than the lilting, hula-inflected Hawaiian music that was popular at the time.

FIGURE 11.1

Sound Tour: Hawaii,
Verve V6-50003;
photo by Davis Drew Zingg.

STEREO

V6-50003

VERVE RECORDS AND
SOUND TOUR:
Impressions In Sound

ESQUIRE MAGAZINE
HAWAII
Of An American On Tour

The cover of **SOUND TOUR: FRANCE** includes an aerial photograph of the magnificent Château de Chambord in the Loire Valley, begun in 1519 by a French king for a hunting lodge, and used during World War II to store art treasures from the Louvre. Depicting this chateau, although famous, conveys the album's message of sophistication—it's not the Eiffel Tower, after all. Richard Joseph's notes are sprinkled with references to "the Guide Michelin," "a fast Dubonnet," and "Gare Lazare," and urges the reader to visit Courbevoie, "probably unvisited by any American since Black Jack Pershing." Joseph makes a game attempt to link the music with his itinerary: "on this trip, you'll want to use the same fine taste and discrimination of Kenyon Hopkins' lovely music," as he suggests that "bongos, percussion and harp will lead you into 'Place Elégante' via Claire de Lune." Writing for an in-the-know listener, Joseph describes a sound tour of France with shimmers of savior faire, and insists "you'll find that your off-trail itinerary—away from the usual tourist orbit—will pay handsomely." The back cover promises that the LP presents "the France sophisticated travelers savor. Esquire travel guide tells how to do France the smart way … everything but the tickets inside."

Of course, *Sound Tour: France—Impressions in Sound of an American on Tour* evokes composer George Gershwin's *An American in Paris*, which aimed to capture an American traveler's experience in 1920s Paris. As Gershwin told it, "My purpose here is to portray the impressions of an American visitor in Paris as he strolls about the city, listens to the various street noises, and absorbs the French atmosphere."[7] The *Sound Tour: France* LP incorporates sounds of a train whistling down the tracks, women talking *en français*, and snatches of conversation that veers from the left to the right channel, demonstrating the stereo mix. The instrumentals are very good, with catchy saxophone solos and bouncy beat that bear repeat listening.[8]

FIGURE 11.2

Sound Tour: France,
Verve V6-50000;
photo by Louis Renault.

V6-50000

VERVE RECORDS AND ESQUIRE MAGAZINE
SOUND TOUR: FRANCE
Impressions In Sound   Of An American On Tour

Italy's contribution to the Sound Tour series offers a somewhat barren looking photograph on its cover, capturing classical ruins, perhaps Pompeii, with several Roman
columns and an ancient wall among grass-covered buildings. SOUND TOUR: ITALY
offered a sophisticated soundtrack for the man who knew Chianti from Chardonnay.
A-list architectural monuments, including the Colosseum, the Roman Forum, and
Pompeii receive guidebook quality description and a song for each site. This album
captures the romance of Rome, the seductions of Sicily, and the virility of Venice,
helping to pave the way for a rapprochement with the former Axis enemy.

Sound Tour: Italy's notes confront recent history right away: "It's sometimes
hard to remember that Italy was enemy territory throughout most of the last war.
In 1945, its railroads, steamship piers, hotels and sections of its great cities were
shelled by Allies and Germans into blackened piles of rubble." The *Esquire* voice
suffuses the notes with offhand comments about Italian gender dynamics: such as
this observation about Milanese males: "Being Italians after all, chances are that
they're also distributing painless pinches where they will do the most good," and
"like all Italians, the Venetian has a strongly developed appreciation of female beauty."
The booklet brims with advice—when to visit, how to hire a gondolier, and what to
eat. Complementing the notes' cultivated air, "the music avoids the tourist route;
instead it wanders, happily at random, up and down the Italian boot." Once again,
"street" noises mix with the music, and credited trumpet solos from Doc Severinsen
and Joe Wilder, and an alto saxophone solo by Phil Woods, complement the selections, which hint at Italy: "Arrival Milano *(Funiculi, funicula)*," "L'Autobus (*O sole
mio*)," and "Arrivederci Roma."

FIGURE 11.3

Sound Tour: Italy,
Verve V6-50002;
photo by John Ross.

STEREO

V6-50002

VERVE RECORDS AND ESQUIRE MAGAZINE
SOUND TOUR: ITALY
Impressions In Sound Of An American On Tour

The gothic Segovia Cathedral in northwest Spain graces the cover of **SOUND TOUR: SPAIN**. Now a world heritage site, the cathedral looms between trees, perched proudly overlooking the Plaza Mayor in Segovia. Bullfighting references open the text of the album's enclosed travel guide, with its description of the "blood-red glare of the bullring." Despite exhortations not to rush through and attempt to "see everything," the guide provides a whirlwind driving tour through much of Spain, starting with Madrid, working down to the southern sites of Andalucía, roving over to Basque country, and winding up in Granada and Valencia. Mention of Spain's recent history intervenes with pleasant thoughts of travel: "divided by politics, economics, even language, they live with the memory of the blood bath of their Civil War a quarter century ago, which killed millions of Spanish men."[9]

We are told not to expect Spanish music "that usually expresses the anguished dissonances of flamenco ballads," as "Kenyon Hopkins transposes traditional Spanish melody into a contemporary American idiom" as classical Spanish melodies and instrumentation "are augmented by the instruments of modern jazz: a romping piano, saxophones, clarinet, bass, percussion, drums." Side one's opener, "Madrid (*Espana of Emile Waldteufel*)," promises authenticity with rhythmic castanets and Latin-flavored trumpet but morphs into more typical lounge jazz, with tinkling piano and walking bass. This Sound Tour includes ambient sounds, too, including the throaty exhaust notes of an Alfa Romeo sports car on "Parador," girls' voices, and the claps of a flamenco dancer. Overall, the music sounds fine, but seems to have only vague Spanish connection.

FIGURE 11.4

Sound Tour: Spain,
Verve V6-50001;
photo by Peter Buckley.

VERVE RECORDS AND
SOUND TOUR:
Impressions In Sound

ESQUIRE MAGAZINE
SPAIN
Of An American On Tour

V-50001

12 ADVENTURES IN SOUND

Columbia Records' Adventures in Sound included albums from around the world, creatively packaged to appeal to American consumers eager to hear an international selection of sounds. Building on the growing interest in folk and "exotic" music, the series presented LPs from established American and British folksingers as well as from far-flung lands, such as the Caribbean, Paraguay, and the Russian Steppes. The series earned a reputation for authenticity and quality in recording and sound, as well as presentation of difficult to capture, rarely heard music. Adventures in Sound, promoted as "a revolutionary concept in recording designed especially for the adventurous listener," included dozens of records, some of which might be considered cult classics, such as *Sorcery!* However, the series has received relatively little attention—even within Columbia's own histories, including the lavishly illustrated chronicle of their first 125 years, *360 Sound: The Columbia Records Story*, and their extensive "125 Years of Columbia Records" website, which focus mainly on star performers in the company's recording pantheon[1]

A January 1958 article in *Billboard* announced Adventures in Sound as "a series of pop packages priced at $4.98."[2] Shortly thereafter, a review for the *Jamaican Drums* LP exclaimed, "an exciting and varied set with excellent sound. This ranks high in the folk category, and hi-fi bugs should also find it to their liking."[3] The following year, Columbia began running Adventures in Sound as a separate operation; and despite *Billboard*'s early designation of the series as pop, a broader vista emerged as new albums were released.

Renowned blues musician Big Bill Broonzy contributed his album *Big Bill's Blues*, named after his 1928 hit song, that was also reviewed under "folk"—along with Burl Ives and *The Wandering Minstrel*—though the reviewer notes, "Lovers of blues will find this hard to resist."[4] It seems Adventures in Sound courted a certain amount of genre confusion.

Making a keen promotional point, Columbia advertising executive Art Schwartz approached Adventures in Sound from another angle. He explained: "Today, a customer can buy a Sinatra, Mathis or a Mitch Miller record in grocery stores or chains. Thus a record dealer who wants to keep his clientele has to become a specialty store, and the 'Adventures' line is perfect for this."[5] In other words, stocking LPs from a series known for unusual music could make a record store a desirable destination, and record labels used this claim to get their vinyl onto shelves.

For the Adventures in Sound series, the expanded size of the twelve-inch LP, both in terms of the capacity to include more music and the larger size of the cover was advantageous. The longer format made it easier to market international stars—the album could include several songs that "gave Americans listeners time to absorb the work of that artist who, more likely than not, was getting only limited airplay; and the album format accommodated extensive notes, so an American listener could learn about [foreign performers]."[6]

In the early releases, block capital letters, often in thematic colors, each in its own square, run around the four sides of the album covers, spelling out the words Adventures in Sound. This design element, reminiscent of crossword puzzles or Scrabble word patterns, creates a visual coherence and a consistent frame for each album's thematic image—often a photograph, but sometimes a drawing or painting. On the back cover, the name of the album and the featured artists appear with the list of song titles in the album's appropriate language.

Typically, the liner notes include two or three paragraphs explaining the LP's context, including geographical, cultural, or biographical information. Then, songs are listed again with description of the arrangements, story, or sometimes a line of translation. Often more ethnographic in approach than Capitol's Capitol of the World albums, and with more colorful covers than Folkways records, this series was an adventurous effort to capture authentic performances and introduce different sounds and traditions to the American public.

ALBUMS

FIESTA LINDA's border of party pinks, oranges, and reds and the close-up photo of the striking white and black "toucan: a long-beaked bird in the Paraguayan forests" creates expectations of an upbeat experience; and the orange-billed bird naturally becomes an iconic element by which to recall the fauna of Paraguay. With harp representing "the typical instrument of the Paraguayan people" and featured artist Digno Garcia designated an authentic exemplar of a harp player—Digno Garcia built his own harp and "In the manner of the minstrels of old, he carries it with him wherever he goes"—the Western listener can feel an insider access to music and song a world away.

FIGURE 12.1

Digno Garcia and His Paraguayan Trio,
Fiesta Linda,
Columbia WL 122;
photo by Three Lions Inc.

ADVENTURES IN SOUND *

WL 122 **DIGNO GARCIA HIS HARP AND HIS PARAGUAYAN TRIO** COLUMBIA
GUARANTEED HIGH-FIDELITY

FIESTA LINDA

TOUCAN: A LONG-BEAKED BIRD IN THE PARAGUAYAN FORESTS

ADVENTURES IN SOUND *

CARIBBEE places us somewhere in the "Indies" where dense green foliage includes palm trees and Juan Serrano and His Caribbean Combo serenade with songs and "simple words expressing natural thoughts and uninhibited ideas common to the natural environment of these uncomplicated people." Tropical hues of yellow, orange, and pink frame the cover photograph of a native woman and two boys as they tend a stand heaped with vegetables as they look toward a white woman in a sundress who appears to ready her camera. Lyrics communicate an "innocent" life of avoiding work, as in "El negrito del Baley," dancing and drinking sugar cane juice in "Cana brava," and, of course, inflamed passion; however, an emphasis on simple joys cannot erase the presence of poverty and hunger in the song "China."

FIGURE 12.2

Juan Serrano and His Caribbean Combo,
Caribbee: Songs of the Indies,
Columbia WL 103;
photo by Henry Wolf.

Finding "Minuet in G" on the album **JAMAICAN DRUMS** among "Jamaica Jump-Up," popularized in the Bond film *Dr. No*'s calypso party scene, and "Soja Man," a folk song in the mento style, expresses a "delicious impertinence"—which according to the liner notes reflects a "Caribbean frame of mind." A classical piece becomes a "percussive exercise." This is not Vienna, after all. The cover photo of dark-skinned young men navigating hand-built-looking wooden canoes and diving into dark blue water fails to support a vision of compositional or improvisational musical genius on the part of the featured steel band, but more a notion of unschooled, unspoiled, natural abilities. Described as "ingratiating," "gifted," "highly polished," and capable of "interpretative overtones," the ensemble's main work here seems to be conjuring up "a languorous picture of palms and surf," appealing to an armchair traveler in Omaha or Orlando.

FIGURE 12.3

Royal Steel Band of
Kingston, Jamaica,
Jamaican Drums: Steel Band in Hi-Fi,
Columbia WL 121;
cover drawing by Russell Hoban;
photo by Henry Wolf.

A turquoise blue wall and door—from what appears to be a traveling musician's claus-trophobic room that reveals a coat, a bottle of booze, and a guitar perched on a low daybed—compose two-thirds of the cover photo and provide the background for the LP title **BIG BILL'S BLUES**, in orange. The remainder of the photo is black, as though a dark curtain has been drawn, providing a strong vertical line, and a graphic back-drop to the yellow letters spelling out "Big Bill Broonzy." In a rare example of music from the United States being collected in a series like Adventures in Sound, *Big Bill's Blues* features performances from Broonzy and captures the in-country exotic, with "original American negro music." Broonzy was born in Mississippi in 1893 and moved to Chicago's South Side in the 1920s. He became a successful professional blues performer and toured the world. In the liner notes, the definition of "blues" denotes "depressed in spirits," with no mention of the influential musical interval, or "blue note," found in West Africa-originating musical scales; and black slavery in America becomes indiscernible from poverty and generally grueling work. A new musical form began, we are told, with "the 'Field Holler,' the cry of the negro, possibly a slave, in a deserted landscape, cutting a tree or looking for a lost cow. A lonely human being, frightened by the awe-inspiring silence enveloping him, shouting to dispel the silence and his fears like a child in the dark." The sublime existential angst, and the infantilized response, described here as the root of a "primitive" musical inspiration might well have been portrayed as having more concrete origins such as dehuman-ized living conditions, regular beatings, or threat of brutal death. In case we need

FIGURE 12.4

Big Bill Broonzy,
Big Bill's Blues,
Columbia WL 111;
photo by Roy DeCarava.

further confirmation of the abyss between the pioneers of blues and the audience for this album: "Big Bill is a natural-born musician. He never 'learned' music as we do, but discovered for himself how to play the guitar and how to sing." With increasingly suburban lifestyles that emphasized nuclear family homes, each with an individually purchased piano, the notion that "we" learn music differently is not a stretch.

....

The vivid red of the pale model's lips and fingernails match the lettering that spells out the title of **DARK EYES: SONGS OF THE STEPPES**. The green and blue of the Adventures in Sound lettering evokes a kind of pastoral calm. This LP celebrates Russia's contrasts and vastness, reflecting a story prior to "the turn of modern politics." The notes are dense with history, geography, and diverse culture, as well as details of an unconquerable human emotional depth illustrated by quotes from Chekov and Tolstoy. Included are dances such as the *lezghinka* and the Ukrainian *gopak*, as well as the iconic song "Volga Boatman," a bit of Romanian folk music with "Doina," and the traditional "Bublitschki," evoking the misery of a hot bagel seller.

FIGURE 12.5

Boris Sarbek and His Orchestra,
Dark Eyes: Songs of the Steppes,
Columbia WL 118;
photo by Normand Menard/Graham Associates.

WL 118

COLUMBIA
GUARANTEED HIGH-FIDELITY

lp

DARK EYES

SONGS OF THE STEPPES
BY BORIS SARBEK
AND HIS ORCHESTRA

ADVENTURES IN SOUND

Soaked in smoky, shadowy greys and browns, the cover of **SORCERY!**, featuring Sabu and His Percussion Ensemble, portrays glamorous, animal aspects lightly veiled in contemporary civilized woman; and horizontal rectangles of black and white frame the titles and graphically represent these dual natures. The anonymous liner notes achieve a rare level of poetically gruesome description—apparently to match the primordial struggles sorcery entails: "Life grows apace in lands where men still know the joys of being eaten alive by other men and/or by small fishes in furious clusters." Appreciatively hearing this musical chaos, from "giant crocodiles crunching the bones of careless waterfowl" to lice that "violate in aimless joy the matted fur of some dead, cold, warm-blooded species," Sabu creates music and through the magic of modern sound technology takes the listener from the comfortable safety of the domestic sphere to someplace other: "The rhythmic cadences of nature's boiler room are here, the aural history of the sex life of a cosmic corn popper, the wail and chime and gong sound of the eternal SORCERY."

FIGURE 12.6

Sabu and His Percussion Ensemble,
Sorcery!,
Columbia WL 101;
photo by Murray Laden.

ADVENTURES IN SOUND *
ADVENTURES IN SOUND

WL 101

sorcery!

sabu
and his percussion ensemble

COLUMBIA
GUARANTEED HIGH-FIDELITY
LP

PHOTO: MURRAY LADEN

ADVENTURES IN SOUND

13　CAPITOL OF THE WORLD

The Capitol of the World series, introduced in 1956 and active into the 1970s, encompassed a wide range of titles, from its early best-selling *German Beer Drinking Songs* and *Honeymoon in Rome* to more "exotic" titles such as *Australian Aboriginals* and *Kasongo!: Modern Music of the Belgian Congo*. Produced by Dave Dexter, Capitol of the World included over 400 albums. Each introduced listeners to music, images, and cultural highlights from around the globe. Some featured dual language texts, including Chinese characters and Arabic script. Today, these LPs appear as earnest attempts to offer listeners exposure to often unfamiliar cultural traditions, as well as opportunities to recall experiences from a trip abroad or tour of duty.

In 1957, Capitol released a Capitol of the World promotional album *A Musical Journey to Far Off Lands* to radio stations to promote the fledging effort. The liner notes capture the goals of the series:

> In far-off lands, as here, musical taste takes many forms: romantic ballads, "pop" novelty tunes, swinging instrumentals and every other conceivable type of music. Many of the tunes from other countries have found a place in the hearts of listeners here in America. Conversely, much of our music has become popular with the people overseas. Capitol's exciting series of outstanding international albums

features music from abroad—music that is played, loved and listened to in foreign countries.

Some Capitol of the World titles focused on faraway places, and seemed intent on moving US citizens out of wartime biases about Axis enemies, and to begin thinking of travel to these countries, appreciating their cultures and foods, and, most important, music, again, as tourism and airlines enjoyed a postwar boom. As the notes for the 1958 Capitol of the World album *The War Years* state, "Regardless of where one now lives, about the only good memory of The War Years is the music—the songs that were popular when the world was afire." Treading a fine line between memories of popular music and the miseries of war, *The War Years* recorded singer Eve Boswell "in a more serious mood. For weren't we all a bit more serious in those troubled times when *I'll Walk Alone* topped the international hit parades?" Wounds from the war in the Pacific were still fresh when Capitol released several Japanese-themed albums, including *Japanese Sketches* and *Japan Revisited*, both recorded in Tokyo and featuring "authentic Japanese instruments and songs."

Four subcategories were designed to bring particular aspects of a country's music and culture to the listener: "modern song stylists" for "popular tunes of the day presented by the top stars of foreign lands"; "folk songs" for "authentic music of the people, handed down from generation to generation"; "folk dances" for "traditional dance music that captures the living spirit of distant lands"; and "unusual recordings" for "exotic instruments and unique musical groups rarely heard" in the United States.[1]

Capitol of the World represented an early foray into what now might be called world music. As an early review exclaimed:

Dave Dexter Jr., brilliant and imaginative executive at Capitol Records in Hollywood, has for the past two years been releasing a sensational series of pop albums—the most exciting, entertaining, exotic music the world has to offer. His *Capitol of the World* series, now 150 albums strong, has captured on record the musical moods of all nations–from the sensual Egyptian dances, wild African chants, Mexican fiestas to Parisienne melodies and Italian tremulos … recorded on the spot by excellent local musicians.[2]

A sales report from the early days of the Capitol of the World series revealed the importance of export to its success: one out of every five Capitol of the World albums was exported. Clearly, markets existed outside the United States, suggesting that Capitol's musical vision of many counties touched not only those living in the States but also listeners living abroad. In other words, not only a listener in Louisville, Kentucky, but also in Beirut, Lebanon, may have come to "understand" the music of Lebanon or Sweden through the lens of Capitol of the World records.

Capitol had enjoyed success with "foreign" music: "[e]ven before the Beatles, the label had stunned the industry (and perhaps itself) by taking a Japanese-language number by Kyu Sakamoto, changing the title (translatable as 'I Look Up When I Walk') to the completely irrelevant but Occidentally recognizable 'Sukiyaki,' and reaching No. 1 in 1963."[3] The *Sukiyaki and Other Japanese Hits* LP was one of the best-selling Capitol of the World titles, but, unfortunately for Capitol, no "Japanese Beatles" emerged.

Despite its success, the Capitol of the World series seemed to inhabit a difficult, contested space at the growing record company. On one hand, after the enormous breakthrough of the Beatles, the search was on for more "foreign" bands to follow in their footsteps. As *Billboard* magazine reported in 1965: "with foreign material enjoying its greatest successes domestically through the British rock invasion, the Capitol of the World series takes on growing importance as an exposure barometer."[4] On the other hand, most Capitol of the World releases were clearly not destined for platinum status—many sold less than 1,000 copies. However, some sold over 100,000, including *German Beer Drinking Music*, *Christmas in Germany*, and *In London, in Love* (by Norrie Paramor).

Capitol of the World producer Dave Dexter, Jr., notoriously rejected the Beatles' first three singles, which were sent over from England to him by Capitol's majority owner, EMI. When he did agree to release Beatles records on Capitol, he altered the running order of the albums, dropped some songs altogether, changed the cover design and LP titles, and even remixed the master tapes to produce what he thought was a better sound. A respected jazz critic and jazz producer in the early 1950s, Dexter embraced the possibilities and profit potential of rereleasing "foreign" music, as he grew to resent much of the growing influence of rock and roll in the sales charts. At the time, he apparently thought the Beatles' music was "too foreign" for the US market. Dexter was roundly criticized for meddling with the Fab Four. For example, rock critic Dave Marsh excoriates

Dexter in his book on the *Beatles' Second Album*, taking him to task for "butchering" the Beatles records, and calling him the "man who hated the Beatles."[5]

The reason Dexter oversaw the Beatles in the first place was due to his role with Capitol's international artists and repertoire—the Beatles, from England, were at first considered "foreign" music. Dexter, the driving force behind the Capitol of the World series for most of its existence, thought "that young people should be given the opportunity to be exposed to better music; foreign music and music from other countries is classed as 'better music.'"[6]

Lloyd Dunn, Vice President of Capitol's International Division, who helped found the National Academy of Recording Arts & Sciences, which grants the Grammy Awards, was primarily focused on increasing Capitol of the World sales. Over the years they worked together, Dexter often received pointed memos from Dunn that included numerous ideas of how to package—or in some cases, repackage—recordings, and other ways of improving the Capitol of the World project. A 1964 memo from Dunn titled "Change in C.O.W. status," reflects the shifting terrain of pop music during the period: "We find it necessary to change our method of releasing and marketing certain C.O.W. items. Today it is frequently impossible to distinguish what is "Pops" and what is C.O.W., due to the influx and popularity of foreign artists."[7]

Throughout the life of the series, Capitol seemed to waver about what—and who—the records were produced for, and how best to promote them. Were they for curious American listeners exploring other musical traditions? Ethnic groups within the States? Or people elsewhere in the listening world? In particular, they had trouble deciding if Capitol of the World records should be packaged as "ethnic" or "popular." Some titles were meant for "ethnic" markets, as a 1958 promotional article reports: "Most of our albums are directed for a specific and largely ethnic audience, but some of the albums, particularly the 'German Beer Drinking Songs,' are among Capitol's best sellers."[8]

In 1963, Dexter summarized the scope of Capitol of the World and Capitol's perplexing policy regarding the mix and release of popular and "ethnic" LPs: "Rarely, to add authenticity and exclusivity to our catalog, we issue a Zulu LP, Belgian Congo music, chants of Australian aborigines, etc."[9] And, in an internal analysis of Capitol of the World records from 1964, "ethnic" albums included *Kasongo!: Music from the Belgian Congo*, *German Beer Drinking Music*, and *Cairo: The Music of Modern Egypt*, but not *Slow Boat to Capri*, *When in Rome*, or *Sounds of Old Mexico*.[10] Capitol of the World albums often make it seem as if they are recorded specifically for the American market, yet most were repackaged recordings of foreign performers, often stars in their home country. However, a few were recorded expressly for the series, including the "Sounds of" albums.

Each album includes liner notes that linked performers to the moods and culture of a nation or national capitol. Capitol of the World titles such as *Songs of India* and *Argentina Today* provide hours of interesting listening, as well as an introduction to core aesthetic and cultural elements beyond day-to-day US experience and education.

ALBUMS

MEXICO: ITS SOUNDS AND PEOPLE formed part of the Sounds and People series from Capitol, which included *Italy: Its Sounds and People*, *Japan: Its Sounds and People*, and *Afternoon in Amsterdam*. The front cover shows a beautifully ornate work of art on the front of an otherwise nondescript building. On reading the liner notes, which appear in both English and Spanish, we are informed that the artwork is "the Facade of the Library Building on the Campus of the University of Mexico, one of the Western Hemisphere's Greatest Architectural Wonders." The intricate mosaic, by renowned Mexican artist Juan O'Gorman, includes historical and mythical elements that invoke Aztec motifs as well as Western faith and reason.[11] The "sounds" on the LP include "Children in English Class," "Women Selling Tacos," "Bells of San Francisco Church," and "Race Driver Ricardo Rodriguez (And the Sounds of His Porsche)." The notes, revealing the complicated calculations of market segmentation for the series, conclude: "for all those who speak Spanish, for those who have visited or hope to visit one of the most friendly and colorful lands on the globe, and for those high fidelity filberts who glory in experiencing 'different' sounds from their turntable, *Mexico: Its Sounds and People* is the perfect album to have." The record was given away at travel conventions, as evidenced by a sticker seen on one example, stating: "*Show* magazine and Boeing present this Mexican memento of Asta's [American Society of Travel Agents] 33rd World Travel Congress, Mexico City, 1963."[12]

FIGURE 13.1

Mexico: Its Sounds and People,
Capitol T 10185.

MS-44

RDED IN MEXICO
'CAPITOL' OF THE WORLD

Capitol
RECORDS

MEXICO
its sounds and people

SANTIAGO!: MODERN CHILEAN FOLK MUSIC, "the first of its kind ever to be released in the U.S.A. and Canada," presents a sampling of traditional Chilean music.[13] The notes continue, "rarely is reference made to Chile's music, and its musicians, or to the music-minded Chileans who adore both their classical and 'pop' varieties." The cover photo, courtesy of Pan American World Airways, depicts a rural scene with an impressive snow-capped Andes peak in the background, and shows a traditional ox-drawn cart, and a man and a boy carrying long, pointed sticks for moving the oxen. What appear to be two tourists, with blue jeans and plaid shirts, look on. The liner notes include a brief geographical reminder that Chile is "a South American nation situated between the Andes and the South Pacific ocean." After providing some brief information on the music, the notes shift into travel guide mode:

> Chile in this latter half of the twentieth century has countless attractions. Friendly citizens, modern cities, snow-topped mountains as lovely as Switzerland's, a beautiful "main street" in Santiago incongruously named "Avenida O'Higgins," a fabulous resort known as Viña Del Mar, and as luxuriously beautiful as Nice or Mallorca; a high lake country, the Villarica and Osorno volcanoes, fjords, forests and scenery glorious.

The LP features wonderful music by Violetta Parra, Raul Gardy, and Silvia Infantas and Los Baqueanos—both "authentic" and contemporary—and might sound at home on a world music sampler from Putumayo World Music, available at Starbucks.

FIGURE 13.2

Santiago!: Modern Chilean Folk Music, Capitol T 10020; photo courtesy of Pan American World Airways.

Santiago!

Modern Chilean Folk Music

The liner notes of **ARGENTINA TODAY**, one of the earliest Capitol of the World LPs, advise the reader that "there's a 'new' nation developing today in South America. And along with its ambitious infant government and youthful expansion and growth there is emerging an engaging, distinctive, new music which contains all the required ingredients for acceptance in North America." The striking cover, photographed in Buenos Aires's historic square Plaza de Mayo, includes the imposing Obelisk, a national historical monument, built to celebrate Argentina's founding, and a Ferrari 225 Sport car (perhaps in town for the 1956 Argentine Grand Prix, won by the Ferrari team). The notes tout the musical talents of Vlady, who was "rewriting his nation's music, expertly combining the ancient folk melodies with the urgency and modernity of life in busy Buenos Aires." When *Argentina Today* was released in 1956, Argentina had recently suffered through the Argentine military bombing of Plaza de Mayo, part of a coup attempt, which threw the government into turmoil and helped precipitate President Juan Perón's resignation and exile. The LP, however, focuses on the "bright new country," reflecting optimism, perhaps, that Argentina would become more open to US interests with the fall of the labor-backed Perón regime. The musical selections offer easy-listening melodies, strong on strings and flute.

FIGURE 13.3

Vlady and His Buenos Aires
Orchestra,
Argentina Today,
Capitol T 10019;
photo courtesy of Pan American
World Airways.

RECORDED IN
BUENOS AIRES
Capitol
RECORDS
HIGH FIDELITY
ARGENTINA
TODAY
VLADY AND HIS BUENOS AIRES ORCHESTRA

The cover of **BERLIN BEI NACHT—BERLIN BY NIGHT: SONGS IN GERMAN LED BY HORST KUDRITZKI** presents an atmospheric nighttime photograph of the famous Kurfürstendamm in the then West Berlin, with bright red neon lights advertising Mercedes Benz, Graetz Radio, and Victoria, a large German insurance company. The street's wet surface reflects the blue, red, yellow and white lights, adding action to the image. A few pedestrians appear, but generally the scene seems quiet. The famous Kaiser Wilhelm Memorial Church, badly damaged in World War II, looms darkly in the distance. Bright blue and red typography resonate with the neon colors in the shot. Released in 1961, the year the Berlin Wall went up, the liner notes, presented in both English and German, carefully bring up politics: "Berlin is the most discussed city in the world today. But why go into that? This album ignores the delicate political situation of Berlin. It is, instead, designed to reflect the distinctive music of the city—music closely identified with the great German metropolis." With over thirty songs, many reminiscent of German cabaret, the album provides an excellent overview of a "modern West German hit parade," with both male and female soloists as well as chorales supported by lush, brass-heavy orchestral arrangements. As the notes optimistically remark: "The music needs no lengthy notes. Just drop the needle, lightly, on the record. This is Berlin of the 1960s. Nor has it changed much in a hundred years!"

FIGURE 13.4

Horst Kudritzki,
Berlin bei Nacht—
Berlin by Night: Songs in
German Led by Horst Kudritzki,
Capitol T 10228.

Berlin bei nacht

BERLIN BY NIGHT

Songs in German led by Horst Kudritzki

'CAPITOL' OF THE WORLD

Capitol RECORDS

HIGH FIDELITY

RECORDED IN GERMANY

Promoted as "an intimate moody recital guaranteed to please," **THE WAR YEARS: MEMORY-MAKING SONGS BY EVE BOSWELL**, with Reg Owen's Orchestra looks back at music that enjoyed popularity during World War II. Boswell, "born in Hungary, educated in Switzerland, married in South Africa," who "sings in *eight* languages, tap dances, juggles and plays saxophone solos" became well-known after performing on the BBC with the English bandleader known as Geraldo. Part of Capitol's Mood Albums series, the LP's selections include popular songs from the 1940s, such as "I'll Walk Alone," a hit for Dinah Shore from the morale-boosting film *Follow the Boys* in 1944, "It's Been a Long, Long Time," a major hit from 1945, and "Besame Mucho," which had been one of Capitol Records' first big hits, as recorded by Mexican singer Andy Russell, who sang it in alternating English and Spanish verses in 1944. The cover photograph shows a kissing couple on a railway platform—he in military uniform, a freight train standing on the tracks, and a sailor looking on as they say a sorrowful goodbye.[14] The back cover follows this theme with an illustration of a pensive woman writing to her absent soldier, his framed picture nearby.

FIGURE 13.5

Reg Owen and His Orchestra,
The War Years: Memory-Making Songs by Eve Boswell,
Capitol T 10140.

THE WAR YEARS
'CAPITOL' OF THE WORLD
Capitol
RECORDS
RECORDED IN ENGLAND
HIGH FIDELITY
Memory-Making Songs by Eve Boswell with Reg Owen's Orchestra
T10140
P940-5
7

The 1958 LP, **A VISIT TO FINLAND**, celebrates the capital city of Helsinki and offers a "smörgåsbord of Finnish pops by famous Helsinki artists" designed to guide Americans into the Helsinki music scene of the day. Although Finland at that time was emerging as a center for modernist design, with ex-pat Eliel Saarinen leading the way as the Director of the Cranbrook Academy of Art in Michigan, the rural scene on the cover belongs to the tradition of representing the Nordic countries as "natural" and "pure," steeped in romantic, pastoral traditions. Shot by Dave Forbert, longtime head of the photography department at *Reader's Digest* magazine, the photograph shows several couples dancing in traditional dress, accompanied by a fiddler. Bright red vests, hats, and skirts pop out of the winsome image, as a two story historic wooden building sets the stage for the dance performance. The music, "friendly and honest as the Finnish people themselves," includes folk songs, "rollicking dances" such as the *jenkka*, which "has a bouncy lilt as refreshing as a Finnish summer," and pop music, "sung by the very blonde and very blue-eyed Miss Rantanen, a gracious tourist guide in any latitude." The notes include a brief summary in Finnish, and all titles are listed in Finnish with English translations.

FIGURE 13.6

Maanantaikuoro,
Tuula-Anneli Rantanen,
Urpo Pylvänäinen,
and Yrjö Saarnio's Band,
A Visit to Finland,
Capitol T 10270;
photo by Dave Forbert.

a
Visit
to
Finland

MAANANTAIKUORO · RANTANEN · PYLVÄNÄINEN · YRJÖ SAARNIO'S BAND

RECORDED IN HELSINKI
'CAPITOL' OF THE WORLD

Capitol
RECORDS

HIGH FIDELITY

In May 1958, Dave Dexter sent a letter to a producer with an idea for making another recording in the vein of *Mexico: Its Sound and People*: "if you are stationed in or near Tokyo for the next few months, and if you have access to a tape recorder … perhaps we could cook up a 'Japan: Its Sounds and People.' Dexter explained: "It would require at least 50 and possibly 60 different sequences of sounds and sound effects including Tokyo traffic, street salesmen hollering in Japanese, a Japanese guide describing the imperial palace in broken English, and many other such sequences."[15]

The result was **JAPAN: ITS SOUNDS AND PEOPLE** (or, in Japanese characters that appeared on the cover, *Japan According to the Expression of Sound*), which resembles a *National Geographic* documentary soundtrack. The cover shows the colorful "Ching-Dong-Ya," street musicians advertising a store's grand opening. Japanese characters appear in different styles and sizes adding to a chaotic energy, with "Japan" rendered in a calligraphic red font. Six black-and-white thumbnail photos on the back cover picture music ensembles, a street cart, geishas, and a woodland shrine. The LP presents music as well as ambient noise: sumo wrestlers bellow, a Buddhist priest plays flute, fire engines scream to the Ginza, and "150 worshippers play the hand drums simultaneously and recite Nammyo Horen Geikyo in unison."[16] In a favorite album moment, Rose Okagawa, our recorded tour guide, tells about geisha training. Geishas are taught to serve food and tea, dance and sing, converse skillfully, and "that's all." The liner notes describe the contexts and details of the diverse sounds, creating an interesting acoustic time capsule.

JAPANESE SKETCHES presents a cover of strong red and yellow—the title font evoking bamboo brush strokes—and a crowd of children in clear focus and near enough that we can identify their individual features: their hair is cut short, they appear healthy and curious, as they gather around a *kamishibai* (paper theater) performance. Back cover liner notes report that this is "one of the few authentic Japanese long-playing records—in magnificent high fidelity—to emanate from the world's largest (and most colorful) city." The Shin Ensemble of Tokyo play compositions by Dorothy Guyver Britton, a Brit born in Tokyo, schooled in England and the United States, who returned to Japan in 1949.[17] Notes give intimate, detailed descriptions of places, sights, and events evoked in each song, such as, "Carnival at Asakusa"—"where vendors sell everything from magic lanterns to goldfish"; "Hanami"—the Spring cherry blossom festival that "gives the Japanese a good excuse for outings complete with food and *sake* (rice wine)"; or from side two, "Geisha," evoking artists' renditions of "the innocence of Harunobu's young beauties to the more voluptuous women of Utamaro."

On **JAPAN REVISITED**, two traditionally dressed young women in colorful *yukata*—summer kimonos—with coordinated parasols stand on a red bridge amid green shrubs and trees in a formal garden. The album title font evokes the calligraphic brush stroke, with "Japan" appearing in a calming grass green and "Revisited" in pale turquoise: these match the small Capitol banner and oval logo in the lower right corner. On the back cover, in three small black-and-white photos, Mamoru Miyagi and the Graduates of Tokyo's University of the Arts display their instruments, such as the taiko drum, the flute-like yokobue, and samisen guitars, as this LP reveals the sounds and stylings of traditional Japanese music. Each song title is printed in a slim font echoing calligraphic writing; and notes explaining the instrumentation or meaning of each number follow. From "Sakura Sakura" ("Cherry Blossoms") to "Nozakimura" (associated with Japanese puppet plays), the ensemble offers virtuoso authenticity.

THE STREETS OF TOKYO: TOP POPS SUNG IN JAPANESE BY NIPPON'S FAVORITE RECORD STARS dispenses with traditional dress and archaic instruments, instead offering a cover photo of young people in what appear to be school uniforms strolling by a movie theater covered with huge colorful film posters for Japanese films *Spectacular Showdown* and *The Legend of the Eight Samurai*, as well as Disney's *Pinocchio* and *Old Yeller*.[18] Contemporary culture has come to Japan: "These then are the songs you might hear on the streets of Tokyo, piped out of the record shops and theaters." In explaining the absence of what one might expect on a record of Japanese music, the notes explain: "The older Japanese style, always fresh to Western ears for its rhythmic brightness and its supple vocal style, is represented in this album by 'The Nikko Folksong' and 'Farewell to Tokyo.'" The main current of Japanese pop music, with its characteristically "minor" keys and dark moods, is typified by "Lullaby of the Birds" and "Cigarette Blues," while a strong American pop feel is apparent in "Black Flower Petal" and "Brown Leaves." Pen and ink drawings on the back cover portray jazz musicians with sax, clarinet, and guitar, while elegant Japanese women, more traditionally clad than those on the cover, dance to this new music, edging their way into the modern world.

FIGURE 13.7

Japan: Its Sounds and People,
Capitol ST 10230.

FIGURE 13.8

Dorothy Guyver Britton's
Japanese Sketches,
The Shin Ensemble of Tokyo
conducted by Ikuma Dan,
Capitol T 10123.

FIGURE 13.9

Mamoru Miyagi and the graduates
of Tokyo's University of Arts,
Japan Revisited,
Capitol T 10195;
photo by Col. Jack Novak.

FIGURE 13.10

The Streets of Tokyo:
Top Pops Sung in Japanese by
Nippon's Favorite Record Stars,
Capitol T 10250.

FULL DIMENSIONAL STEREO

RECORDED IN JAPAN

'CAPITOL OF THE WORLD'

Capitol
RECORDS

HIGH FIDELITY

JAPAN
ITS SOUNDS AND PEOPLE

音目による
日本の表情

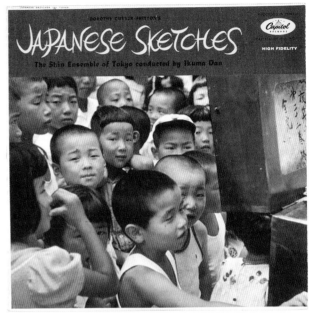

DOROTHY CUYLER BRITTON'S

JAPANESE SKETCHES

Capitol
RECORDS

HIGH FIDELITY

The Shin Ensemble of Tokyo conducted by Ikuma Dan

JAPAN REVISITED

RECORDED IN TOKYO
'CAPITOL OF THE WORLD'

Capitol
RECORDS

HIGH FIDELITY

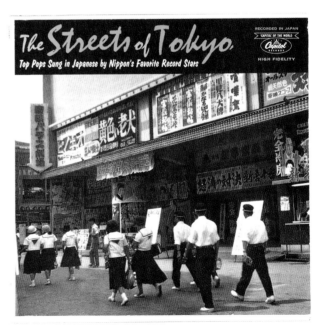

The Streets of Tokyo

RECORDED IN JAPAN
'CAPITOL OF THE WORLD'

Capitol
RECORDS

HIGH FIDELITY

Top Pops Sung in Japanese by Nippon's Favorite Record Stars

AUTHENTIC AUSTRALIAN ABORIGINALS!: NATIVE CHANTS, SONGS, AND DANCES
RECORDED IN ARNHEM LAND presents "rare and authentic performances of the
Aborigines." A. P. Elkin, a prominent Australian anthropologist, provided both the
recordings and the notes for the album. Elkin, who served as president of the Associ-
ation for the Protection of Native Races, was an advocate for the assimilation and bet-
ter treatment of the Aborigines. The LP follows in the footsteps of the distinguished
Folkways Records catalog of ethnographic recordings, which had produced *Tribal
Music of Australia* in 1949, the first recording of Aboriginal music (also recorded by
Elkin), and *Australia: Australian Aborigines: Corroboree Song* in their Music of the
World's People series in 1952. The notes acknowledge Elkin's pioneering work, "until
he attempted the task, music of these primitives had never before been recorded,"
but neglect to mention much about who wrote the pieces, or copyright issues.[19] For
example, the performers are described, but not named: "This gossip song is sung
by the same young man as the Indji-Indji. He is exceptionally gifted." Arnhem Land
forms part of Australia's mostly Aboriginal Northern Territory, and the music derives
from a *corroboree,* an Aboriginal ceremony that acts out the mythical history of their
tribal ancestors, although the notes indicate merely that they "usually consist of
music and dancing." Instruments include "rhythm sticks," or clapsticks, hand clap-
ping, feet dancing, and didgeridoos—the distinctive Aboriginal wind instrument used
to provide a constant, low sound as a kind of *basso continuo* for the other musical
parts. The cover, reminiscent of an anthropologist's ethnographic field photograph,
shows a group of Aboriginals preparing for a corroboree, with body paint and ceremonial regalia.

FIGURE 13.11

Authentic Australian Aboriginals!:
Native Chants, Songs, and Dances
Recorded in Arnhem Land,
Capitol T 10086;
photo courtesy John Thompson of
the Australian Broadcasting Commission.

authentic

AUSTRALIAN ABORIGINALS!

CAPITOL OF THE WORLD

Capitol
RECORDS

HIGH FIDELITY

native chants, songs and dances recorded in **ARNHEM LAND**

HONG KONG!: EXOTIC CHINESE POP MUSIC RECORDED IN KOWLOON has a muddy picture of a small Chinese "junk" boat steered by two young boys on the cover, with the LP title spelled out in vaguely Chinese-like typography. In the distance are the hills of Kowloon Bay, dotted with a small number of buildings compared to today. The liner notes provide both English and Chinese characters, as they tell a tale about Hong Kong, which "teems with unbelievable contrasts: poverty and wealth, ugliness and beauty, modern commercialism and a culture that is thousands of years old." Hong Kong, which means "Fragrant Harbor," serves as a major international port and leading financial center, and has often stood at the crossroads of global political currents: "Like Hong Kong itself, the music in this album is a fascinating fusion of east and west, old and new." The notes highlight the instruments used on the LP, including the *p'-p'a*, an ancient form of lute, the *hu ch'in*, "the Chinese fiddle," and the *lo*—the cherished Chinese gong. Yao Ming, described as "a prominent musician and composer, resident in Hong Kong since 1950," composed and arranged most of the selections. We hear a version of "The Sorrows of Meng Chiang Nu," which "tells of a woman whose husband was forced to labor in building the Great Wall of China." On "Swatting Butterflies," we hear of a young girl "dancing for her lover beside a lily pond, and swatting butterflies with her fan. The fan falls into the water, and while she looks for it her lover disappears." The song, based on one of China's Four Great Folktales, also appears on the Capitol of the World LP *China!: Popular Songs Sung by Li Li Hua and Tong Pei Pei*.[20]

FIGURE 13.12

Hong Kong!: Exotic Chinese Pop Music Recorded in Kowloon, Capitol T 10267.

HONG KONG!

EXOTIC CHINESE POP MUSIC RECORDED IN KOWLOON

CHINA!: POPULAR SONGS SUNG BY LI LI HUA AND TONG PEI PEI, "recorded
in the Orient," features a night scene, moodily lit with Chinese character neon signs
rising up above dark streets.[21] Li Li Hua, who was featured in a 1947 *Life* magazine article, was a principal for the Peking Opera before she became a well-known
movie actress, eventually moving to Hollywood, and starring in the 1958 film *China
Doll*, with Victor Mature.[22] Tong Pei Pei was also a successful actress in the Hong
Kong movie industry. This unusual LP—few major label albums released music from
recently communist China—offered a glimpse of popular music of the day: "thus, in
the sensitive sentimental voices of Li Li Hua and Tong Pei Pei, is the mighty heart of
modern China tenderly exposed to the world." The liner notes focus on explaining
the songs, providing Chinese character translations for each song title, as well as
an image of Chinese musical notation. The LP steers clear of any discussion about
the contemporary scene in China, focusing instead on ancient and imperial themes
in the music. For example, in "The Sorrowful Wife," "Li Li Hua sings of the young
bride whose husband has left home for a remote city," and goes on to "compare the
bride's difficulty with similar troubles experienced by Chinese wives, among them
Man Chiang-nui, the legendary girl whose husband was seized by Emperor Ching
Sze Huang to help build the Great Wall of China."

FIGURE 13.13

Li Li Hua and Tong Pei Pei,
*China!: Popular Songs Sung by
Li Li Hua and Tong Pei Pei*,
Capitol T 10087,
photo by Ricciardi, F. T. G.

HIGH FIDELITY

CAPITOL OF THE WORLD

RECORDED IN THE ORIENT

China!

popular songs sung by LI LI HUA and TONG PEI PEI

Even though the album's songs derive from the booming Indian movie industry, the front cover of **SONGS OF INDIA** shows a photograph of two traditionally dressed Indian women carrying iconic brass water pots on their heads. In visual terms, they "stand in" for all the diversity of India, from the teeming cities to the high Himalayas to the vast coastline. The cover spells out *Songs of India* with decorative, vaguely Sanskrit-like letters. The notes assure us that "Indian popular music is far less complicated melodically and far more approachable to Westerners than its classical music." Released in 1968, the year of the Beatles' famous visit with Maharishi Mahesh Yogi, the LP joins several other Indian records in the series, including *Dance Music of India, Drums of India,* and *Six Ragas* by Ravi Shankar. Side one features Utpala Sen, a popular "playback" singer—her singing provided the voice for many Indian movie actresses, who would lip-synch her songs. Shyamal Mitra, another well-known playback singer, performs on side two: "they both possess a popular style that is easily enjoyable and yet highly exotic." "For many this album will be a musical adventure into magical new sounds. Those who have visited India will treasure it as a vivid souvenir of a great and gentle people." *Songs of India* showcases a certain type of song from India, nevertheless, musically, this is a standout.

FIGURE 13.14

Utpala Sen and Shyamal Mitra,
*Songs of India: The Voices of Utpala
Sen and Shyamal Mitra,*
Capitol T 10246;
photo by Baldev Kapoor.

Songs of India

RECORDED IN CALCUTTA

'CAPITOL' OF THE WORLD

HIGH FIDELITY

CAR CITY RECORDS
GUARANTEED
$ 3.80

the
voices of
Utpala Sen
and
Shyamal Mitra

This LP invites the listener to imagine **AN EVENING IN BEIRUT** as it might play out
on a pleasant holiday: after settling in at the hotel, one heads out to a picturesque
location, perhaps a seafront restaurant, to get a bit of food and hear some contemporary music (side one); then stepping away from the urban bustle, the visitor wanders
into more "traditional" environments, coming across singing country girls, and an
outdoor party where one is invited to join in the eating, singing and dancing (side
two). The record, and the evening, conclude by dancing the *dabka* to a song that
ends, "You have visited us, and we are honoured by your visits. You are very welcome and welcome again and again." The liner notes offer this narrative, as well as
song titles and musicians' names in both English and Arabic.

Bright orange Arabic script that matches the Capitol of the World banner and
an English translation in off-white announce "An Evening in Beirut." The featured
artists' names appear in the lower left corner, also in both languages and distinct colors. In the cover photo, darkness settles and city lights spread out from the curved
shoreline. Fringes of foliage against a gray sky form the ceiling of this view from
high above the water and two thin tree trunks, likely cypress, rather than the legendary cedars of Lebanon, break the panorama's unity. The shot is taken north of
Beirut, across Jounieh Bay, in an area associated with a majority Christian population. Perhaps in line with the cover photo's perspective, and the photographer's own
religion,[23] most, if not all, of the singers on this album were Christian, including the
awe-inspiring Fairuz. Throughout her long and dedicated carrier, Fairuz displayed
diplomatic flexibility and often tread a delicate political line: she performed light
dance songs with Western aspects, as she does on this album; but she also drew on

FIGURE 13.15

An Evening in Beirut,
Capitol T 10189;
photo by Manoug.

ليالى بيروت

An Evening in Beirut

فـيـروز   **FAIRUZ**

شيـراز   **SHIRAZ**

سعـاد هـاشم   **SU'AD HAŞHIM**

صبـاح   **SABAH**

نـور الهدى   **NUR AL-HUDA**

نجـاح سـلام   **NAJAH SALAM**

وديـع الصافى   **WADI AL-SAFI**

Photo: Manoug

'CAPITOL' OF THE WORLD

Capitol RECORDS

RECORDED IN LEBANON

her knowledge of "how to chant verses from the Koran according to what is known as *tajwid*, the high style of Koranic intonation in classic Arabic."[24] In 1957, around the time this LP was released, Lebanese President Camille Chamoun "presented Fairuz with the 'Cavalier,' the highest medal ever conferred on a Lebanese Artist."[25] Most of the musicians included here—some of whom went on to act in film and television—also managed long-lasting, prominent, if sometimes controversial, careers: Sabah, Najah Salam, and Wadi' Al-Safi. The lives of Nur Al-Huda and Shiraz are more difficult to trace.

....

CAIRO!: THE MUSIC OF MODERN EGYPT's cover photograph shows an iconic Egyptian scene—kneeling camels amid a crowd of tourists and guides at the foot of the Great Sphinx of Giza with the Pyramid of Khafre in the distance.[26] The album provides enthusiastic descriptions of Egypt's abundant tourist attractions, "which no other city in the world can hope to match." The album's slightly arabesque typography announces: "'*Ahlan wa Sahlam*,' cries the dragoman from his camel as he approaches the age-old Sphinx of Giza on the outskirts of Cairo … and his bright 'welcome' in Arabic leads you to the mighty attractions of Egypt—and its music." The liner notes focus on tourism, not tunes, with generic descriptions, such as: "this is what Cairoans are singing and whistling these days, a sort of Nile-land Hit Parade" and "although Cairo is about the size of Detroit, musicians and singers of professional calibre are hardly as numerous as those of America's Motor City." The selections include several spoken introductions to the music of Ahmed Jabor, Nagah Salamar,

FIGURE 13.16

Cairo!: The Music of Modern Egypt,
Capitol T 10021;
photo by Max Tatch.

T-10021

Capitol
RECORDS

Cairo!

the music of modern Egypt

Laila Matar, and Tariq Abdul Hakem—who, born in Saudi Arabia but trained in Egypt, has been called "the father of Saudi Music."[27] Upon its release in 1956, *Billboard's* reviewer was a bit mystified by the LP, apparently, calling it "an esoteric package" whose "melodies have a bizarre quality; some are in quarter tones. An interesting set of notes will help the Brill Building aficionados dig this stuff."[28] The music is haunting, and certainly sounds "recorded in Egypt," as the cover reports. In closing, the anonymous scribe, who clearly admires the Egyptian musical scene of the day, writes: "There, in a darkened room above Adly Pacha street awaiting sleep, one is likely to hear the distant, exotic voice of Laila Matar from a still-gay cafe. For this is Cairo, the ancient; the musical metropolis in the shade of the Great Pyramid and history. There's nothing quite like it anywhere else in the world."

Part of the Unusual Sounds segment of the Capitol of the World series, **KASONGO!: MODERN MUSIC OF THE BELGIAN CONGO**, from 1957, features Watusi (now known as Tutsi) ceremonial dancers, with headdresses meant to resemble lion's manes, elaborate beaded regalia, spears, and traditional bells on their ankles that provided rhythmic accompaniment to their movements.[29] They appear mid-dance, and the photo is drenched in a muted orange cast. The Kasongo of the LP's title refers to a midsize city in the east of the country, but the LP was recorded in Leopoldville (renamed Kinshasa in 1966), named for King Leopold II of Belgium who disastrously presided over the Congo as his private domain from 1885 to 1908. The

FIGURE 13.17

Kasongo!: Modern Music of the Belgian Congo, Capitol T 10005; photo courtesy of Sabena Airlines.

liner notes offer a brief and circumspect background on the Belgian Congo, now the Democratic Republic of the Congo: "Home of the gigantic Watusi tribesman, the explosive Nyamuragira Volcano and some of the world's most enchanting music" and mention its colonial history: "The big holidays in the Congo are the King's birthday, the annual fete commemorating the declaration of the Congo as a colony of Belgium." However, they also offer enlightening details on the album's music, including information about the *likembe* "a truly native instrument found only in Africa, and made of a flat wooden sound-box on which are attached thin bamboo or metal keys," and "the vocal 'style' heard on most of the album's selections here … is in parallel thirds, and is, the experts say, also found commonly in French Guinea and the northern part of Madagascar." Performers include Boniface Koufoudila, "the top man on the pole," playing "contemporary representative popular music of the Congo." Despite the focus on the Watusi and their traditional ceremonies, the album features modern sounding songs, a bit like today's Afropop, and in particular, internationally acclaimed Congolese recording artists such as Papa Wemba and Lokua Kanza. The liner notes conclude with the potentially optimistic thought that the Belgian Congo might emerge as "one of the world's great tourist attractions of the 1980s."[30]

Although the content of **MUSIC OF THE AFRICAN ZULUS!** consists of late 1950s pop music, "recorded in Johannesburg, in modern, superbly-equipped studios," the cover features a striking color photograph of Zulu women performing outdoors, in traditional dress, barefoot on dry grass.[31] The notes describe the LP's selections this way: "This long-playing record presents a collection of contemporary hit songs—a

FIGURE 13.18

Music of the African Zulus!,
Capitol T 10114.

'CAPITOL' OF THE WORLD

RECORDED IN JOHANNESBURG

music of the
African Zulus!

sort of Zulu hit parade—as well as standard jazz selections sung in the various languages and South African dialects, and all are self-composed by the artists themselves." For example, track two, "New Year Rock," "was a smash 1956–57 hit" for
11-year-old performer Little Kid Lex. Entertaining excerpts of spoken word mingle
with the songs. Side one closes with "Skhanda Mayeza" by Suzie and Grace, which
sounds similar to fellow South African singer Miriam Makeba's "Pata Pata," originally recorded in 1957, and an international hit in 1967. Other standouts include
"Drums of Africa," a song of a Zulu Chief, by the Globe Trotters, and "Kamohlaba," by
Jackson Ngobeni, "a traditional praise song." Although patronizing comments mar
the liner notes, such as "The Zulus have a knack for music," and "Zulu tribal dances
may appear meaningless and repetitious to the Caucasian audience," listening to
this remarkably up-to-date sounding LP today, one can hear connections to Makeba, trumpeter Hugh Masekela, and other successful South African musical groups
such as Ladysmith Black Mambazo and the Boyoyo Boys, as well as South African–
inspired American musicians such as Paul Simon and Vampire Weekend.

FIGURE 13.19

Music of the African Zulus!,
Capitol T 10114,
back cover.

T
1
0
1
1
4

MUSIC OF THE

AFRICAN ZULUS!

Side One

1—DRUMS OF AFRICA
The Globe Trotters
2—NEW YEAR ROCK
Little Kid Lex
3—SEETA
Lefu Mokoena
4—TOM HARK
Elias and his Jazz Flutes
5—K.B.
Country Jazz Band
6—SKHANDA MAYEZA
Suzie and Grace

Side Two

1—WAMBAMBA LOMFAAN
The Goli Sisters
2—A UPINDE MZALA
The Sharpetown Swingsters
3—MANYAUSA
The Globe Trotters
4—KAMOHLABA
Jackson Ngobeni
5—SIYA GIYA
The Melotone Brothers
6—HOLOM TOE
The Globe Trotters

GONE ARE the days when an African native could produce elementary musical sounds only by beating on a crude drum. Today, in busy, modern South Africa, the music-loving Zulu is more likely to have his own set of modern percussion instruments, a snare and bass drum, cymbals, cowbells, woodblocks — the works. He is even more likely to be plaguing the various record companies constantly, attempting to land a recording contract.

The music in this album was recorded in Johannesburg, in modern, superbly-equipped studios. Each song was recorded by Negro artists, men and young women who regularly come to the city to make hit records. The market for phono discs is large in South Africa. And the influence of North American jazz, blues and even rock 'n' roll is emphatic.

The Zulus hear American records on the radio. Nat "King" Cole is no stranger to them. Nor are Duke Ellington, Elvis Presley, Woody Herman and Count Basie unknown.

The Zulus have a knack for music. They will pick up any simple instrument — a guitar, a pennywhistle flute, a tiny concertina — and walk the streets playing simple little melodies in a matter of minutes.

They express their emotions in music constantly. The Zulu tribal dances may appear meaningless and repetitious to the Caucasian audience, but to the Zulu it is all important, even vital, to his way of life. Without any formal training or coaching, with no ability to "read the notes," the Zulu handles his instrument and voice with an amazing and remarkable craftsmanship.

This long-playing record presents a collection of contemporary hit songs — a sort of Zulu Hit Parade — as well as standard jazz selections sung in the various languages and South African dialects, and all are self-composed by the artists themselves.

LITTLE KID LEX. Lex is one of the more popular pennywhistle virtuosi. He is only 11 years old, and a rabid fan of North American jazz. *New Year Rock* was a smash 1956-57 hit in South Africa — it's still a big seller, moreover!

LEFU MOKOENA. Lefu is of the Sesotho tribe (also known as the Basuto). The little concertina is featured here as accompaniment to the lyric describing the homeland.

ELIAS AND HIS JAZZ FLUTES. Before an African makes music, he (or she) likes to talk and "warm up." They also enjoy a little gambling, and are frequently seen on the streets of Johannesburg huddled over dice and decks of cards. The pennywhistle again dominates the instrumentation in *Tom Hark*.

COUNTRY JAZZ BAND. K.B. is a drink, and a potent one, and it inspired this performance and song title. In the vocal versions, one of the lines in the lyrics, when translated, comes out like this:

"It is time to go pub-crawling."

GOLI SISTERS. "Goli" means gold. *Wambamba Lomfaan* is sung by the Golis in both Zulu and Sotho and tells of the boy who was arrested, handcuffed and thrown into a dark cell. He suffered, but his people took him bananas and mangoes and he became happier.

THE SHARPETOWN SWINGSTERS. Another example of modern, progressive African jazz. Here the audience shouts and pleads for the "Swingsters" to repeat their exciting performance.

JACKSON NGOBENI. *Kamohlaba* is a traditional Shangaan praise song. Ngobeni is accompanied by guitar as he praises a tribal chief for his benevolence and good treatment.

THE MELOTONE BROTHERS. The singers ask, in Zulu, for the listeners to relax while they perform. Typical African jazz with undeniable New Orleans overtones. The Melotone Brothers are big record stars throughout the Jo'burg area.

THE GLOBE TROTTERS. A vocal group singing in Zulu. Here they are featured on three selections, *Drums of Africa, Manyausa* and *Holom Toe.* The first tells of the Zulu chief, Tshaka, and the young Zulus who chanted and danced for him to the beat of drums. The second is a song, sung in Xhosa dialect, about a cousin who is lost and perhaps wandering about, afraid and alone. *Holom Toe* is a jazz classic. "Hold me closely and kiss me," the Globe Trotters sing, "for I am going to catch the train to

'CAPITOL' OF THE WORLD

A SERIES OF OUTSTANDING INTERNATIONAL RECORDINGS

SUZIE AND GRACE. *Skhanda Mayeza* is the witch doctor who grows herbs and plays an important part in the life of the African Negro. Sung in Zulu, the girls confide that "my sweetheart is a witch doctor. They all laugh at me but I don't care. I love my witch doctor."

Photos by Pictone, Johannesburg

14

The final frontier of our midcentury vinyl voyage—space—will focus on the quest for the moon and beyond. Graphically modern, these LPs narrate the US ambition to lead the world into the outer reaches, even as they offer domesticated visions complete with cartoon astronauts and childlike renderings of spaceships. If the typical American had no chance of taking this particular trip abroad, these albums helped wrap space exploration into what it meant to be a cosmopolitan US citizen in the postwar era, and created visions for the ultimate in armchair travel. As these albums represent the farthest "away," they make a fitting end to our journey into the realm of the midcentury vinyl LP.[1]

The Apollo space program, in its role as the preeminent scientific mission of its day, fired the popular imagination, intersecting with Cold War tensions and animating marketing and public relations campaigns.[2] Space exploration and related technology and design innovations evoked the future, at the same time that home entertainment and music equipment rooted earthly musical styles popular for record connoisseurs. Many albums explicitly compare technological processes of sound reproduction with aeronautic advances, as travel to faraway places, discourses of US identity, and hi-fi sets come together on dozens of albums promoting the music, mystery, and global significance of space.

Vinyl LPs joined a wide variety of popular media that fueled the space race, including television shows such as *Space Patrol* and Disney's "Man in Space," "Man and the Moon," and "Mars and Beyond" *Disneyland* broadcasts; a proliferating series of articles in *Collier's, Life*, and *Time* magazine; as well as numerous popular books, such as Isaac Asimov's best-selling children's book, *Satellites in Outer Space*, from 1960.[3] Ignited by President Kennedy's bold announcement of Project Apollo in 1961, and fanned by Project Gemini's successful space walk in 1965, space came to occupy a central place in popular culture. Space LPs, now celebrated as "Space Age Pop," and "Space Age Bachelor Pad" music, continue to inspire.[4]

ALBUMS

THE CONQUEST OF SPACE, a "spoken arts" album directed by Arthur Luce Klein, resembles a contemporary podcast about the space race. The cover shows the pale blue Earth partially covered in white cloud resting in a black star-filled galaxy. The LP, narrated by controversial *New York Times* science editor William L. Laurence—depicted on the back cover by famous photographer Arnold Newman—presents a technical introduction to space travel, exploring, as the print along the cover's bottom edge proclaims, "scientific horizons on the threshold of space."[5] The liner notes soar with the optimism of the era, as well as a peculiar sense of entitlement: "With the harnessing of atomic power," Mr. Laurence assures us, "we are now on the threshold of a world of plenty—a world where there will be no 'have-nots' to covet the possessions of the 'haves'; a world without poverty, without war and without disease … a world in which men will have the opportunity for the first time in their history to realize to the full their unlimited intellectual, spiritual and creative potential."

FIGURE 14.1

William L. Laurence,
The Conquest of Space,
Spoken Arts 775.

THE CONQUEST OF SPACE
WILLIAM L. LAURENCE
SCIENCE EDITOR · The New York Times.

775

SPOKEN ARTS

...directed by Arthur Luce Klein

SCIENTIFIC HORIZONS ON THE THRESHOLD OF SPACE

MAN ON THE MOON presents "The Flight of *Apollo 11*," which was "recorded live at Mission control … manned spacecraft center, Houston, Texas." The cover shows an iconic photograph of the successful *Apollo 11* mission that reached the moon on July 20, 1969: astronaut, US flag, and lunar lander on the moon's surface against the inky darkness of space. The LP is narrated by Roy Neal from NBC News, and "produced with official NASA voice tapes and photographs." The back cover includes short, baseball card–like biographies of the *Apollo 11* astronauts, Neil Armstrong, Edwin "Buzz" Aldrin, Jr., and Michael Collins, including their height, weight, hair color, marital status, and hobbies. The elaborate gatefold package contains an eight-page booklet, with color photographs from the mission, and a lengthy story written by Vic Petkoff. Upon listening, one easily moves from sincere interest to excitement as the recordings of the moon landing unfold. For those who remember the moon landing from television, it provides a striking memento of the momentous event; for those who were not yet born in 1969, it represents a remarkable time capsule from another era.

FIGURE 14.2

Man on the Moon:
The Flight of Apollo 11,
Evolution STAO 91999;
designed by Jack Purtle.

SPECIAL COLLECTORS EDITION · WITH FULL COLOR 8-PAGE COMMEMORATIVE BOOKLET

MAN
ON THE MOON

The Flight of Apollo 11

Evolution
a stereo dimension recording

RECORDED LIVE AT MISSION CONTROL...MANNED SPACECRAFT CENTER, HOUSTON, TEXAS Narrated by Roy Neal, NBC News PRODUCED WITH OFFICIAL NASA VOICE TAPES AND PHOTOGRAPHS

STEREO 3004

STRINGS FOR A SPACE AGE, from the Study in High Fidelity Sound series in 1959, features a blue cover; but this is an eerie midnight cerulean gray glow that tints the darkened half-moon and an alien-looking blue-blond as they frame a slim red, white, and blue rocket propelled aloft a bed of flame and steam. According to the imaginative and allegorically minded liner notes, familiar favorites, such as "Autumn in New York" and "How High the Moon" are "cast in a predominantly outer-space mold." Side two's *Space Suite* is composed of tones, rhythms, and melodies that invoke "counterparts in specific space terms. For example, the music actually seems to suggest words like *apogee* (ceiling in the orbit of a satellite) and *perigee* (point nearest the earth in a satellite orbit), air resistance, acceleration, cosmic wind, circular motion, jet thrust, luminescent coatings, magnetic field," and so on, "mirrored" in featured musician Bobby Christian's composition. "The Beautiful Girl above the Clouds," in a section titled *The Call*, tempts one to "compare the attraction exerted on the astronaut by the beautiful girl with the electronic and gravitational pull exerted on an artificial satellite by man-made controls and the gravitational attraction of the earth." The magic of sound engineering combined with "unusual orchestrations, suggest the effects of all kinds of astral bodies whizzing along at high speed and in various stages of visibility." A highlighted gray box of "Technical Data" on the back cover provides the mastering details intended to achieve "the ultimate in signal to noise ratio" as well as a listing of the high and low frequencies on the LP. Although some are outside "the range of ordinary human hearing," the liner notes contend that "if these frequencies were omitted from this record a certain warmth of tone that is felt and sensed rather than heard would be lost." Recording and exploring these extremes is presented as a key aspect of the Study in High Fidelity Sound series.

FIGURE 14.3

Bobby Christian and His Orchestra,
Strings for a Space Age,
Audio Fidelity AFLP 1959.

©AUDIO FIDELITY INC. Printed in U.S.A.
AUDIO FIDELITY
AF a study in high fidelity sound
AFLP 1959
STRINGS FOR A SPACE AGE
SPACE SUITE
OUT OF THIS WORLD
BLUE STAR
OUT OF NOWHERE
MIDNIGHT SUN
HOW HIGH THE MOON
AUTUMN IN NEW YORK
BOBBY CHRISTIAN & HIS ORCHESTRA
A STUDY IN HIGH FIDELITY SOUND

As soon as the Soviet Union launched *Sputnik*, the recording industry responded. RCA Victor's **ADVENTURES IN SOUND AND SPACE** LP, which appeared in 1958, just a few months after *Sputnik*'s successful orbit, takes listeners on an imagined journey into outer space, with stops on the moon and Mars. The story, "while fiction, is based solidly upon accepted physical and scientific principles and theories," and was written by prolific liner note author C. E. "Chick" Crumpacker. Aimed at younger listeners, and part of RCA Victor's Bluebird Children's Record catalog, which offered "Fun and Entertainment for Growing Girls and Boys," the album resembles a radio drama and includes several voice actors, including Staats Cotsworth, well-known for radio work, playing mission leader Col. Frank Erhardt, with occasional dissonant musical accompaniment by Marty Gold to enhance the tension. The entertaining album follows a space crew as they crash, battle unknown dangers, and ultimately return safely to Earth. Pressed into service after equipment failure, one astronaut protests "our training was only simulated!" The cover features an imaginative scene of an orbiter close to the moon.

FIGURE 14.4

C. E. Crumpacker,
Adventures in Sound and Space,
RCA Victor LBY-1013.

ADVENTURES IN SOUND AND SPACE

COL. FRANK ERHARDT & CAST

**BLAST OFF...FREE FALL...SPACE STATION...
MOON CRASH...SPACE STORM...
MARS AND THE SECRET OF THE CANALS**

RPM
1.98

RCA VICTOR
LBY-1013
BLUEBIRD CHILDREN'S RECORDS
A HIGH FIDELITY RECORDING

1.98

Mfr's. Nat'l Adv. Price Optional with Dealer

MUSIC FROM ANOTHER WORLD, from the Jay Gordon Concert Orchestra, offers "the ultimate in Hi-Fidelity excellence." In a bit of a tangent, the liner notes begin, "Jet-propulsion, man-made satellites, rockets to the moon—all bring us within reach of another world!" The vibrant cover captures a young couple captivated by vividly colored gyroscopic lines, reminiscent of those made with the popular Spirograph drawing toy, hovering above their heads. The bold white typography announces a list of tunes whose "melodic dreaminess will soothe your senses and truly uplift you from the mundane cards of life on this planet and transport you over the threshold into a land of musical enchantment." The energetic liner notes keep to the theme: "If you are seeking a new adventure in music, let this mystical, exciting compilation of scintillating tunes carry you right out of the world!" Gordon takes his musicians through familiar, easy-listening fare, devoid of "space" sounds, such as eerie echo, reverberation, or theremin, typical of many space records. This comes as no surprise, as other Gordon albums from the era include *Strictly for Lovers* and *Time on My Hands*, straightforward lounge music.

FIGURE 14.5

Jay Gordon Concert Orchestra,
Music from Another World,
Tops L1552.

33⅓ RPM LONG PLAYING

L1552

HI-FI TOPS

MUSIC FROM ANOTHER WORLD

From Another World
Deserted Ballroom
Prelude To Love
Dance Of The Elves
You Haunt Me
Chant Of The Amazon
Nightingale
Starlight Interlude
Nocturnal Mood
Lotus Land
March Of The Pink Elephants
Intermezzo For A Day In May

THE JAY GORDON CONCERT ORCHESTRA

The airplane has served as a "symbol of the history and advance of modern man" coinciding with the notion that "every advance in aviation necessarily has reflected our changing times and world."[6] The cover of **AIR POWER**, an LP of symphonic music from the television show of the same name that premiered on CBS in 1956, features a clear blue background encompassing a near-full moon and a fighter plane edging ever further into space. The TV show began with footage among the clouds and, made "in full cooperation with the U.S. Air Force," featured test flights, crash landings, and "never-seen-before" film retrieved from former enemies to support notions of flight as a weapon and air power as the most important defense.[7]

FIGURE 14.6

Norman Dello Joio,
Air Power,
Philadelphia Orchestra
with Eugene Ormandy,
Columbia ML 5214.

COLUMBIA
MASTERWORKS
GUARANTEED HIGH FIDELITY

DELLO JOIO

AIR
POWER
(SYMPHONIC SUITE)
THE
PHILADELPHIA
ORCHESTRA,
EUGENE ORMANDY,
CONDUCTOR

Many LPs released during the height of the space race adopted a space theme, no matter how tangential it might have been to the album's content. Against dark space specked with white stars, three heavenly bodies, one blue with a yellow ring and two shadowed and pale green, anchor the delightfully simple cover of **SOUNDS IN SPACE**. Thin white lines map partial elliptical and circular orbits and add lightness to the design, which prominently displays the famous "Living Stereo" designation. The album, an RCA Victor "Stereophonic Sound Demonstration Record" begins with narrator Ken Nordine—who had recently released the cult favorite *Word Jazz* album—announcing: "The age of space is here. And now RCA Victor brings you *Sounds in Space*." The LP includes excerpts from high-profile RCA recordings, such as Stravinsky's "The Rite of Spring," Lena Horne's "Day In … Day Out," and Julie Andrews's "Little Old Lady," along with classic stereo demonstrations of a train puffing and a racetrack car zooming, as these sounds move between stereo channels. And, Nordine's distinctive, charismatic commentary "travels" from one channel to another, as he explains "the miracle of RCA stereophonic sound."

FIGURE 14.7

Sounds in Space,
RCA Victor SP-33-13.

LIVING STEREO

RCA VICTOR
SP-33-13

Stereo-Orthophonic High Fidelity Recording

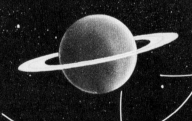

SOUNDS
IN SPACE

© RCA Printed in U.S.A.

In a muddle of space and place, the cover of **TROPICAL ORBIT: INTO SPACE WITH LATIN RHYTHMS!** is a riot of red, green, blue, and yellow, reminiscent of Kodak Hula Show colors. Small line drawings of instruments, such as saxophones, trumpets, maracas, and bongos, float in a Caribbean blue spiral, evoking the swirl of an ocean whirlpool, more than the darkness of space. Amid the musical tidal debris are names of dance styles, such as merengue, cha-cha, and bossa nova, offering clues to the music within. Lettering suggestive of jungle foliage frames the tiny black and white photo of a man dressed in white jacket and dark pants, posed at a small keyboard. This must be "Luther" who is taking the listener "into space with Latin rhythms." Other than the title, the album, from West Indies Records Limited, has no apparent connection to space or orbits, rather it offers a selection of touristy numbers ranging from "Orbitito," to "Never on Sunday."

FIGURE 14.8

Luther in Tropical Orbit:
Into Space with Latin Rhythms!,
West Indies Records,
WIRL 1004;
designed and produced by
Advertising Art Limited, Trinidad.

LAUNCHING A NEW SOUND IN MUSIC, by Terry Gibbs and His Orchestra, show-cases Gibbs, an accomplished vibraphone player as well as a band leader. Other than the cover photograph, which shows a Thor-Able rocket launch—the type of booster used in an unsuccessful attempt to send a US Pioneer spacecraft into lunar orbit in 1958—no attempt has been made to link the album with rockets, space, or the moon. On the back cover, Pete Rugolo, a recording engineer at Mercury Records, provides copious notes about the recording technology, listing which microphones were used for each set of instruments, and reporting that the "monaural track was cut on an Ampex tape recorder (300), while stereo was cut on an Ampex tape recorder (350)." Further listings include each of the session musicians, the recording dates (February 18 and 19, 1959), and Gibbs's commentary on the selections. The big band music sounds fine, if a bit out of date for the time period, and includes abundant jaunty vibraphone solos with a widely dispersed stereo separation.

FIGURE 14.9

Terry Gibbs and His Orchestra,
Launching a New Sound in Music,
Mercury SR 60112.

HI-FI STEREO

Mercury RECORDS

LAUNCHING
A
NEW SOUND
IN
MUSIC

TERRY GIBBS

and his
ORCHESTRA

The front cover painting for Ron Goodwin's **MUSIC IN ORBIT** depicts a classic space
age pop theme: against a deep velvety purple atmosphere a small rocket blasts off
from an otherworldly lunar landscape, including a rock arch straight out of Utah's
Zion National Park. The earth, with the North American continent strangely prominent, floats off in the distance. The back cover includes a proto-psychedelic illustration by Burt Shonberg, whose work also appeared in several early 1960s Roger
Corman films.[8] "Out of the World Instrumentals" promises the cover, but the notes
reveal, "Music in Orbit is, admittedly, only a theme—a peg—around which Goodwin
has fashioned a dozen extremely listenable and entertaining fresh melodies." The
notes go on to reveal "it is descriptive music, listening music, with the inimitable
Goodwin touch. Ron expects few listeners to take the themes seriously." To set the
scene, "Departure" opens with eerie strings, followed by the boom of kettle drums
and whirling glissandos, then settles down to rather conventional easy-listening
orchestra music. Other numbers include "Sally the Satellite," "The Venus Waltz," and
"Martians on Parade." The album notes suggest similarities to Holst's "The Planets"
as "Goodwin opines that there is ample room for original mood-provoking music in
any field." Listening to *Music in Orbit* today, the music sounds perfect for a science
fiction film, despite its tenuous connections to the space age, and might be appreci-
ated more for the cover than the record within.

FIGURE 14.10

Ron Goodwin's *Music in Orbit:
Out of the World Instrumentals by
London's Finest Orchestra*,
Capitol ST 10188;
painting by George Akimoto.

CAPITOL STEREO THE FULL SPECTRUM OF SOUND
Ron Goodwin's MUSIC IN ORBIT
Out of the World Instrumentals by London's Finest Orchestra
RECORDED IN ENGLAND
'CAPITOL' OF THE WORLD
Capitol
RECORDS
HIGH FIDELITY

NOTES

INTRODUCTION

1. Katherine Bussard and Lisa Hostetler, *Color Rush: American Color Photography from Stieglitz to Sherman* (New York and Milwaukee: Aperture/Milwaukee Art Museum, 2013), 44–47.

2. For elaboration, see ibid., 52–63 and 72–76, which also discusses related work of Condé Nast photographer Anton Bruehl. During World War II, Bruehl created a series for *Esquire* magazine, producing vibrant color "photographs that would specifically offer a space of escapism for the men of the armed forces," 58.

3. Pygmalion Karatzas, "Hedrich Blessing Photographers," *Arcspace*, October 26, 2015, http://www.arcspace.com/the-camera/hedrich-blessing-photographers.

4. See Robert A. Sobieszek, ed., *The Architectural Photography of Hedrich-Blessing* (New York: Henry Holt & Co., 1988).

5. Greg Castillo, *Cold War on the Home Front: The Soft Power of Midcentury Design* (Minneapolis: University of Minnesota Press, 2010), xviii.

6. With thanks to Lisa Hostetler, Photography Curator at the George Eastman Museum, for examples from her lecture at Rochester Institute of Technology, Rochester, New York, October 14, 2014.

7. Jacob Smith, *Spoken Word: Postwar American Phonograph Culture* (Berkeley: University of California Press, 2011), 1.

8. Ibid., 202–203.

9. Kier Keightley, "Long Play: Adult-Oriented Popular Music and the Temporal Logics of the Post-War Sound Recording Industry in the USA," *Media, Culture & Society* 26, no. 3 (Autumn 2004), 375–391. Rock and jazz LP covers generally constitute the bulk of those deemed worthy of reproduction in books and articles; for analyses of the cultural work of classical albums, see Nicholas Cook, "The Domestic *Gesamtkunstwerk*, or Record Sleeves and Reception," in *Composition—Performance—Reception: Studies in the Creative Process in Music*, ed. Wyndham Thomas (Aldershot, UK: Ashgate, 1998), 105–117; and Evan Eisenberg, *The Recording Angel: Music, Records and Culture from Aristotle to Zappa*, 2nd ed. (New Haven, CT: Yale University Press, 2005).

10. Dianne Harris, *Little White Houses: How the Postwar Home Constructed Race in America* (Minneapolis: University of Minnesota Press, 2013), 9.

11. Asbjørn Grønstad and Øyvind Vågnes, eds. "Introduction," in *Coverscaping: Discovering Album Aesthetics* (Copenhagen: Museum Tusculanum Press, 2010), 11.

12. See Dominik Bartmanski and Ian Woodward, "The Vinyl: The Analogue Medium in the Age of Digital Reproduction," *Journal of Consumer Culture* 15, no. 1 (January 2013): 3–17. One might argue that these LPs supported "training the young for life at the frontiers of consumption," as cultural theorist Andrew Ross suggested in his work on culture and the Cold War. Andrew Ross, "Containing Culture in the Cold War," *Cultural Studies* 1, no. 3 (1987), 337.

13. Mike Evans, *Vinyl: The Art of Making Records* (New York: Sterling, 2015).

14. Paul Théberge, Kyle Devine, and Tom Everett, "Introduction: Living Stereo," in *Living Stereo: Histories and Cultures of Multichannel Sound*, ed. Paul Théberge, Kyle Devine, and Tom Everett (London: Bloomsbury, 2015), 1–34.

15. Dominic Bradbury, *Mid-Century Modern Complete* (New York: Abrams, 2014), 6.

16. Jennifer McKnight-Trontz, *Exotiquarium: Album Art from the Space Age* (New York: St. Martin's, 1999), 3. See also Rob Chapman, "Introduction," in *Album Covers from the Vinyl Junkyard* (London: Booth-Clibborn Editions, 1997).

17. Dominik Bartmanski and Ian Woodward, *Vinyl: The Analogue Record in the Digital Age* (London: Bloomsbury, 2015), 176.

18. Steven Heller and Veronique Vienne, *100 Ideas that Changed Graphic Design* (London: Laurence King Publishing, 2012), 47.

19. Steven Heller, "Historical Critique: For the Record," *Critique: The Magazine of Graphic Design* 7 (Winter 1998): 36–45. See also Jennifer McKnight-Trontz and Alex Steinweiss, *For the Record: The Life and Work of Alex Steinweiss* (New York: Princeton Architectural Press, 2000).

20. Quoted in Steven Heller, "Alex Steinweiss, Who Made Album Covers Artful, Dies at 94," *New York Times*, July 20, 2011, A20.

21. In the case of ethnographic collections or "ethnic" music, "album" evokes the (white) colonialist potential of a medium that begins as a blank slate and treats the observed exotic native, often dark-skinned, as an object to be reported on and recorded by the outside observer. See Janet L. Borgerson and Jonathan E. Schroeder, "Ethical Issues of Global Marketing: Avoiding Bad Faith in Visual Representation," *European Journal of Marketing* 36, nos. 5/6 (May–June 2002): 570–594.

22. See Richard Evans, *The Art of the Album Cover* (New York: Chartwell Books, 2010); Nick de Ville, *Album: Classic Sleeve Design* (London: Mitchell Beazley, 2003); V. Vale and Andrea Juno, eds., *Incredibly Strange Music, Volume 1* (San Francisco: RE/Search, 1993); and Sean O'Hagan, "The Photographers Who Revolutionised Album Art," *The Guardian*, July 10, 2015, http://www .theguardian.com/artanddesign/2015/jul/10/the-photographers-revolutionised-pop-album-artwork.

23. Kevin Reagan, *Alex Steinweiss: The Inventor of the Modern Album Cover* (Cologne: Taschen, 2010). See also Steven Heller, "Waxing Chromatic: An Interview with S. Neil Fujita," *AGIA: The Professional Association for Design* [blog], Sept 18, 2007, http://www.aiga.org/waxing-chromatic -an-interview-with-s-neil-fujita.

24. Carissa Kowalski Dougherty, "The Coloring of Jazz: Race and Record Cover Design in American Jazz, 1950 to 1970," *Design Issues* 23, no. 1 (Winter 2007), 48–49.

25. Benjamin Cawthra, *Blue Notes in Black and White: Photography and Jazz* (Chicago: University of Chicago Press, 2011), 9. Cawthra provides an insightful analysis of the cultural roles of musical imagery:

> As LPs served to market the music to fans around the country, and indeed, around the globe, the obscure genre of jazz photography flowered into a full-blown visual culture with its own stylistic variations, its own special photographic conditions, and its own iconic subjects. Many of the most important of these subjects were African American, and as jazz on LP reached wider audiences in the late 1950s, African American musicians were depicted as serious artists at the very time that black Americans' demands for equality could no longer be ignored. (Ibid., 8)

See Graham Marsh and Glyn Callingham, *The Cover Art of Blue Note Records: The Collection* (London: Collins & Brown, 2010) for a rich compendium of Blue Note covers.

26. Ashbjørn Grønsted and Øyvind Vågnes, "Introduction," in *Coverscaping: Discovering Album Aesthetics*, ed. Ashbjørn Grønsted and Øyvind Vågnes (Copenhagen: Museum Tusculanum Press, 2010), 12.

27. Quoted in Paul Grein, *Capitol Records: Fiftieth Anniversary 1942–1992* (Hollywood, CA: Capitol Records, 1992), 9. Tommy Steele, Vice President of Art and Design at Capitol, adds:

> The history of visual art from the halls of Capitol Records reads like a veritable who's who of graphic design. Beginning with the godfather of music company art departments,

Marvin Schwartz. As Capitol's first art director starting in 1947, he spawned thousands of eye-catching packages, nurtured illustrious young talent, won three Grammy awards for best album package, and even designed the actual Grammy award itself… cover art is the closest thing that we get to fine art in the commercial design world." (Ibid., 179)

In an amusing note from 1964, a Capitol executive writes to musician Norrie Paramour, "Incidentally, while your picture is quite handsome and representative, if you ever have any real sexy ones wearing a tiger skin or with low key lighting, pass them along. Don't forget that all albums today are competing with the Beatles!" (Lloyd Dunn, "Letter to Norrie Paramour," March 24, 1964. Dave E. Dexter, Jr. Collection, LaBudde Special Collections Department, University of Missouri-Kansas City University Libraries).

28. Ted Poyser, "Capitol Album Covers," *CA: The Journal of Commercial Art*, 2 (September, 1960), 43.

29. Dougherty, "The Coloring of Jazz," 49.

30. Hilary Moore, "Painting Sound, Playing Color: The Multiple Voices of Ornette Coleman's *Free Jazz* and Jackson Pollock's *White Light*," in *Coverscaping: Discovering Album Aesthetics*, ed. Asbjørn Grønstad and Øyvind Vågnes (Copenhagen: Museum Tusculanum Press, 2010), 193.

31. "To provide striking cover art for the company's five hundred annual releases, Capitol's art director, Marvin Schwartz, cultivated not only renowned graphic designers like [Saul] Bass but also photographers and illustrators, most notably William Claxton and Robert Guidi." Jeremy Aynsley, "Graphic Design in California," in *California Design 1930–1965: Living in a Modern Way*, ed. Wendy Kaplan (Cambridge, MA: MIT Press/Los Angeles County Museum of Art, 2011), 280.

32. Diane Boucher, *The 1950s American Home* (Oxford: Shire Publications, 2013), 59.

33. Ibid., 59. Given the roles of key creators in American modernism—for example, George Nelson, Charles and Ray Eames, Eero Saarinen—note the connections to chapter 2, "Modern Art and Design."

34. See Laura Belmonte, *Selling the American Way: US Propaganda and the Cold War* (Philadelphia: University of Pennsylvania Press, 2008). For further analysis of how such contrasts play out more broadly throughout 500 years of history, see Judith Flanders, *The Making of Home: The 500-Year Story of How Our Houses Became Our Homes* (New York: St Martin's Press, 2014).

35. Lizbeth Cohen, *A Consumers' Republic: The Politics of Mass Consumption in Postwar America* (New York: Vintage, 2003), 8.

36. Ibid., 13–14.

37. Andrea Carosso, *Cold War Narratives: American Culture in the 1950s* (Bern: Peter Lang, 2012), 10. He writes that the related "master rhetoric"

> was mostly aimed at countering that discomfort with intimations of national wholeness and prosperity. In other words, 1950s America was pervaded by conflicting and contradictory narratives, whose convergence within a continuum of either idealized presentation of a prosperous and confident nation, or within a troubled agenda of fear, rebellion, and inequality appears problematic and inappropriate.

38. Alan Nadel, *Containment Culture: American Narratives, Postmodernism, and the Atomic Age* (Durham, NC: Duke University Press, 1995), 3. He argues, "The story of containment had derived its logic from the rigid major premise that the world was divided into two monolithic camps, one dedicated to promoting the inextricable combination of capitalism, democracy, and (Judeo-Christian) religion, and one seeking to destroy that ideological amalgamation by any means."

39. Elaine Tyler May, *Homeward Bound: American Families in the Cold War Era* (New York: Basic Books, 2008), 156.

40. Don Slater, *Consumer Culture and Modernity* (Cambridge: Polity, 1997), 35.

41. Ibid., 31. See also, Janet L. Borgerson, "The Flickering Consumer: New Materialities and Consumer Research," *Research in Consumer Behavior* 15 (2013), 125–144. In the context of consumption studies, we recognize the way concepts like *materiality* and *agency* inform how people become who they are, and we think of this book as a case study on the intersections of identity creation and material culture, concentrating on a set of vintage vinyl albums.

42. Carosso, *Cold War Narratives*, 56.

43. Ibid., 80.

44. Ruth Oldenziel and Karin Zachmann, "Kitchens as Technology and Politics: An Introduction," in *Cold War Kitchen: Americanization, Technology, and European Users*, ed. Ruth Oldenziel and Karin Zachmann (Cambridge, MA: MIT Press, 2009), 6. See also Susan E. Reid, "'Our Kitchen Is Just as Good': Soviet Responses to the American National Exhibition in Moscow, 1959," in *Cold War Modern: Design 1945–1970*, ed. David Crowley and Jane Pavitt (London: Victoria and Albert Museum, 2008), 154–162.

45. Greg Barnhisel, *Cold War Modernists: Art, Literature, & American Cultural Diplomacy* (New York: Columbia University Press, 2015), 2. See also Walter L. Hixson, *Parting the Curtain: Propaganda, Culture, and the Cold War* (New York, St. Martin's Press, 1998), and Danielle Fosler-Lussier, *Music in America's Cold War Diplomacy* (Berkeley: University of California Press, 2016).

46. May, *Homeward Bound*, 12.

47. David Attwood, *Sound Design: Classic Audio and Hi-Fi Design* (London: Octopus, 2002), 25. George Nelson and Henry Wright's highly influential book *Tomorrow's House*, from 1945, discussed radio-phonographs, record players, speakers, and record storage as essential ingredients. George Nelson and Henry Wright, *Tomorrow's House: How to Plan Your Post-War Home Now* (New York: Simon & Schuster, 1945).

48. Elizabeth Armstrong, "The Square and the Cool: California Art, Design, and Culture at Midcentury," in *Birth of the Cool: California Art, Design, and Culture in Midcentury*, ed. Elizabeth Armstrong (Newport Beach, CA: Orange County Museum of Art and Prestel, 2007), 56.

49. Maud Lavin, *Clean New World: Culture, Politics, and Graphic Design* (Cambridge, MA: MIT Press, 2001), 6.

50. In particular, we are indebted to Henry Giroux's work on pedagogy and popular culture, Susan Bordo's analysis of cultural images, and Stuart Hall's scholarship on representation. See, for example, Henry A. Giroux, *Disturbing Pleasures: Learning Popular Culture* (New York: Routledge, 1994); Susan Bordo, *Twilight Zones: The Hidden Life of Cultural Images from Plato to O.J.* (Berkeley: University of California Press, 1997); Stuart Hall, Jessica Evans, and Sean Nixon, eds. *Representation: Cultural Representations and Signifying Practices* (London: Open University Press/Sage, 2013).

PART I: HOME

1. Richard K. Popp, *The Holiday Makers: Magazines, Advertising, and Mass Tourism in Postwar America* (Baton Rouge: Louisiana State University Press, 2012), 24.

2. James A. Jacobs, *Detached America: Building Houses in Postwar Suburbia* (Charlottesville: University of Virginia Press, 2015), 136.

3. Ruth Oldenziel and Karin Zachmann, "Kitchens as Technology and Politics: An Introduction," in *Cold War Kitchen: Americanization, Technology, and European Users*, ed. Ruth Oldenziel and Karin Zachmann (Cambridge, MA: MIT Press, 2009), 2.

4. Ibid., 2.

5. The 1959 American National Exhibition in Moscow was designed to "demonstrate the joys of American consumption." Eric J. Sandeen, *Picturing an Exhibition: The Family of Man and 1950s America* (Albuquerque: University of New Mexico Press, 1995), 128.

6. Witold Rybczynski, *Home: A Short History of an Idea* (New York: Penguin, 1987), 43.

7. Ibid., 49.

CHAPTER 1: BEING AT HOME

1. See Sam Gosling, *Snoop: What Your Stuff Says about You* (New York: Basic Books, 2009), and Daniel Miller, *The Comfort of Things* (London: Polity, 2009).

2. Gideon Bosker, "Introduction: Cocktail Nation," in *Atomic Cocktails: Mixed Drinks for Modern Times*, by Karen Brooks, Gideon Bosker, and Reed Darmon (San Francisco: Chronicle Books, 1998), 9.

3. After World War II, US Department of State officials considered it important to contest stereotypes of Americans: these included that every American housewife had a maid to wait on her. Thus, this small detail in describing a perfect dinner party seems less random. See Laura Belmonte, *Selling the American Way: U.S. Propaganda and the Cold War* (Philadelphia: University of Pennsylvania Press, 2008), 137.

4. See for example, the sports clothing designs by Varvara Stepanova, discussed in Evgenia Dorofeeva, "Constructivism in Russia in the 1920s," *The Russian Fashion Blog*, June 2013, http://www.russianfashionblog.com/index.php/2013/06/constructivism-russia-1920s /#axzz3ysc60RUA. See also Christina Klaer, "Into Production! The Socialist Objects of Russian Constructivism," European Institute for Progressive Cultural Policies [blog], March 2009, http://eipcp.net/transversal/0910/kiaer/en.

5. Dale DeGroff, "Cocktails," in *Oxford Companion to American Food and Drink*, ed. Andrew F. Smith (Oxford: Oxford University Press, 2007), 135.

6. The cover of *Cocktail Time* was shot by Leombruno-Bodi, the well-known team of fashion photographers Joe Leombruno and Jack Bodi, who "used natural light to produce photographs of extreme clarity that showed off the details of the clothes." Bernadine Morris, "Jack Bodi, Designer and Photographer of French Couture," *New York Times*, September 27, 1986, http://www.nytimes .com/1986/09/27/obituaries/jack-bodi-designer-and-photographer-of-french-couture.html.

7. Billboard, "Album and LP Record Reviews: *Cocktail Time*, The Dell Trio," *Billboard*, January 21, 1950, 40.

8. Richard Harris, *Building a Market: The Rise of the Home Improvement Industry, 1914–1960* (Chicago: University of Chicago Press, 2012), 313–325. Harris emphasizes the gendering of home construction, home improvement, and women's roles on the rise of the industry.

9. Russel Wright apparently considered the table as the center of the modern American home. As an element of US postwar imaginings, the privately owned single family home's kitchen table forming the center here stands in interesting contrast to visions of the kitchen hovering in the background on the other side of the Cold War. In *Cold War on the Home Front*, historian Greg Castillo writes of the "communal kitchen, a facility celebrated in Soviet modernist utopias as an incubator of social collectivity." Castillo, *Cold War on the Home Front: The Soft Power of*

Midcentury Design (Minneapolis: University of Minnesota Press, 2011), 14. The presence of alternative visions for living and design just over the border in East Berlin provided some inspiration, no doubt, for the noncommunal future demonstrated on the cover of *March around the Breakfast Table*.

10. For a thoughtful discussion of stereo demonstration LPs, see Tim J. Anderson, "Training the Listener: Stereo Demonstration Discs in an Emerging Consumer Market," in *Living Stereo: Histories and Cultures of Multichannel Sound*, ed. Paul Théberge, Kyle Devine, and Tom Everett (London: Bloomsbury, 2015), 107–124.

11. For more detailed information on the Moods in Music series, see Joseph Lanza, *Elevator Music: A Surreal History of Muzak, Easy-Listening, and Other Moodsong* (New York: Picador, 1994), and John Connell and Chris Gibson, *Sound Tracks: Popular Music, Identity, and Place* (London: Routledge, 2003).

CHAPTER 2: MODERN ART AND DESIGN

1. The notion of "US origins" is understood broadly, and in these examples suggests a strong connection to African American cultural developments.

2. Sanka Knox, "Abstract Art Is Going to Europe to Represent American Culture," *New York Times*, March 11, 1958, 31.

3. Quoted in Laura A. Belmonte, *Selling the American Way: U.S. Propaganda and the Cold War* (Philadelphia: University of Pennsylvania Press, 2008), 146.

4. Phil Ford, *Dig: Sound and Music in Hip Culture* (Oxford: Oxford University Press, 2013), 135.

5. Lisa Phillips, "Introduction," in *High Styles: Twentieth-Century American Design* (New York: Whitney Museum of American Art, 1985), ix.

6. Dominic Bradbury, *Mid-Century Modern Complete* (New York: Abrams, 2014), 11.

7. From a wonderful catalog about a 2015–16 Eames retrospective at London's Barbican. John Winter, "Eames House," in *The World of Charles and Ray Eames*, ed. Catherine Ince and Lotte Johnson (London: Thames & Hudson/Barbican, 2015), 110–121. [Originally published in John Winter, *Great Buildings of the World: Modern Buildings* (London: Paul Hamlyn, 1969).

8. John Anderson, "Designs for Living," *Playboy*, July 1961, 46–52, 108–109. See plans for such a bachelor pad in "*Playboy*'s Penthouse Apartment: A High Haven for the Bachelor in Town," which reproduced a 1956 *Playboy* article, complete with blueprints, in Joel Sanders, ed., *Stud: Architectures of Masculinity* (New York: Princeton Architectural Press, 1996), 54–67. A quote from the original magazine article: "This is the kind of pre-planning in design and furnishing

which makes *Playboy*'s penthouse apartment a bachelor haven of virile good looks, a place styled for a man of taste and sophistication. This is *his* place, to fit his moods, suit his needs, reflect his personality." Thus, the bachelor pad aesthetic places men within the realm of interior design and decoration, fostering consumption of design objects to express taste and build a home. For more on the relationship between architecture and consumption in this vein, see Beatriz Preciado, *Pornotopia: An Essay on* Playboy*'s Architecture and Biopolitics* (New York: Zone Books, 2014).

9. Steven Guarnaccia and Bob Sloan, *Hi-Fi's and Hi-Balls: The Golden Age of the American Bachelor* (San Francisco: Chronicle Books, 1997), 52.

10. "Space age bachelor pad music" or just "music for bachelors" emerged in the 1980s and 1990s as terms for a popular, collectible genre of midcentury vinyl LPs. The hi-fi formed a key element of such a "pad": "the altarpiece in this cathedral of leisure was the hi-fi. From it issued forth musical sermons testifying to the supremacy of bachelorhood." Guarnaccia and Sloan, *Hi-Fi's and Hi-Balls*, 14.

11. Bradbury, *Mid-Century Modern Complete*.

12. Bertoia recorded his own music on the Sonambient label, combining his interest in "sonambient" sculpture and tonal music, created by "playing" his wire sculptures. Bertoia's recordings are available from Important Records, which released an eleven-CD box set from his original LPs. "Harry Bertoia: Sonambient: Recordings of Harry Bertoia," Important Records, http://importantrecords.com/imprec/imprec419. His son, Val Bertoia, continues to play his "sound sculptures," which resemble a cross between church bells and Lou Reed's *Metal Machine Music*. See Mark Masters, "Sculptures You Can Hear: Why Harry Bertoia's 'Sonambient' Art Still Resonates," *Washington Post*, March 27, 2015. https://www.washingtonpost.com/news/arts-and-entertainment/wp/2015/03/27/sculptures-you-can-hear-why-harry-bertoias-sonambient-art-still-resonates.

13. Perhaps one reason why the covers of *Relaxing with Perry Como* and *Let's Listen* look so timeless and appealing is that they resemble reclining nudes from classical painting, with modernist furniture replacing Ottoman beds or Renaissance interiors. The reclining nude—interestingly, the model is not always depicted without clothing—has served for centuries as a way to represent ideal female beauty, as well as offer a titillating image. A key example might be Modigliani's *Reclining Nude*, which sold for $170 million in 2015, making it one of highest prices yet realized for a painting. These LP covers echo the fine art tradition of reclining nudes, as they update them by incorporating modern settings, including midcentury chairs. For consumers, then, they may represent a beautiful example of modernist-inspired "art" now; they are collectible as cheesecake covers and sought out for their visual appeal as frameable objects of desire. Even if consumers weren't proud owners of midcentury furniture classics, they could possess images of them on their LP covers.

14. Esther McCoy, "The Rationalist Period," in *High Styles: Twentieth-Century American Design* (New York: Whitney Museum of American Art, 1985), 135.

15. Quoted in Cara Greenberg, *Mid-Century Modern: Furniture of the 1950s* (New York: Harmony Books, 1995), 78. Eames chairs placed in the "high-brow" category of art historian and editor at *Harper's* magazine Russell Lynes's famous and controversial "High-Brow, Low-Brow, Middle-Brow" chart in *Life* magazine. Russell Lynes, "High-Brow, Low-Brow, Middle-Brow," *Life*, April 11, 1949, 99–101.

16. Sam Jacob, "Context as Destiny: The Eameses from Californian Dreams to the Californiafication of Everywhere," in *The World of Charles and Ray Eames*, ed. Catherine Ince (London: Thames & Hudson/Barbican, 2015), 164–167.

17. From an interview on the JazzWax blog, Marc Myers, "Nancy Wilson on Shearing," *JazzWax* [blog], February 11, 2011, http://www.jazzwax.com/2011/02/nancy-wilson-on-shearing.html.

18. Particularly poignant as Shearing, of course, could not "see" Wilson's blackness.

19. Not to be confused with the guitarist Herb Ellis's 1956 LP of the same title on the Norgan label, a precursor to Norman Granz's famous Verve Records.

20. Victor Moscoso turned Josef Alber's color theory on its head. Moscoso used the "irritating" and "affronting" qualities of vibrating color, forcing "the viewer into a throbbing and kinetic relationship with the two-dimensional picture surface that fostered a more dynamic relationship than flatness could achieve." Steven Heller and Véronique Vienne, *100 Ideas That Changed Graphic Design* (London: Laurence King Publishing, 2012), 118.

21. As Eames's biographer Pat Kirkham observed, their shell chair "was used extensively in public spaces, so much so that it took on a certain invisibility, and was taken for granted by many who used it, day in and day out, in restaurants, schools, and office buildings." Pat Kirkham, *Charles and Ray Eames: Designers of the Twentieth Century* (Cambridge, MA: MIT Press, 1995), 236.

22. Award-winning graphic designer and art director at MGM Records and RCA Records, Acy Lehman, designed the *Animalization* cover. Lehman did art direction for a number of Velvet Underground and Lou Reed albums, including the famous *The Velvet Underground and Nico* "banana" cover—typically attributed to Andy Warhol, who provided the banana image for the cover. "Uses Designed by Acy Lehman," Fonts in Use, http://fontsinuse.com/designers/2119/acy-lehman.

23. From the description of the Womb chair on Knoll's website: "Womb Chair," Knoll Corporation, http://www.knoll.com/product/womb-chair.

24. The cover of *All of You* was photographed by Don Bronstein, the first staff photographer for *Playboy*.

25. Bradbury, *Mid-Century Modern Complete*, 72. MAA stands for medium-height armchair adjustable-back. Thanks to Andreas Nutz at Vitra Design Museum for spelling out this acronym.

26. Kelsey Smith, "Mr. Chair by George Mulhauser for Plycraft," *Dwell*, July 7, 2014, http://www .dwell.com/product/article/mr-chair-george-mulhauser-plycraft.

27. In a 2016 Nespresso advertising campaign, Hollywood star George Clooney relaxes in an Eames lounge in a pose reminiscent of these LP covers, revealing and reinforcing the masculinity and the staying power of this iconic image.

28. This was one of the first albums produced in the famous round "stack of records" Capitol headquarters, and marked a departure for the top recording artist. As one Sinatra biographer put it: "Given his commercial and artistic success in so many media, Sinatra's choice of *Tone Poems of Color* to inaugurate the new Capitol studios is a fascinating one." Gilbert L. Gigliotti, *A Storied Singer: Frank Sinatra as Literary Conceit* (Westport, CT: Greenwood Press, 2002), 22.

29. Jennifer Bass and Pat Kirkham, *Saul Bass: A Life in Film and Design* (London: Lawrence King, 2013), 53.

30. Archive of fonts from website Fonts in Use: An Independent Archive of Typography, http:// fontsinuse.com/tags/266/record+cover/5.

31. From the book *Saul Bass: A Life in Film and Design*, 53. The book was designed by Bass's daughter Jennifer Bass and written by prolific design writer Pat Kirkham.

32. Bass, celebrated for virtually creating a veritable new art form with his innovative and stylish film title sequence designs, such as *The Man with the Golden Arm*, and *Psycho*, was an early freelance designer of album covers, such as 1956's *Blues and Brass*, by Elmer Bernstein for Decca. In his film work, he helped create what would now be called integrated marketing campaigns, with titles, posters, advertising, and soundtracks sharing the same visual style. He remained active as an album cover designer into the 1990s, with a late effort producing the artwork for rock group the Smithereens' LP, *Blow Up*.

33. The cover for *Tone Poems of Color* remains contemporary—the dust jacket of a 2011 book from the MIT Press, *Living in a Modern Way: California Design 1930–1965*, ed. Wendy Kaplan, perfectly emulates the LP design, with credits "Designed after Saul Bass" in small type, right where "Designed by Saul Bass" appeared on the original cover.

34. As interviewed by Steven Heller in 2007. Steven Heller, "Waxing Chromatic: An Interview with S. Neil Fujita," *AIGA: The Professional Association for Design* [blog], September 18, 2007, http://www.aiga.org/waxing-chromatic-an-interview-with-s-neil-fujita. Design historian Victor Margolin assesses Fujita's influence this way: "For albums by Charles Mingus and Dave Brubeck, Fujita illustrated the music with his own paintings—playful lyrical abstractions with swirling shapes on different colored fields. Fujita brought a modern design sensibility to album covers,

making the typography as important as visual images in the overall design of a cover." Victor Margolin, "American Jazz Album Covers in the 1950s and 1960s," *Print*, June 29, 2015, http://www.printmag.com/design-culture-2/american-jazz-album-covers-in-the-1950s-and-1960s.

35. Edward Lucie-Smith, *Art Now: From Abstract Expressionism to Superrealism* (New York: William Morris & Co., 1977), 61.

36. See Louis Menand's essay, "Unpopular Front: American Art and the Cold War," *The New Yorker*, October 17, 2005, http://www.newyorker.com/magazine/2005/10/17/unpopular-front, as well as Eva Cockcroft "Abstract Expressionism, Weapon of the Cold War," *Artforum* 15, no 10. (October 1974): 39–41.

37. Serge Guilbaut, *How New York Stole the Idea of Modern Art: Abstract Expressionism, Freedom, and the Cold War* (Chicago: University of Chicago Press, 1983), 201. See also Greg Barnhisel, *Cold War Modernists: Art, Literature, and American Cultural Diplomacy, 1946–1959* (New York: Columbia University Press, 2015), and Nicholas J. Cull, *The Cold War and the United States Information Agency: American Propaganda and Public Diplomacy, 1945–1989* (Cambridge: Cambridge University Press, 2009).

38. On the liner notes for *Countdown: Time in Outer Space*, Brubeck also wrote against the "Europeanization" of jazz, and the loss of "a great deal of the rhythmic drive which African music offers. … New and complex rhythm patterns, more akin to the African parent, are the natural direction for jazz to develop. This new interest in the African heritage of jazz is but one of many awakening forces."

39. Amah-Rose Abrams, "Jazz Innovator and Jackson Pollock Lover Ornette Coleman Dies at 85," *Artnet News*, June 12, 2015, https://news.artnet.com/people/jackson-pollock-lover-ornette-coleman-dies-307565. For more on the connections between Coleman and Pollock, see Terry Kattelman, "Ornette Coleman and Jackson Pollock: Black Music, White Light," *Jazz Diplomacy* [blog], 2013, http://federaljazzpolicy.com/?p=369.

40. Hilary Moore, "Painting Sound, Playing Color: The Multiple Voices of Ornette Coleman's *Free Jazz* and Jackson Pollock's *White Light*," in *Coverscaping: Discovering Album Aesthetics*, ed. Asbjørn Grønstad and Øyvind Vågnes (Copenhagen: Museum Tusculanum Press, 2010), 193.

41. The label's records exemplified the emerging easy-listening category, but its recording technology was more progressive, and included early use of 35mm film to record sound for LPs. Command helped pioneer the marketing of LPs to audiophiles who were interested in innovations in recording technology and high fidelity.

42. See "Albers in Command," http://albersincommand.com, and an accompanying article: Alexander Tochilovsky, "Albers in Command," *Medium*, January 28, 2015, https://medium.com/vvvvvv-studio/albers-in-command-b3184edd7746#.5lces2rwl [credited to the Herb Lubalin Study

Center]. Referenced in Steven Heller, "When Bauhaus Met Lounge Music," *The Atlantic*, January 15, 2015, http://www.theatlantic.com/entertainment/archive/2015/01/when-bauhaus-met-lounge -music/384711.

43. The gallery was run by Felix Landau, whose background included managing Pete Seeger and working in public relations for Folkways Records. Suzanne Muchnic, "Felix Landau, 78; His L.A. Art Gallery Was Showcase in 1960s," *Los Angeles Times*, March 5, 2003, http://articles.latimes .com/2003/mar/05/local/me-landau5.

CHAPTER 3: MUSIC FOR GRACIOUS LIVING

1. One observer keenly remarked that Hedrich Blessing "did in color in Columbia's 'Gracious Living' series what it did in their black & white architectural photography. They took a subject, in the case of 'Gracious Living,' a common suburban family trope, and perfected it like they did their images of buildings." Brian F. Coffey, "Gracious Blessings from Hedrich Blessing,*" The Incredulous Pithecanthrope* [blog], January 10, 2008, https://tancred62.wordpress.com/2008 /01/10/gracious-blessings-from-hedrich-blessing/#comments.

2. When the Music for Gracious Living series was released, the recently launched Columbia Record Club offered four musical divisions "to please every taste: Classical, Listening and Dancing, Broadway, Movies, Television and Musical Comedies, and Jazz." The Listening and Dancing division included "music for gracious living, for relaxation, for dancing." Columbia Records, "Columbia Record Club" [advertisement], *Life*, September 19, 1955, 22–23.

3. Billboard, "Music for Gracious Living" [review], *Billboard*, October 15, 1955, 24.

4. Richard Harris, *Building a Market: The Rise of the Home Improvement Industry, 1914–1960* (Chicago: University of Chicago Press, 2012), 1.

5. Kristin L. Matthews, "One Nation over Coals: Cold War Nationalism and the Barbecue," *American Studies* 50, no. 3 (Fall–Winter 2009), 6.

6. Harris, *Building a Market*, 341. From a gender perspective, DIY can be seen as a form of relaxation for men more than women. Men traditionally worked outside the home, and do-it-yourself was not considered paid work or necessary chores, in contrast to women, who were expected to perform the bulk of the housework. See Ellen Lupton, *Mechanical Brides: Women and Machines from Home to Office* (New York: Cooper-Hewitt National Museum of Design and Princeton Architectural Press, 1993).

7. Legendary collector and pop culture enthusiast Mickey McGowan insightfully remarks on albums such as Music for Gracious Living's *After the Dance*: "The story of America for the past 40 years could be told by a chronological layout of all these LPs. You could infer the social

mores, the fads, and see how this country has changed—just by laying out all these records on a wall." V. Vale and Andrea Juno, *Incredibly Strange Music, Volume 1* (San Francisco: RE/Search, 1993), 117.

8. Fred Patterson, at the Archive of Contemporary Music in New York, described the LP this way: "The cover photo on *Do-It-Yourself* depicts a very square family in their neatly appointed den working on home projects. It definitely looks as if Rock 'n' Roll had not come to this town yet. Ten years after this photo was taken, I'll bet the boy in the picture was rockin' to The Beatles!" Fred Patterson, "What Is Music Good For?," *The ARChive of Contemporary Music* [blog], October 4, 2014, http://arcmusic.org/blog/what-is-music-good-for.

9. "It's hard to believe that barbecuing as an industry has been around only since the 1950's, when Weber-Stephens Products marketed the first version of its phenomenally successful kettle-shaped charcoal grill." David Tuller, "What's New in Barbecue," *New York Times*, September 6, 1987, http://www.nytimes.com/1987/09/06/business/what-s-new-in-barbecue.html.

10. Then, as now, barbecue was "widely seen to be a man's job, with its connections to the outdoors and hunks of raw meat." Tim Miller, *Barbecue: A History* (Lanham, MD: Rowman & Littlefield, 2014), 149. During the 1950s, barbecue "worked to 'stabilize' the home in ways only it could, for barbecue's division of labor—'dad' is the chef whereas 'mom' is on prep and clean-up duty—clarified gender roles and reasserted the postwar male's position." Matthews, "One Nation Over Coals," 7.

CHAPTER 4: LET'S HAVE A DINNER PARTY!

1. Bernie Hodes, "Victor Aid to Gourmet Digestion," *Billboard*, April 20, 1959, 40.

2. Despite the name, Wendy Hilty was a male photographer, originally from Switzerland, who photographed many LP covers as well as advertisements.

3. These LPs were also marketed to "ethnic" groups in the US: "Italian-Americans, of course, were also one of the biggest ethnic minorities in the United States and presented a ready-made audience for LPs of Italian songs." Travis Elborough, *The Long-Player Goodbye: The Album from Vinyl to iPod and Back Again* (London: Sceptre, 2008), 88.

4. Peter Moruzzi, *Classic Dining: Discovering America's Finest Mid-Century Restaurants* (Layton, UT: Gibbs Smith, 2012), 10.

5. Ibid., 12.

CHAPTER 5: MUSIC FOR HI-FI LIVING

1. Musical excerpts from the Music for Hi-Fi Living series are available at: Mark Betcher, "Hi-Fi Living," *Unearthed in the Atomic Attic* [blog], May 12, 2014, http://artworkbymanicmark .blogspot.com/2014/05/hi-fi-living.html.

2. For a marvelous look at record collecting and record collectors, see Elion Paz, *Dust & Grooves: Adventures in Record Collecting* (New York: Dust & Grooves Publications, 2014).

3. See Sarah Bray's Valentine's Day feature in *Elle Decor* for a discussion about the continued popularity of Dalí's design. Sarah Bray, "The Most Romantic Sofa of All Time," *Elle Decor*, February 14, 2014, http://www.elledecor.com/design-decorate/a5795/salvador-dali-lip-sofa.

4. Robert McG. Thomas, Jr., "George Wright, 77, Theater Organist with a Cult Following," *New York Times*, May 30, 1998, http://www.nytimes.com/1998/05/30/arts/george-wright-77-theater -organist-with-a-cult-following.html.

PART II: AWAY

1. For example, Capitol Records executive Dave Dexter, Jr., writes that Capitol of the World planned to produce "an extremely lush and attractive Tahiti package with an 8-page insert for release next May to tie in with the start of jet flights from Los Angeles to Pipette [capital city of Tahiti]." In 1961, *Tahiti Dream Island* came out with a bright pink cover featuring an "ethnic" model in a pond up to her neck in lily pads and pink blossoms. The album insert contains color photographs, mostly of girls, or "wahine," in bikinis, with liner notes focused on their beauty and availability, and how these characteristics led to "mixed blood lines." Dave Dexter, "Memo to Lloyd W. Dunn," December 1, 1960. Dave E. Dexter, Jr. Collection, LaBudde Special Collections Department, University of Missouri–Kansas City University Libraries.

2. "A typical and rather obvious idea would be a trip through Europe, using Holiday pictures and educational material and tying in a track or two from each country. Or a trip around the world. Or something." In such albums, distinction was made between a "real native package" and something recorded in the USA. Lloyd W. Dunn, "Memo to Dave Dexter, Jr.," November 29, 1960. Dave E. Dexter, Jr. Collection, LaBudde Special Collections Department, University of Missouri-Kansas City University Libraries.

3. For a discussion of the United States' push for postwar consumption in Europe, see Sheryl Kroen, "Negotiations with the American Way: The Consumer and the Social Contract in Post-War Europe," in *Consuming Cultures, Global Perspectives: Historical Trajectories, Transnational Exchanges*, ed. John Brewer and Frank Trentmann (Oxford: Berg, 2006), 251–278.

4. Orvar Löfgren, *On Holiday: A History of Vacationing* (Berkeley: University of California Press, 1999), 7. Löfgren reveals how the tourist phenomenon was created, and how tourists came to expect certain experiences.

5. Richard K. Popp, *The Holiday Makers: Magazines, Advertising, and Mass Tourism in Postwar America* (Baton Rouge: Louisiana State University Press, 2012), 82–83. There are rules and rituals for travel. How do we organize and make sense of what we see? Sociologist John Urry outlines several aspects of "consuming places" that shed light on the complex interconnections between travel and consumer culture. First, places are reinvented as sites of consumption, providing an arena for shopping, hanging out, using goods, and photographing or videotaping friends and family. Second, places themselves are in a sense consumed visually. Third, places can be literally consumed; what people take to be significant about a place—industry, history, buildings, literature, environments—is over time depleted, devoured, or exhausted by use. John Urry, *Consuming Places* (London: Routledge, 1995).

6. Löfgren, *On Holiday*, 5. Löfgren views vacationing as a kind of cultural laboratory in which travelers explore new aspects of their identities and relationships. He contrasts the vacation with work to understand the wants and needs of the vacationer.

CHAPTER 6: AIRLINES

1. Advertising executive Mary Wells spearheaded Braniff's design efforts. Girard had curated an influential 1949 exhibition for the Detroit Institute of Arts called "For Modern Living," that celebrated postwar modernism. Herman Miller, Inc., "Designers: Alexander Girard," http://www .hermanmiller.com/designers/girard.html.

2. Jim Heimann and Allison Silver, *20th Century Travel: 100 Years of Globe-Trotting Ads* (Köln: Taschen, 2015), 257, 292, 299, 311; see also Matthias C. Hahn, *Airline Visual Identity, 1945–1975* (Cherry Hill, NJ: Calisto, 2015).

3. "Holiday Abroad Promotion" [advertisement], *Billboard*, November 10, 1958, 21.

4. Nick Keppler, "An Exhibit Showcases Classic Album Covers by a Forgotten Local Artist," *Pittsburgh City Paper*, October 29, 2014, http://www.pghcitypaper.com/pittsburgh/an-exhibit -showcases-classic-album-covers-by-a-forgotten-local-artist/Content?oid=1787449. One of the few African American artists at a major label in the 1950s and 1960s, Thompson produced well-known covers for RCA's 1951 version of *Porgy and Bess* and MGM's *The Lonesome Sound of Hank Williams*, as well as the five-volume Black America spoken-word series for Buddha Records. However, he faced discrimination, and was often fired when commissioning employers found out he was black.

5. Mike Dicecco, "A History of 16-RPM Records, Part Two: Audio Books," *Antique Phonograph News* [blog], Canadian Antique Phonograph Society, May–June 2010, http://www.capsnews.org /apn2010-3.htm.

6. "No dictatorship can tolerate jazz," Brubeck said at one performance. "[Jazz] is the first sign of a return to freedom." David Brent Johnson, "Jazz Impressions of Brubeck," *Night Lights: Classic Jazz with David Brent Johnson* [radio program], May 3, 2008, http://indianapublicmedia .org/nightlights/jazz-impressions-of-brubeck.

7. Embassy of the United States of America, "The Real Ambassadors: America Exports Jazz," Meridian International Center's *Jam Session* exhibition pamphlet, March 21, 2013, http:// iipdigital.usembassy.gov/st/english/pamphlet/2013/03/20130320144471.html#axzz405mFbXav.

CHAPTER 7: HONEYMOON

1. Kris Bulcroft, Richard Bulcroft, Linda Smeins, and Helen Cranage, "The Social Construction of the North American Honeymoon, 1880–1995," *Journal of Family History* 22, no. 4 (October 1997), 467.

2. Richard Bulcroft, "Honeymoon," in *Encyclopedia of Human Relationships*, ed. Harry T. Reis and Susan Sprecher (Thousand Oaks, CA: Sage, 2009), 812.

3. "The tropical beach hotel was a Hawaiian invention. The honeymoon couple did not need to leave the grounds of the hotel, since there they could enjoy fine dining, daytime and evening activities, bars, and special events at the pool or on the beach." Cele C. Otnes and Elizabeth H. Peck, *Cinderella Dreams: The Allure of the Lavish Wedding (*Berkeley: University of California Press, 2003), 152.

4. Janet L. Borgerson and Jonathan E. Schroeder, "Ethical Issues of Global Marketing: Avoiding Bad Faith in Visual Representation," *European Journal of Marketing* 36, nos. 5/6 (May–June, 2002): 570–594. See also Otnes and Peck, *Cinderella Dreams*, 151–152; Bulcroft, et al., "The Social Construction of the North American Honeymoon, 1880–1995," 474.

5. Kris Bulcroft, Linda Smeins, and Richard Bulcroft, *Romancing the Honeymoon: Consummating Marriage in Modern Society* (Thousand Oaks, CA: Sage, 1999), 3.

6. Communication theorist Lorna Roth has studied the ways that visual reproduction technologies reproduce skin color and tone,

> emphasizing the technical challenges presented by the limitations within imaging technologies and the ways in which an ensemble of practices emerged to address these deficiencies with reference to human skin tone reproduction quality. These deficiencies include the difficulty of imaging high contrasts in skin tones within the same screen

shot—for example, a very dark-skinned person sitting next to a very pale-skinned person—and the lack of establishment and design of appropriate lighting and make-up for peoples of darker skin colours. (Lorna Roth, "Looking at Shirley, the Ultimate Norm: Colour Balance, Image Technologies, and Cognitive Equity," *Canadian Journal of Communication* 34, no. 1 [Winter 2009], 115)

7. Billboard, "Honeymoon in Mexico" [Reviews and Ratings of New Popular Albums], *Billboard*, March 24, 1956, 26.

8. Thanks to Cele Otnes for her illuminating insights into the honeymoon albums.

CHAPTER 8: NEW YORK CITY

1. Clive Scott, *Street Photography: From Atget to Cartier-Bresson* (London: I. B. Tauris, 2007).

2. Joseph Lanza, *Elevator Music: A Surreal History of Muzak, Easy-Listening, and Other Moodsong* (New York: Picador, 1994).

3. Lee Friedlander, *American Musicians* (New York: Distributed Art Publishers, 1998).

4. See Lee Israel, *Kilgallen* (New York: Delacorte Press, 1979).

5. Peggy Roalf, *Colorama: The World's Largest Photographs from Kodak and the George Eastman House Collection* (New York: Aperture, 2004).

6. For a comprehensive look at Christmas records, see Joel Whitburn, ed. *Christmas in the Charts, 1920–2004* (Menomonee Falls, WI: Record Research, Inc., 2004).

CHAPTER 9: CUBA

1. Rosalie Schwartz, *Pleasure Island: Tourism and Temptation in Cuba* (Lincoln: University of Nebraska Press, 1997), xiv.

2. Ibid., 87. For a rich history of the Afro-Cuban drum, see Roberto Nodal, "The Social Evolution of the Afro-Cuban Drum," *The Black Perspective in Music* 11, no. 2 (Autumn 1983), 157–177.

3. The success of Ry Cooder's *Buena Vista Social Club* LP and Wim Wenders's Academy Award–winning film in the late 1990s, named after a famous Havana nightclub, gathered an all-star lineup of Cuban musicians and helped spur a revival of interest in Cuban music; many classic Cuban LPs from the 1950s and 1960s have been reissued on compact disc as well as vinyl.

4. Louis A. Pérez, Jr., *On Becoming Cuban: Identity, Nationality, and Culture* (Charlotte: University of North Carolina Press, 2012), 211.

5. Peter Moruzzi, *Havana before Castro: When Cuba was a Tropical Playground* (Salt Lake City, UT: Gibbs Smith, 2008), 10.

6. Popular entertainment fed the Cuba craze, too. Hollywood films such as *Week-end in Havana*, featuring Carmen Miranda and Cesar Romero, was a hit in 1941, and 1949's *Holiday in Havana* included music by Desi Arnaz, who famously went on to play a Cuban bandleader in the top TV show *I Love Lucy* with Lucille Ball. See Philip D. Beidler, *The Island Called Paradise: Cuba in History, Literature, and the Arts* (Tuscaloosa: University of Alabama Press, 2014). For a concise history of Cuban music, see Ned Sublette, *Cuba and Its Music: From the First Drums to the Mambo* (Chicago: Chicago Review Press, 2007).

7. Alan Hess, "Built by Becket," *Los Angeles Forum for Architecture and Design* [blog], January 10, 2010, http://laforum.org/article/built-by-becket/.

8. Srinath Perur, "The Habana Libre Hotel, Pawn in Castro's Battle against the US," *The Guardian*, May 12, 2015, http://www.theguardian.com/cities/2015/may/12/havana-habana-libre-castro-cuba-us-history-cities-50-buildings-day-34. For an enlightening study of the association of Hilton Hotels and the US government during the Cold War, see Annabel Jane Wharton, *Building the Cold War: Hilton International Hotels and Modern Architecture* (Chicago: University of Chicago Press, 2001).

9. Perur, "The Habana Libre Hotel."

10. Ibid.

11. The official White House announcement emphasized travel as a key aspect of the "new course" on Cuba: "With expanded travel, Americans will be able to help support the growth of civil society in Cuba more easily, and provide business training for private Cuban businesses and small farmers. Americans will also be able to provide other support for the growth of Cuba's nascent private sector." The White House, "Charting a New Course on Cuba," President Barack Obama Official White House website, https://obamawhitehouse.archives.gov/issues/foreign-policy/cuba. It is still illegal to visit Cuba merely as a US tourist; one must qualify for one of twelve categories, such as family visits, education, or religious activity, and humanitarian projects.

12. Christopher Muther, "Cuba Opens Its Creaky Doors to US Tourists, Seeking to Connect," *Boston Globe*, August 8, 2015, https://www.bostonglobe.com/lifestyle/travel/2015/08/08/cuba-opens-its-creaky-doors-tourists/FzGcUA3vstgrK7l6yjtjqL/story.html.

13. Elizabeth Pineau and Dominique Vidalon, "Cuban Rum Is Coming to America as Trade Embargo Lifts," *Business Insider*, May, 19, 2015, http://www.businessinsider.com/r-pernod-prepares-to-take-cuban-made-rum-to-the-united-states--2015-5.

14. Nick Allen, "Cuba's Revolution Comes Full Circle with a Hilton in Havana," *The Telegraph*, March 15, 2015, http://www.telegraph.co.uk/news/worldnews/centralamericaandthecaribbean/cuba/11443590/Cubas-revolution-comes-full-circle-with-a-Hilton-in-Havana.html.

15. Charles Sinclair, "Cap Adds Fine Supplement to '57 Christmas Series," *Billboard*, November 3, 1958, 18, 53.

16. Writing about how Latin music was often lost in translation, world music scholar and record producer John Storm Roberts complained:

> As played by most American bands, in fact, the chachacha's features were so exaggerated that it was almost a novelty number, and—like all novelty numbers—it burned out as fast as it flared up. A few years of lumpy rhythm sections, mooing sax sections, and musicians raggedly chanting CHAH! CHAH! CHAH! were enough. (John Storm Roberts, *The Latin Tinge: The Impact of Latin American Music on the United States* [Oxford: Oxford University Press, 1999], 132–133)

17. Helio Orovio, *Cuban Music from A to Z* (Durham, NC: Duke University Press, 2004).

18. Moruzzi, *Havana before Castro*.

19. See Andrew Williamson, *The Golden Age of Travel: The Romantic Years of Tourism in Images from the Thomas Cook Archive* (Cambridge: Thomas Cook Publishing, 1998).

20. Billboard, "Travel Albums by Vox-Cook," *Billboard*, March 31, 1956, 23.

21. Roberts, *The Latin Tinge*, 10.

22. Mike Callahan, David Edwards, and Patrice Eyries, "Tops/Mayfair Story," *Both Sides Now Stereo Newsletter* [blog], April 15, 2007, http://www.bsnpubs.com/pri/tops.html.

CHAPTER 10: HAWAII

1. We have used "Hawaii" to refer to the common name of the state, rather than Hawai'i, which denotes the orthographic spelling of the name.

2. Philippa Pollenz, "Changes in the Form and Function of Hawaiian Hulas," *American Anthropologist* 52, no. 2 (April–June, 1950), 225.

3. Janet L. Borgerson and Jonathan E. Schroeder, "Ethical Issues of Global Marketing: Avoiding Bad Faith in Visual Representation," *European Journal of Marketing* 36, nos. 5/6, (May/June 2002), 570–594. See also, Susan Smulyan, "Live from Waikiki: Colonialism, Race, and Radio in Hawaii, 1934–1963," *Historical Journal of Film, Radio and Television* 27, no. 1 (March 2007), 63–75.

4. For an insightful overview of so-called "exotica" music, see Philip Hayward, ed. *Widening the Horizon: Exoticism in Post-War Popular Music* (London: John Libbey & Co., 1999).

5. Indeed, "Hawai'i was one of a few iconic places, exotic or nostalgic, celebrated as important destinations in virtual music tourism." John Connell and Chris Gibson, "'No Passport Necessary': Music, Record Covers and Vicarious Tourism in Post-War Hawai'i," *Journal of Pacific History* 43, no. 1 (June 2008), 59.

6. Hawaiian music served as a sonic resource that lends the Hawaii brand an "authentic" history that draws on cultural, mythical, and stereotypical resources—about Hawaiian natives, paradise, and fallen monarchies. Hawaii and her "lilting and undulating call," lure us to what we have called the ultimate "retro-escape." Janet L. Borgerson and Jonathan E. Schroeder, "The Lure of Paradise: Marketing the Retro-escape of Hawaii," in *Time, Space, and the Market: Retroscapes Rising*, ed. Stephen Brown and John F. Sherry (Armonk, NY: M. E. Sharpe, 2003), 219–237.

7. The genre of Hawaiian record albums provides a spectacular site for analysis of the way aesthetics, identity, and representation cooperate in cultural production, appropriation, and imperialism. Marketers use the album cover as a conveyor of visual representation to sell products, but more than just attractive packaging these visions have played a significant part in constructing the meaning of Hawaii.

8. Jonathan E. Schroeder and Janet L. Borgerson, "Packaging Paradise: Organizing Representations of Hawaii," in *Against the Grain: Advances in Postcolonial Organization Studies*, ed. Anshu Prasad (Copenhagen: Copenhagen Business School Press, 2012), 32–53.

9. Garrison worked in Hollywood, and was known for his use of colored gelatins to enhance his trademark glamorous publicity shots. See Editor, "Lighting in Color," *Popular Photography*, August 1950, 34–37, 107.

10. Adria L. Imada, *Aloha America: Hula Circuits through the US Empire* (Durham, NC: Duke University Press, 2012), 4. She argues:

> Hawaiians become legible and largely desirable to Americans through what I term "hula circuits"—popular tours of hula performers that crisscrossed both the Atlantic and Pacific, performing for largely Euro-American audiences in Western metropolitan centers, rural outposts, and small towns. … Hawai'i became familiar and assimilable to American audiences through the alluring female bodies those spectators saw circulating on the continent. (Ibid., 5)

11. Billboard, "Album Reviews: *Your Musical Trip around the Island of Hawaii with the 'Hilo Kalimas,'*" *Billboard*, April 16, 1966, 42.

12. Thinking about the role of color in picturing Hawaii:

> The colors that most clearly identified the show itself could be found in the iconic, oversized letters brought out by dancers at the show's beginning and end—in red and yellow and spelling out the words "HAWAII" and "ALOHA." Significant is the fact that

these very same two colors are not only the ones chosen by the Kodak company in the 1930s for their own logo but that, for centuries within the Hawaiian Islands, red and yellow had also been the distinguished colors designating royalty, or the *ali'i* status, of many of the islands' people. As such, even in a commercial sense, times of the past once again became linked to the present. (Karyl Reynolds, "Picture Perfect," *Waikiki Magazine*, July 1, 2014, http://www.waikikivisitor.com/2014/ilove-waikiki /picture-perfect)

13. See, for example, Elizabeth Buck, *Remaking Paradise* (Philadelphia: Temple University Press, 1993); Jane C. Desmond, *Staging Tourism: Bodies on Display from Waikiki to Sea World* (Chicago: University of Chicago Press, 1999); Jonathan E. Schroeder, "Consuming Representation: A Visual Approach to Consumer Research," in *Representing Consumers: Voices, Views, and Visions*, ed. Barbara B. Stern (New York: Routledge, 1998), 193–230, and Borgerson and Schroeder, "Ethical Issues of Global Marketing."

14. "Both men and women performed hula, but Hawaiian women were spectacularized on colonial stages and became metonyms for the nation of Hawai'i. Hawaiian women thus bore the responsibility for reproducing national knowledge for their people as they were commodified within U.S. tourist economies." Imada, *Aloha America*, 13.

15. See Fred E. Baston and Charles Phoenix's celebratory compendium *The Lure of Hawaii in the Fifties* (Waipahu, HI: Island Heritage Publishing, 1999).

CHAPTER 11: SOUND TOUR

1. Billboard, "Verve Works Tie with *Esquire* on 'Sound Tour' Sets," *Billboard Music Week*, May 26, 1962, 6. For a lavishly illustrated history of Verve Records, see Richard Havers, *Verve: The Sound of America* (London: Thames & Hudson, 2013).

2. Ren Grevatt, "Albums Just Right for Travel Buffs," *Billboard Music Week*, June 9, 1962, 5.

3. "Esquire," *Encyclopædia Britannica*, http://www.britannica.com/topic/Esquire-American -magazine.

4. Kenon Breazeale, "In Spite of Women: 'Esquire' Magazine and the Construction of the Male Consumer," *Signs* 20, no. 1 (Autumn 1994): 1–22. In the 1960s, *Esquire* achieved widespread recognition for the cover art of George Lois, whose work was often controversial.

5. Steven Guarnaccia and Bob Sloan, *Hi-Fi's and Hi-Balls: The Golden Age of the American Bachelor* (San Francisco: Chronicle Books, 1997), 88.

6. Bob Porter, "Jazz at the Philharmonic: The Complete Recordings on Verve: 1944–1949," *Jazztimes* [blog], January–February 1999, http://jazztimes.com/articles/7867-the-complete

-recordings-on-verve-1944-1949-jazz-at-the-philharmonic. See also Richard Havers, "Verve Records Helped Spread Jazz around the World," *Telegraph*, November 8, 2013, http://www .telegraph.co.uk/culture/music/worldfolkandjazz/10425647/Verve-Records-helped-spread -jazz-around-the-world.html.

7. Howard Pollack, *Gershwin: His Life and Work* (Berkeley: University of California Press, 2007), 433. *An American in Paris*, a jazz-inflected symphonic poem, which includes the sound of car horns meant to represent Parisian street noise, went on to become the basis for an Oscar-winning movie in 1951, famously starring Gene Kelly as "the American" and Leslie Caron as his French love interest, as well as a Tony Award–winning Broadway play in 2015.

8. For a brief discussion of the Sound Tour series, see C. Andrew Hovan, "Kenyon Hopkins: Verve/Esquire Sound Tour," *All about Jazz* [blog], August 16, 2004, http://www.allaboutjazz.com /kenyon-hopkins-verve-esquire-sound-tour-by-c-andrew-hovan.php.

9. Of course, the Spanish Civil War also killed women, both civilians and combatants. See Lisa Lines, "Female Combatants in the Spanish Civil War: Milicianas on the Front Lines and in the Rearguard," *Journal of International Women's Studies* 10, no. 4 (December 2009): 168–187.

CHAPTER 12: ADVENTURES IN SOUND

1. Sean Wilentz, *360 Sound: The Columbia Records Story* (San Francisco: Chronicle Books, 2012); Sony Music Entertainment, "125 Years of Columbia Records," http://www.columbiarecords .com/timeline/#!date=1882-11-09_08:17:04!

2. Billboard, "Columbia's 1958 Tee-Off Cues Big Product Campaign: Program Set to Tie in with LP Disk's 10th Anniversary Year," *Billboard*, January 6, 1958, 15.

3. Billboard, "Sound: Review of *Jamaican Drums*," *Billboard*, March 3, 1958, 10.

4. Billboard, "Album Review: *Big Bill's Blues*," *Billboard*, March 3, 1958, 6.

5. Billboard, "Col 'Adventures' Line to Get Intense Hypo," *Billboard*, April 13, 1959, 137.

6. Gary Marmorstein, *The Label: The Story of Columbia Records* (New York: Thunder's Mouth Press, 2007), 231. In his otherwise exhaustive account of Columbia's story, Marmorstein does not mention the Adventures in Sound series. For an extensive online album of Adventures in Sound titles, see Ruud Verkerk, "Columbia Adventures in Sound Series," *musiceureka* [blog], October 29, 2014, https://musiceureka.wordpress.com/category/columbia-adventures-in-sound-series.

CHAPTER 13: CAPITOL OF THE WORLD

1. For a comprehensive website about Capitol Records, see Mark Heimback-Nielsen, *popculturefanboy* [blog], http://popculturefanboy.blogspot.com.

2. Marilyn Lee, "Dexter's World of Albums," *Los Angeles Examiner*, July 13, 1958, 22.

3. Paul Grein, *Capitol Records: Fiftieth Anniversary 1942–1992* (Hollywood, CA: Capitol Records, 1992), 216.

4. Billboard, "Capitol Foreign Language Album Series Is Exposure Barometer," *Billboard*, February 6, 1965, 6. The Capitol of the World series was also favorably mentioned in Eliot Tiegel, "Entertainment Fields Sparkle with Diversity! Record Companies Emphasize Standard Sounds While Embracing the Big Beat," *Billboard*, December 16, 1967, M4–M5, M26.

5. Dave Marsh, *The Beatles' Second Album* (New York: Rodale, 2007).

6. John G. Houser, "Capitol's Dave Dexter Is a 'Worldly' Fellow," *Los Angeles Herald-Examiner*, June 10, 1967, A-10. Capitol repeatedly tried to link Capitol of the World titles with popular music trends. For example, to capitalize on the folk music boom in the early 1960s, they released *Finnish Folk Songs*, *The Toshiba Singing Angels*, and *Music of Norwegian Fjords*, each packaged as "authentic" folk music from around the world. Capitol of the World also included an International Starline series, with LPs by Maurice Chevalier and Edith Piaf, and an International Celebrity series, presenting performers such as Marlene Dietrich. In debating the appeal of Capitol of the World amid plans to increase sales, Capitol staffers went back and forth deciding how to segment an "international star line," general pop music, and those LPs that contained "authentic foreign music," which in Capitol's National Sales Manager Bill Tallant's mind included music "such as 'Music of the Austrian Alps,' 'Streets of Tokyo,' 'German Schlagers,' or any album recorded in a native tongue or with native instruments." Bill Tallant, "Memo to Alan Livingstone," April 10, 1962. Dave E. Dexter, Jr. Collection, LaBudde Special Collections Department, University of Missouri–Kansas City University Libraries.

7. Lloyd Dunn, "Change in C.O.W. [Capitol of the World] Status: Memo from Lloyd Dunn," September 14, 1964. Dave E. Dexter, Jr. Collection, LaBudde Special Collections Department, University of Missouri–Kansas City University Libraries. Dunn frequently clashed with Dexter over the Capitol of the World series.

8. Lee, "Dexter's World of Albums," 22. In retrospect, Capitol's promotion reflected the emerging art of market segmentation, as practiced by the growing legion of advertising agencies: "Despite concern among cultural critics of the fifties that the standardization inherent in mass consumption was breeding social conformity and homogeneity, the Madison Avenue they reviled was moving by the end of the decade in the opposite direction: toward acknowledging, even

reifying, social differences through an embrace of market segmentation." Lizbeth Cohen, *A Consumers' Republic: The Politics of Mass Consumption in Postwar America* (New York: Vintage, 2003), 306.

9. Internal Memo, "Capitol of the World," Capitol Records, January 31, 1963. Dave E. Dexter, Jr. Collection, LaBudde Special Collections Department, University of Missouri–Kansas City University Libraries.

10. Dave Dexter, "C.O.W. Unit Sales: Internal Memo," December 1963. Dave E. Dexter, Jr. Collection, LaBudde Special Collections Department, University of Missouri–Kansas City University Libraries.

11. "UNAM Library," Great Buildings online, http://www.greatbuildings.com/buildings/UNAM _Library.html.

12. A *Mexico: Its Sounds and People* album with such a sticker can be seen at: Ruud Verkerk, "Capitol of the World Series 10100-10199," *musiceureka* [blog], October 29, 2014, https:// musiceureka.wordpress.com/category/capitol-of-the-world-series-10100-10199.

13. Several of the more unusual Capitol of the World album titles include exclamation points, and boldly colored, childlike typography, lending an exoticized excitement to the titles, akin to the science fiction films of the era that featured Space Invaders! Mutants! and Cannibals!— further reinforcing the sense that this music was alien.

14. The soldier appears to be from the United States Army's 8th Armored Division, which fought in France at the end of World War II and is considered a liberating unit. United States Holocaust Memorial Museum, "The 8th Armored Division," *The Holocaust Encyclopedia*, https://www .ushmm.org/wlc/en/article.php?ModuleId=10006149.

15. Letter from Dave Dexter to John Reynolds, May 14, 1958. Dave E. Dexter, Jr. Collection, LaBudde Special Collections Department, University of Missouri–Kansas City University Libraries.

16. This Buddhist chant, sometimes called the *Lotus Sutra*, expresses the ability of all to overcome suffering.

17. Britton—who married and became Lady Bouchier and was appointed Member of the Order of the British Empire—was a translator and a poet, and studied at Mills College in Oakland, California, with Darius Milhaud, with whom the likes of Dave Brubeck, Philip Glass, Joan Tower, and Steve Reich also studied.

18. Thanks to Cobus van Staden for insight and identifications on the Japanese LPs.

19. See Sophia Sambono, "Tribal Music of Australia: Curator's Notes," *Australian Screen*, National Film and Sound Archive, http://aso.gov.au/titles/music/tribal-music-of-australia/notes.

20. Although four is considered one of the unlucky numbers in China, groupings of four are common in the Chinese arts. See Patricia Bjaaland Welch, *Chinese Art: A Guide to Motifs and Visual Imagery* (Rutland, VT: Tuttle, 2008).

21. "Recorded in the Orient" probably indicates that the LP was recorded in Hong Kong, not mainland China. At the time, Hong Kong remained a British colony.

22. Anonymous, "Chinese Movie: Comedy about an Amorous Barber Is Breaking Records in Shanghai," *Life*, October 27, 1947, 75, 77.

23. The cover photographer for *An Evening in Beirut*, Manoug Alemian, of Armenian descent, was born in Syria and moved to Lebanon. He became known for his iconic shots of the country's ancient sites, ports, and landscapes; but also for his portraits of Jordanian, Saudi Arabian, and Syrian leaders, as well as portraits of the heads of the Armenian Apostolic Church. Harry L. Koundakjian, "Manoug Alemian," One Fine Art, http://www.onefineart.com/en/artists/manoug _alemian/index.shtml.

24. Sargon Boulos, "The Origin of a Legend," Al Mashriq: The Levant [website], http://almashriq .hiof.no/lebanon/700/780/fairuz/legend/biography.html. See also Fairuz, "Fairuz Legend and Legacy Tour Book," Maqam: Caravan to Culture, http://www.maqam.com/Fairuz-Legend-And -Legacy-Tour-Book-P3481.html.

25. Fairuz Online, "A Legend: Biography," FairuzOnline.com, http://www.fairuzonline.com /alegend.htm.

26. The cover of the *Cairo!* album was shot by Max Tatch, an accomplished landscape and architecture photographer, who was the uncle and teacher of Sid Avery, a well-known midcentury Hollywood photographer and occasional album cover artist.

27. Lisa Urkevich, *Music and Traditions of the Arabian Peninsula: Saudi Arabia, Kuwait, Bahrain, and Qatar* (London: Routledge, 2014), 213.

28. Billboard, "*Cairo!*" [review], *Billboard*, May 5, 1956, 28.

29. This type of dance was filmed for the Academy Award–winning film *King Solomon's Mines* from 1950, and has been claimed to be an inspiration for the popular 1960s Watusi dance fad.

30. Although this "unusual" LP offered some information about its "exotic" recording locale, and does an admirable job showcasing talented musicians, it provided little relevant information about the Central African country of its title. The Congo was particularly plagued by colonialism, and its effects haunt the republic today: "The official Belgian attitude was paternalism: Africans were to be cared for and trained as if they were children. In the late 1950s, when France and the United Kingdom worked with their colonies to prepare for independence, Belgium still portrayed the Congo as an idyllic land of parent-child relationships between Europeans and Africans." *Encyclopædia Britannica*, "Belgian Congo," http://www.britannica.com/place/Belgian

-Congo. A few years after *Kasongo! Modern Music of the Belgian Congo* was released, the Congo revolted against its Belgian rulers.

31. Produced in the height of the apartheid era, the cover of *Music of the African Zulus!* seems caught in a tourist gaze, and from a postcolonial perspective might be critiqued as objectifying the culture as much as celebrating it. See Jonathan Schroeder, *Visual Consumption* (New York: Routledge, 2002). Thanks to Mehita Iqani for insight about this LP.

CHAPTER 14: SPACE

1. For an interesting analysis of space themes on jazz LPs, see Morris B. Holbrook and Barbara B. Stern, "The Use of Space-Travel and Rocket-Ship Imagery to Market Commercial Music: How Some Jazz Albums from the 1950s, 1960s, and 1970s Burned Brightly but Fizzled Fast," *Extrapolation* 41, no. 1 (Spring 2000): 51–62. See also the Space Age Pop music website, http://www.spaceagepop.com/index.htm.

2. Indeed, the mission to the moon has been conceived of as a lesson in promotion: "Apollo is the largest, and we believe the most important, marketing and public relations case study in history." David Meerman Scott and Richard Jurek, *Marketing the Moon: The Selling of the Apollo Lunar Program* (Cambridge, MA: MIT Press, 2014), ix.

3. Ibid.; Isaac Asimov, *Satellites in Outer Space* (New York; Random House, 1960).

4. For example, RCA released the *History of Space Age Pop* series of compact discs in the 1990s; and Capitol offered *Jet Set Swingers!* as part of their "Ultra Lounge" reissues. In the mid-1990s, the French pop group Stereolab and legendary Mexican musician Esquivel each put out LPs entitled *Space Age Bachelor Pad Music*. British electronic group Lemon Jelly sampled transmissions from the 1965 Gemini spacewalk for their 2002 *Lost Horizons* album, and more recently, in 2015, the band Public Service Broadcasting released *The Race for Space*, which mixes John F. Kennedy's uplifting speeches announcing the Apollo program and radio chatter from the moon missions with contemporary electronic pop soundscapes. See Mike Katzif, "Review: 'Public Service Broadcasting: The Race for Space,'" *NPR*, February 15, 2015, updated June 23, 2015, http://www.npr.org/2015/02/15/385549238/first-listen-public-service-broadcasting-the-race-for-space.

5. Laurence became embroiled in controversy after winning a Pulitzer Prize in 1946 for his reporting on the atomic bombing of Hiroshima and Nagasaki. (Laurence was the only reporter allowed to fly on the atomic bomb mission over Nagasaki.) It was later revealed that he was on the War Department's payroll at the time and was criticized for downplaying the dangers of

radiation. See Leslie R. Groves, *Now It Can Be Told: The Story of the Manhattan Project* (New York: Da Capo Press, 1983).

6. For a similar perspective on air travel and contemporary life, see Nathan Heller, "Air Head: How Aviation Made the Modern World," *New Yorker*, February 1, 2016, 62–67.

7. In episode four of *Air Power*, "Pearl Harbor," US mainlanders arrive on the Matson *Lurline*, greeted with leis and kisses, as Hawaiian music forms the soundtrack. As the voiceover intones a further warning of the breakdown between US and Japanese negotiations leading to potential aggressive action, smiling beachcombers frolic on the Waikiki Beach front, diving into the sea, with Diamond Head in the distance; and outrigger canoes full of white tourists head out to sea in front of the iconic Royal Hawaiian Hotel as the scene shifts to Japanese spies pulling out and focusing cameras, casing the American fleet at Pearl Harbor.

8. Shonberg was part of the Café Frankenstein artistic group in late 1950s and 1960s Los Angeles. His illustration for the LP *Music in Orbit* has been described this way: "a pen and ink drawing of an Oz-like craft whose physiology combines a floating balloon apparatus with attached woodwind instruments and preternatural symbols, operating like a steam era piece of machinery. Childlike and esoteric at once, Shonberg's imaginative genius saw its full consummation of influences in one fell swoop: Outer-space, inner-mysticism and bohemian abstraction." Brian Chidester, "A Declaration of Independents," Café Frankenstein, http://www.cafefrankenstein.com. [Originally published in the *Outre Gallery Journal* 1, (July 2012)].

BIBLIOGRAPHY

Abrams, Amah-Rose. "Jazz Innovator and Jackson Pollock Lover Ornette Coleman Dies at 85." *Artnet News*, June 12, 2015. https://news.artnet.com/people/jackson-pollock-lover-ornette -coleman-dies-307565.

Adinolfi, Francesco. *Mondo Exotica: Sounds, Visions, Obsessions of the Cocktail Generation.* Trans. K. Pinkus. Durham, NC: Duke University Press, 2008.

Allen, Nick. "Cuba's Revolution Comes Full Circle with a Hilton in Havana." *The Telegraph*, March 15, 2015. http://www.telegraph.co.uk/news/worldnews/centralamericaandthe caribbean/cuba/11443590/Cubas-revolution-comes-full-circle-with-a-Hilton-in-Havana.html.

Anderson, John. "Designs for Living." *Playboy*, July 1961, 46–52, 108–109.

Anderson, Tim J. "Training the Listener: Stereo Demonstration Discs in an Emerging Consumer Market." In *Living Stereo: Histories and Cultures of Multichannel Sound*, edited by Paul Théberge, Kyle Devine and Tom Everett, 107–124. London: Bloomsbury, 2015.

Anonymous. "Chinese Movie: Comedy about an Amorous Barber Is Breaking Records in Shanghai." *Life*, October 27, 1947, 75, 77.

Armstrong, Elizabeth. "The Square and the Cool: California Art, Design, and Culture at Midcentury." In *Birth of the Cool: California Art, Design, and Culture in Midcentury*, edited by Elizabeth Armstrong, 23–62. Newport Beach, CA: Orange County Museum of Art and Prestel, 2007.

Asimov, Isaac. *Satellites in Outer Space.* New York: Random House, 1960.

Attwood, David. *Sound Design: Classic Audio & Hi-Fi Design.* London: Octopus, 2002.

Aynsley, Jeremy. "Graphic Design in California." In *California Design 1930–1965: Living in a Modern Way*, edited by Wendy Kaplan, 263–288. Cambridge, MA: MIT Press/Los Angeles County Museum of Art, 2011.

Barhnisel, Greg. *Cold War Modernists: Art, Literature, and American Cultural Diplomacy, 1946–1959*. New York: Columbia University Press, 2015.

Bartmanski, Dominik, and Ian Woodward. "The Vinyl: The Analogue Medium in the Age of Digital Reproduction." *Journal of Consumer Culture* 15 (1) (January 2013): 3–17.

Bartmanski, Dominik, and Ian Woodward. *Vinyl: The Analogue Record in the Digital Age*. London: Bloomsbury, 2015.

Bass, Jennifer, and Pat Kirkham. *Saul Bass: A Life in Film and Design*. London: Lawrence King, 2013.

Baston, Fred E., and Charles Phoenix. *The Lure of Hawaii in the Fifties*. Waipahu, HI: Island Heritage Publishing, 1999.

Beidler, Philip D. *The Island Called Paradise: Cuba in History, Literature, and the Arts*. Tuscaloosa: University of Alabama Press, 2014.

Belmonte, Laura A. *Selling the American Way: US Propaganda and the Cold War*. Philadelphia: University of Pennsylvania Press, 2008.

Betcher, Mark. "Hi-Fi Living." *Unearthed in the Atomic Attic* [blog], May 12, 2014. http://artworkbymanicmark.blogspot.com/2014/05/hi-fi-living.html.

Billboard. "Album Review: *Big Bill's Blues*." *Billboard*, March 3, 1958, 6.

Billboard. "Album and LP Record Reviews: *Cocktail Time*, The Dell Trio." *Billboard*, January 21, 1950, 40.

Billboard. "Album Reviews: *Your Musical Trip around the Island of Hawaii with the 'Hilo Kalimas.'*" *Billboard*, April 16, 1966, 42.

Billboard. "*Cairo!*" [review]. *Billboard*, May 5, 1956, 28.

Billboard. "Capitol Foreign Language Album Series Is Exposure Barometer." *Billboard*, February 6, 1965, 6.

Billboard. "Col 'Adventures' Line to Get Intense Hypo." *Billboard*, April 13, 1959, 137.

Billboard. "Columbia's 1958 Tee-Off Cues Big Product Campaign: Program Set to Tie in with LP Disk's 10th Anniversary Year." *Billboard*, January 6, 1958, 15, 20.

Billboard. "Holiday Abroad Promotion." *Billboard*, November 10, 1958, 21.

Billboard. "Honeymoon in Mexico" [Reviews and Ratings of New Popular Albums]. *Billboard*, March 24, 1956, 26.

Billboard. "Music for Gracious Living" [review]. *Billboard*, October 15, 1955, 24.

Billboard. "Sound: Review of *Jamaican Drums*." *Billboard*, March 3, 1958, 10.

Billboard. "Travel Albums by Vox-Cook." *Billboard*, March 31, 1956, 23.

Billboard. "Verve Works Tie with *Esquire* on 'Sound Tour' Sets." *Billboard Music Week*, May 26, 1962, 6.

Bordo, Susan. *Twilight Zones: The Hidden Life of Cultural Images from Plato to O.J.* Berkeley: University of California Press, 1997.

Borgerson, Janet L. "The Flickering Consumer: New Materialities and Consumer Research." *Research in Consumer Behavior* 15 (2013): 125–144.

Borgerson, Janet L., and Jonathan E. Schroeder. "Ethical Issues of Global Marketing: Avoiding Bad Faith in Visual Representation." *European Journal of Marketing* 36 (5–6) (May–June 2002): 570–594.

Borgerson, Janet L., and Jonathan E. Schroeder. "The Lure of Paradise: Marketing the Retro-escape of Hawaii." In *Time, Space, and the Market: Retroscapes Rising*, edited by Stephen Brown and John F. Sherry, Jr., 219–237. Armonk, NY: M. E. Sharpe, 2003.

Borgerson, Janet L., and Jonathan E. Schroeder. "The Pleasures of the Used Text: Revealing Traces of Consumption." In *Consuming Books: The Marketing and Consumption of Literature*, edited by Stephen Brown, 46–59. London: Routledge, 2006.

Bosker, Gideon. "Introduction: Cocktail Nation." In *Atomic Cocktails: Mixed Drinks for Modern Times*, by Karen Brooks, Gideon Bosker, and Reed Darmon, 6–9. San Francisco: Chronicle Books, 1998.

Boucher, Diane. *The 1950s American Home*. Oxford: Shire Publications, 2013.

Boulos, Sargon. "The Origin of a Legend." Al Mashriq: The Levant [website], n.d. http://almashriq.hiof.no/lebanon/700/780/fairuz/legend/biography.html.

Bradbury, Dominic. *Mid-Century Modern Complete*. New York: Abrams, 2014.

Bray, Sarah. "The Most Romantic Sofa of All Time: Some 75 Years after Its Design, Salvador Dalí's Mae West–Inspired 'Lips' Sofa Continues to Make Designers Love Sick." *Elle Decor*, February 14, 2014. http://www.elledecor.com/design-decorate/a5795/salvador-dali-lip-sofa.

Breazeale, Kenon. "In Spite of Women: 'Esquire' Magazine and the Construction of the Male Consumer." *Signs* 20 (1) (Autumn 1994): 1–22.

Brooks, Karen, Gideon Bosker, and Reed Darmon. *Atomic Cocktails: Mixed Drinks for Modern Times*. San Francisco: Chronicle Books, 1998.

Buck, Elizabeth. *Remaking Paradise*. Philadelphia: Temple University Press, 1993.

Bulcroft, Kris, Richard Bulcroft, Linda Smeins, and Helen Cranage. "The Social Construction of the North American Honeymoon, 1880–1995." *Journal of Family History* 22 (4) (October 1997): 462–485.

Bulcroft, Kris, Linda Smeins, and Richard Bulcroft. *Romancing the Honeymoon: Consummating Marriage in Modern Society.* Thousand Oaks, CA: Sage, 1999.

Bulcroft, Richard. "Honeymoon." In *Encyclopedia of Human Relationships*, edited by Harry T. Reis and Susan Sprecher, 811–813. Thousand Oaks, CA: Sage, 2009.

Bussard, Katherine and Lisa Hostetler. *Color Rush: American Color Photography from Stieglitz to Sherman.* New York and Milwaukee: Aperture/Milwaukee Art Museum, 2013.

Callahan, Mike, David Edwards, and Patrice Eyries. "Tops/Mayfair Story," *Both Sides Now Stereo Newsletter* [blog], April 15, 2007. http://www.bsnpubs.com/pri/tops.html.

Carosso, Andrea. *Cold War Narratives: American Culture in the 1950s.* Bern: Peter Lang, 2012.

Castillo, Greg. *Cold War on the Home Front: The Soft Power of Midcentury Design.* Minneapolis: University of Minnesota Press, 2010.

Cawthra, Benjamin. *Blue Notes in Black and White: Photography and Jazz.* Chicago: University of Chicago Press, 2011.

Chapman, Rob. "Introduction." In *Album Covers from the Vinyl Junkyard*, 5–13. London: Booth-Clibborn Editions, 1997.

Chidester, Brian. "A Declaration of Independents." *Cafe Frankenstein*, n.d. http://www .cafefrankenstein.com.

Clifford, John. *Graphic Icons: Visionaries who Shaped Modern Graphic Design.* Berkeley: Peachpit Press, 2014.

Cockcroft, Eva. "Abstract Expressionism, Weapon of the Cold War." *Artforum* 15 (10) (October 1974): 39–41.

Coffey, Brian F. "Gracious Blessings from Hedrich Blessing." *The Incredulous Pithecanthrope* [blog], January 10, 2008. https://tancred62.wordpress.com/2008/01/10/gracious-blessings-from -hedrich-blessing/#comments.

Cohan, Steven. "So Functional for Its Purposes: Rock Hudson's Bachelor Apartment in *Pillow Talk*." In *Stud: Architecture of Masculinity*, edited by Joel Sanders, 28–41. New York: Princeton Architectural Press, 1996.

Cohen, Lizbeth. *A Consumers' Republic: The Politics of Mass Consumption in Postwar America.* New York: Vintage, 2003.

Columbia Records. "Columbia Record Club" [advertisement]. *Life*, September 19, 1955, 22–23.

Connell, John, and Chris Gibson. *Sound Tracks: Popular Music, Identity, and Place*. London: Routledge, 2003.

Connell, John, and Chris Gibson. "'No Passport Necessary': Music, Record Covers, and Vicarious Tourism in Post-War Hawai'i." *Journal of Pacific History* 43 (1) (June 2008): 51–75.

Cook, Nicholas. "The Domestic *Gesamtkunstwerk*, or Record Sleeves and Reception." In *Composition—Performance—Reception: Studies in the Creative Process in Music*, edited by Wyndham Thomas, 105–117. Aldershot, UK: Ashgate, 1998.

Cooper, Laura E., and B. Lee Cooper. "The Pendulum of Cultural Imperialism: Popular Music Interchanges Between the United States and Britain, 1943–1967." *Journal of Popular Culture* 27 (3) (1993): 61–77.

Cull, Nicholas J. *The Cold War and the United States Information Agency: American Propaganda and Public Diplomacy, 1945–1989*. Cambridge: Cambridge University Press, 2009.

DeGroff, Dale. "Cocktails." In *Oxford Companion to American Food and Drink*, edited by Andrew F. Smith, 135. Oxford: Oxford University Press, 2007.

Desmond, Jane C. *Staging Tourism: Bodies on Display from Waikiki to Sea World*. Chicago: University of Chicago Press, 1999.

de Ville, Nick. *Album: Classic Sleeve Design*. London: Mitchell Beazley, 2003.

Dexter, Dave, Jr. *Playback: A Newsman/Record Producer's Hits and Misses from the 1930s to the 1970s*. New York: Billboard, 1976.

Dicecco, Mike. "A History of 16-RPM Records, Part Two: Audio Books." *Antique Phonograph News* [blog]. Canadian Antique Phonograph Society, May–June, 2010. http://www.capsnews.org/apn2010-3.htm.

Dietsch, Deborah K. *Classic Modern: Midcentury Modern At Home*. New York: Simon & Schuster, 2000.

Dorofeeva, Evgenia. "Constructivism in Russia in the 1920s." *The Russian Fashion Blog*, June 2013. http://www.russianfashionblog.com/index.php/2013/06/constructivism-russia-1920s/#axzz3ysc60RUA.

Dougherty, Carissa Kowalski. "The Coloring of Jazz: Race and Record Cover Design in American Jazz, 1950 to 1970." *Design Issues* 23 (1) (Winter 2007): 47–60.

Editor. "Lighting in Color." *Popular Photography*. August 1950, 34–37, 107.

Eisenberg, Evan. *The Recording Angel: Music, Records and Culture from Aristotle to Zappa*, 2nd ed. New Haven, CT: Yale University Press, 2005.

Elborough, Travis. *The Long-Player Goodbye: The Album from Vinyl to iPod and Back Again*. London: Sceptre, 2008.

Embassy of the United States of America. "The Real Ambassadors: America Exports Jazz." Meridian International Center's *Jam Session* exhibition pamphlet. March 21, 2013. http://iipdigital.usembassy.gov/st/english/pamphlet/2013/03/20130320144471.html#axzz405mFbXav.

Encyclopædia Britannica. "Belgian Congo." http://www.britannica.com/place/Belgian-Congo.

Encyclopædia Britannica. "Esquire." http://www.britannica.com/topic/Esquire-American -magazine.

Evans, Mike. *Vinyl: The Art of Making Records*. New York: Sterling, 2015.

Evans, Richard. *The Art of the Album Cover*. New York: Chartwell Books, 2010.

Fairuz. "Fairuz Legend and Legacy Tour Book." *Maqam: Caravan to Culture*, 2016. http://www.maqam.com/Fairuz-Legend-And-Legacy-Tour-Book-P3481.html.

Fairuz Online. "A Legend: Biography." FairuzOnline.com, 2012. http://www.fairuzonline.com /alegend.htm.

Flanders, Judith. *The Making of Home: The 500-Year Story of How Our Houses Became Our Homes*. New York: St Martin's Press, 2014.

Ford, Phil. *Dig: Sound and Music in Hip Culture*. Oxford: Oxford University Press, 2013.

Fosler-Lussier, Danielle. *Music in America's Cold War Diplomacy*. Berkeley: University of California Press, 2016.

Friedlander, Lee. *American Musicians*. New York: Distributed Art Publishers, 1998.

Gigliotti, Gilbert L. *A Storied Singer: Frank Sinatra as Literary Conceit*. Westport, CT: Greenwood Press, 2002.

Giroux, Henry A. *Disturbing Pleasures: Learning Popular Culture*. New York: Routledge, 1994.

Gosling, Sam. *Snoop: What Your Stuff Says about You*. New York: Basic Books, 2009.

Greenberg, Cara. *Mid-Century Modern: Furniture of the 1950s*. New York: Harmony Books, 1995.

Grein, Paul. *Capitol Records: Fiftieth Anniversary 1942–1992*. Hollywood, CA: Capitol Records, 1992.

Grevatt, Ron. "Albums Just Right for Travel Buffs." *Billboard Music Week*, June 9, 1962, 5.

Grønsted, Ashbjørn, and Øyvind Vågnes. "Introduction." In *Coverscaping: Discovering Album Aesthetics*, edited by Ashbjørn Grønsted and Øyvind Vågnes, 9–19. Copenhagen: Museum Tusulanum Press, 2010.

Groves, Leslie R. *Now It Can Be Told: The Story of the Manhattan Project*. New York: Da Capo Press, 1983.

Guarnaccia, Steven, and Bob Sloan. *Hi-Fi's and Hi-Balls: The Golden Age of the American Bachelor*. San Francisco: Chronicle Books, 1997.

Guilbaut, Serge. *How New York Stole the Idea of Modern Art: Abstract Expressionism, Freedom, and the Cold War*. Chicago: University of Chicago Press, 1983.

Hahn, Matthias C. *Airline Visual Identity, 1945–1975*. Cherry Hill, NJ: Calisto, 2015.

Hall, Stuart, Jessica Evans, and Sean Nixon, eds. *Representation: Cultural Representations and Signifying Practices*. London: Open University Press/Sage, 2013.

Harris, Dianne. *Little White Houses: How the Postwar Home Constructed Race in America*. Minneapolis: University of Minnesota Press, 2013.

Harris, Richard. *Building a Market: The Rise of the Home Improvement Industry, 1914–1960*. Chicago: University of Chicago Press, 2012.

Havers, Richard. *Verve: The Sound of America*. London: Thames & Hudson, 2013.

Havers, Richard. "Verve Records Helped Spread Jazz around the World." *Telegraph*, November 8, 2013. http://www.telegraph.co.uk/culture/music/worldfolkandjazz/10425647/Verve-Records-helped-spread-jazz-around-the-world.html.

Hayward, Philip, ed. *Widening the Horizon: Exoticism in Post-War Popular Music*. London: John Libbey & Co., 1999.

Heimann, Jim, and Allison Silver. *20th Century Travel: 100 Years of Globe-Trotting Ads*. Köln: Taschen, 2015.

Heimback-Nielsen, Mark. *popculturefanboy* [blog], n.d. http://popculturefanboy.blogspot.com.

Heller, Nathan. "Air Head: How Aviation Made the Modern World." *New Yorker*, February 1, 2016, 62–67.

Heller, Steven. "Alex Steinweiss, Who Made Album Covers Artful, Dies at 94." *New York Times*. July 20, 2011, A20.

Heller, Steven. "Historical Critique: For the Record." *Critique: The Magazine of Graphic Design* 7 (1998): 36–45.

Heller, Steven. *Pop: How Graphic Design Shapes Popular Culture*. New York: Allworth Press, 2010.

Heller, Steven. "S. Neil Fujita, 1921–2010." *AIGA: The Professional Association for Design* [blog], October 26, 2010. http://www.aiga.org/s-neil-fujita-1921-2010.

Heller, Steven. "Waxing Chromatic: An Interview with S. Neil Fujita." *AIGA: The Professional Association for Design* [blog], September 18, 2007. http://www.aiga.org/waxing-chromatic-an-interview-with-s-neil-fujita.

Heller, Steven. "When Bauhaus Met Lounge Music." *Atlantic*, January 15, 2015. http://www.theatlantic.com/entertainment/archive/2015/01/when-bauhaus-met-lounge-music/384711.

Heller, Steven, and Véronique Vienne. *100 Ideas That Changed Graphic Design*. London: Laurence King Publishing, 2012.

Herman Miller, Inc., "Designers: Alexander Girard," n.d. http://www.hermanmiller.com/designers/girard.html.

Hess, Alan. "Built by Becket," *Los Angeles Forum for Architecture and Design* [blog], January 10, 2010. http://laforum.org/article/built-by-becket.

Hixson, Walter L. *Parting the Curtain: Propaganda, Culture, and the Cold War*. New York: St. Martin's Press, 1998.

Hodes, Bernie. "Victor Aid to Gourmet Digestion." *Billboard*, April 20, 1959, 40.

Holbrook, Morris B., and Barbara B. Stern. "The Use of Space-Travel and Rocket-Ship Imagery to Market Commercial Music: How Some Jazz Albums from the 1950s, 1960s, and 1970s Burned Brightly but Fizzled Fast." *Extrapolation* 41 (Spring 2000): 51–62.

Houser, John G. "Capitol's Dave Dexter Is a 'Worldly' Fellow." *Los Angeles Herald-Examiner*. June 10, 1967, A-10.

Hovan, C. Andrew. "Kenyon Hopkins: Verve/Esquire Sound Tour." *All about Jazz* [blog], August 16, 2004. http://www.allaboutjazz.com/kenyon-hopkins-verve-esquire-sound-tour-by-c-andrew-hovan.php.

Hühne, Matthias C. *Airline Visual Identity, 1945–1975*. Cherry Hill, NJ: Calisto, 2015.

Imada, Adria L. *Aloha America: Hula Circuits through the US Empire*. Durham, NC: Duke University Press, 2012.

Ince, Catherine, and Lotte Johnson, eds. *The World of Charles and Ray Eames*. London: Thames & Hudson/Barbican, 2015.

Israel, Lee. *Kilgallen*. New York: Delacorte Press, 1979.

Jacob, Sam. "Context as Destiny: The Eameses from Californian Dreams to the Californiafication of Everywhere." In *The World of Charles and Ray Eames*, edited by Catherine Ince and Lotte Johnson, 164–167. London: Thames & Hudson/Barbican, 2015.

Jacobs, James A. *Detached America: Building Houses in Postwar Suburbia*. Charlottesville: University of Virginia Press, 2015.

Johnson, David Brent. "Jazz Impressions of Brubeck." *Night Lights: Classic Jazz with David Brent Johnson* [radio program], May 3, 2008. http://indianapublicmedia.org/nightlights /jazz-impressions-of-brubeck.

Jones, Dylan. *Ultra Lounge: The Lexicon of Easy Listening*. New York: Universe, 1997.

Karatzas, Pygmalion. "Hedrich Blessing Photographers." *Arcspace*, October 26, 2015. http:// www.arcspace.com/the-camera/hedrich-blessing-photographers.

Katzif, Mike. "Review: 'Public Service Broadcasting: The Race For Space,'" *NPR*, February 15, 2015. Updated June 23, 2015. http://www.npr.org/2015/02/15/385549238/ first-listen-public-service-broadcasting-the-race-for-space.

Kattelman, Terry S. "Ornette Coleman and Jackson Pollock: Black Music, White Light." *Jazz Diplomacy* [blog], 2013. http://federaljazzpolicy.com/?p=369.

Keightley, Kier. "Long Play: Adult-Oriented Popular Music and the Temporal Logics of the Post-War Sound Recording Industry in the USA." *Media Culture & Society* 26 (3) (Autumn 2004): 375–391.

Keppler, Nick. "An Exhibit Showcases Classic Album Covers by a Forgotten Local Artist." *Pittsburgh City Paper*, October 29, 2014. http://www.pghcitypaper.com/pittsburgh/an-exhibit -showcases-classic-album-covers-by-a-forgotten-local-artist/Content?oid=1787449.

Kirkham, Pat. *Charles and Ray Eames: Designers of the Twentieth Century*. Cambridge, MA: MIT Press, 1995.

Klaer, Christina. "Into Production! The Socialist Objects of Russian Constructivism." *European Institute for Progressive Cultural Policies* [blog], March, 2009. http://eipcp.net /transversal/0910/kiaer/en.

Knox, Sanka. "Abstract Art Is Going to Europe to Represent American Culture." *New York Times*, March 11, 1958, 31.

Koundakjian, Harry L. "Manoug Alemian." One Fine Art, n.d. http://www.onefineart.com/en /artists/manoug_alemian/index.shtml.

Kroen, Sheryl. "Negotiations with the American Way: The Consumer and the Social Contract in Post-war Europe." In *Consuming Cultures, Global Perspectives: Historical Trajectories, Transnational Exchanges*, edited by John Brewer and Frank Trentmann, 251–278. Oxford: Berg, 2006.

Lanza, Joseph. *Elevator Music: A Surreal History of Muzak, Easy-Listening, and Other Moodsong*. New York: Picador, 1994.

Lavin, Maud. *Clean New World: Culture, Politics, and Graphic Design*. Cambridge, MA: MIT Press, 2001.

Leach, Brenda Lynne. *Looking and Listening: Conversations between Modern Art and Music*. Lanham, MD: Rowman & Littlefield, 2015.

Lee, Marilyn. "Dexter's World of Albums." *Los Angeles Examiner*, July 13, 1958, 22.

Levi, Vicki Gold, and Steven Heller. *Cuba Style: Graphics from the Golden Age of Design*. New York: Princeton Architectural Press, 2002.

Lines, Lisa. "Female Combatants in the Spanish Civil War: Milicianas on the Front Lines and in the Rearguard." *Journal of International Women's Studies* 10 (4) (December 2009): 168–187.

Löfgren, Orvar. *On Holiday: A History of Vacationing*. Berkeley: University of California Press, 1999.

Lucie-Smith, Edward. *Art Now: From Abstract Expressionism to Superrealism*. New York: William Morris & Co., 1977.

Lupton, Ellen. *Mechanical Brides: Women and Machines from Home to Office*. New York: Cooper-Hewitt National Museum of Design and Princeton Architectural Press, 1993.

Lynes, Russell. "High-Brow, Low-Brow, Middle-Brow," *Life*. April 11, 1949, 99–101.

Marchand, Robert. *Advertising the American Dream Making Way for Modernity, 1920–1940*. Berkeley: University of California Press, 1986.

Margolin, Victor. "American Jazz Album Covers in the 1950s and 1960s." *Print*, June 29, 2015. http://www.printmag.com/design-culture-2/american-jazz-album-covers-in-the-1950s-and-1960s.

Marmorstein, Gary. *The Label: The Story of Columbia Records*. New York: Thunder's Mouth Press, 2007.

Marsh, Dave. *The Beatles' Second Album*. New York: Rodale, 2007.

Marsh, Graham, and Glyn Callingham. *The Cover Art of Blue Note Records: The Collection*. London: Collins & Brown, 2010.

Masters, Mark. "Sculptures You Can Hear: Why Harry Bertoia's 'Sonambient' Art Still Resonates." *Washington Post*, March 27, 2015. https://www.washingtonpost.com/news/arts -and-entertainment/wp/2015/03/27/sculptures-you-can-hear-why-harry-bertoias-sonambient -art-still-resonates.

Matthews, Kristin L. "One Nation over Coals: Cold War Nationalism and the Barbecue." *American Studies* 50 (3) (Fall/Winter 2009): 5–34.

May, Elaine Tyler. *Homeward Bound: American Families in the Cold War Era*. New York: Basic Books, 2008.

McCoy, Esther. "The Rationalist Period." In *High Styles: Twentieth-Century American Design*, 130–160. New York: Whitney Museum of American Art, 1985.

McKnight-Trontz, Jennifer. *Exotiquarium: Album Art from the Space Age*. New York: St. Martin's, 1999.

McKnight-Trontz, Jennifer, and Alex Steinweiss. *For the Record: The Life and Work of Alex Steinweiss*. New York: Princeton Architectural Press, 2000.

Menand, Louis. "Unpopular Front: American Art and the Cold War." *The New Yorker*, October 17, 2005. http://www.newyorker.com/magazine/2005/10/17/unpopular-front.

Miller, Daniel. *The Comfort of Things*. London: Polity, 2009.

Miller, Tim. *Barbecue: A History*. Lanham, MD: Rowman & Littlefield, 2014.

Moore, Hilary. "Painting Sound, Playing Color: The Multiple Voices of Ornette Coleman's *Free Jazz* and Jackson Pollock's *White Light*." In *Coverscaping: Discovering Album Aesthetics*, edited by Asbjørn Grønsted and Øyvind Vågnes. 179–193. Copenhagen: Museum Tusculanum Press, 2010.

Morgan, Johnny, and Ben Wardle. *The Art of the LP: Classic Album Covers 1955–1995*. New York: Sterling, 2010.

Morris, Bernadine. "Jack Bodi, Designer and Photographer of French Couture." *New York Times*, September 27, 1986. http://www.nytimes.com/1986/09/27/obituaries/jack-bodi-designer-and-photographer-of-french-couture.html.

Moruzzi, Peter. *Havana before Castro: When Cuba was a Tropical Playground*. Salt Lake City, UT: Gibbs Smith, 2008.

Moruzzi, Peter. *Classic Dining: Discovering America's Finest Mid-Century Restaurants*. Layton, UT: Gibbs Smith, 2012.

Muchnic, Suzanne. "Felix Landau, 78; His L.A. Art Gallery Was Showcase in 1960s." *Los Angeles Times*, March 5, 2003. http://articles.latimes.com/2003/mar/05/local/me-landau5.

Muther, Christopher. "Cuba Opens Its Creaky Doors to US Tourists, Seeking to Connect." *Boston Globe*, August 8, 2015. https://www.bostonglobe.com/lifestyle/travel/2015/08/08/cuba-opens-its-creaky-doors-tourists-FzGcUA3vstgrK7l6yjtjqL/story.html.

Myers, Marc. "Nancy Wilson on Shearing." *JazzWax* [blog], February 11, 2011. http://www.jazzwax.com/2011/02/nancy-wilson-on-shearing.html.

Nadel, Alan. *Containment Culture: American Narratives, Postmodernism, and the Atomic Age*. Durham, NC: Duke University Press, 1995.

Nelson, George, and Henry Wright. *Tomorrow's House: How to Plan Your Post-War Home Now*. New York: Simon & Schuster, 1945.

Nodal, Roberto. "The Social Evolution of the Afro-Cuban Drum." *The Black Perspective in Music* 11 (2) (Autumn 1983): 157–177.

Ogata, Amy. *Designing the Creative Child: Playthings and Places in Midcentury America.* Minneapolis: University of Minnesota Press, 2013.

O'Hagan, Sean. "The Photographers Who Revolutionised Album Art." *The Guardian*, July 10, 2015. http://www.theguardian.com/artanddesign/2015/jul/10/the-photographers-revolutionised -pop-album-artwork.

Oldenziel, Ruth, and Karin Zachmann. "Kitchens as Technology and Politics: An Introduction." In *Cold War Kitchen: Americanization, Technology, and European Users,* edited by Ruth Oldenziel and Karin Zachmann, 1–29. Cambridge, MA: MIT Press, 2009.

Orovio, Helio. *Cuban Music from A to Z.* Durham, NC: Duke University Press, 2004.

Osborne, Richard. *Vinyl: A History of the Analogue Record.* Surrey: Ashgate, 2012.

Otnes, Cele C., and Elizabeth H. Peck. *Cinderella Dreams: The Allure of the Lavish Wedding.* Berkeley: University of California Press, 2003.

Patterson, Fred. "What Is Music Good For?" *The ARChive of Contemporary Music* [blog], October 4, 2014. http://arcmusic.org/blog/what-is-music-good-for.

Paz, Elion. *Dust & Grooves: Adventures in Record Collecting.* New York: Dust & Grooves Publications, 2014.

Pérez, Louis A., Jr. *On Becoming Cuban: Identity, Nationality, and Culture.* Charlotte: University of North Carolina Press, 2012.

Perur, Srinath. "The Habana Libre Hotel, Pawn in Castro's Battle against the US." *The Guardian*, May 12, 2015. http://www.theguardian.com/cities/2015/may/12/havana-habana -libre-castro-cuba-us-history-cities-50-buildings-day-34.

Phillips, Lisa. "Introduction." In *High Styles: Twentieth-Century American Design*, ix–xi. New York: Whitney Museum of American Art, 1985.

Pineau, Elizabeth, and Dominique Vidalon. "Cuban Rum is Coming to America as Trade Embargo Lifts." *Business Insider*, May, 19, 2015. http://www.businessinsider.com/r-pernod -prepares-to-take-cuban-made-rum-to-the-united-states--2015-5.

Pollack, Howard. *Gershwin: His Life and Work.* Berkeley: University of California Press, 2007.

Pollenz, Philippa. "Changes in the Form and Function of Hawaiian Hulas." *American Anthropologist* 52 (2) (April-June 1950): 225–234.

Popp, Richard K. *The Holiday Makers: Magazines, Advertising, and Mass Tourism in Postwar America.* Baton Rouge, LA: Louisiana State University Press, 2012.

Porter, Bob. "Jazz at the Philharmonic: The Complete Recordings on Verve: 1944–1949." *Jazztimes* [blog], January/February 1999. http://jazztimes.com/articles/7867-the-complete-recordings-on-verve-1944-1949-jazz-at-the-philharmonic.

Poyser, Ted. "Capitol Album Covers." *CA: Journal of Commercial Art* 2 (September 1960): 42–48.

Preciado, Beatriz. *Pornotopia: An Essay on Playboy's Architecture and Biopolitics*. New York: Zone Books, 2014.

Radcliff, Pamela. *Interpreting the 20th Century: The Struggle over Democracy*. Chantilly, VA: The Teaching Company, 2004.

Reagan, Kevin. *Alex Steinweiss: The Inventor of the Modern Album Cover*. Cologne: Taschen, 2010.

Reid, Susan E. "'Our Kitchen Is Just as Good': Soviet Responses to the American National Exhibition in Moscow, 1959." In *Cold War Modern: Design 1945–1970*, edited by David Crowley and Jane Pavitt, 154–162. London: Victoria and Albert Museum, 2008.

Renwick, Mark, and Carrie Renwick. George Wright Discography, n.d. http://www.tibia.us/main/gwdisc.htm.

Reynolds, Karyl. "Picture Perfect." *Waikiki Magazine*, July 1, 2014. http://www.waikikivisitor.com/2014/ilove-waikiki/picture-perfect.

Roalf, Peggy. *Colorama: The World's Largest Photographs from Kodak and the George Eastman House Collection*. New York: Aperture, 2004.

Roberts, John Storm. *The Latin Tinge: The Impact of Latin American Music on the United States*. Oxford: Oxford University Press, 1999.

Ross, Andrew. "Containing Culture in the Cold War." *Cultural Studies* 1 (3) (1987): 328–348.

Roth, Lorna. "Looking at Shirley, the Ultimate Norm: Colour Balance, Image Technologies, and Cognitive Equity." *Canadian Journal of Communication* 34 (1) (Winter 2009): 111–136.

Rybczynski, Witold. *Home: A Short History of an Idea*. New York: Penguin, 1987.

Sambono, Sophia. "Tribal Music of Australia: Curator's Notes." *Australian Screen*, National Film and Sound Archive, 2016. http://aso.gov.au/titles/music/tribal-music-of-australia/notes.

Sandeen, Eric J. *Picturing an Exhibition: The Family of Man and 1950s America*. Albuquerque: University of New Mexico Press, 1995.

Sanders, Joel, ed. *Stud: Architectures of Masculinity*. Princeton, NJ: Princeton University Press, 1996.

Schoonmaker, Trevor, ed. *The Record: Contemporary Art and Vinyl*. Durham, NC: Duke University Press, 2010.

Schroeder, Jonathan E. "Consuming Representation: A Visual Approach to Consumer Research." In *Representing Consumers: Voices, Views, and Visions*, edited by Barbara B. Stern, 193–230. New York: Routledge, 1998.

Schroeder, Jonathan E. *Visual Consumption*. New York: Routledge, 2002.

Schroeder, Jonathan E., and Janet L. Borgerson. "Packaging Paradise: Organizing Representations of Hawaii." In *Against the Grain: Advances in Postcolonial Organization Studies*, edited by Ashnu Prasad, 32–53. Copenhagen: Copenhagen Business School Press, 2012.

Schudson, Michael. *Advertising, the Uneasy Persuasion: Its Dubious Impact on American Society.* New York: Basic Books, 1984.

Schwartz, Rosalie. *Pleasure Island: Tourism and Temptation in Cuba*. Lincoln: University of Nebraska Press, 1997.

Scott, Clive. *Street Photography: From Atget to Cartier-Bresson*. London: I. B. Tauris, 2007.

Scott, David Meerman, and Richard Jurek. *Marketing the Moon: The Selling of the Apollo Lunar Program*. Cambridge, MA: MIT Press, 2014.

Sinclair, Charles. "Cap Adds Fine Supplement to '57 Christmas Series." *Billboard*, November 3, 1958, 18, 53.

Slater, Don. *Consumer Culture and Modernity*. Cambridge: Polity, 1997.

Smith, Jacob. *Spoken Word: Postwar American Phonograph Culture*. Berkeley: University of California Press, 2011.

Smith, Kelsey. "Mr. Chair by George Mulhauser for Plycraft." *Dwell*, July 7, 2014. http://www.dwell.com/product/article/mr-chair-george-mulhauser-plycraft.

Smulyan, Susan. "Live from Waikiki: Colonialism, Race, and Radio in Hawaii, 1934–1963." *Historical Journal of Film, Radio and Television* 27 (1) (March 2007): 63–75.

Sobieszek, Robert A., ed. *The Architectural Photography of Hedrich-Blessing*. New York: Henry Holt & Co, 1988.

Sony Music Entertainment. "125 Years of Columbia Records," n.d. http://www.columbiarecords.com/timeline/#!date=1882-11-09_08:17:04.

Space Age Pop. Music website, n.d. http://www.spaceagepop.com/index.htm.

Sublette, Ned. *Cuba and Its Music: From the First Drums to the Mambo*. Chicago: Chicago Review Press, 2007.

Taylor, Timothy D. *The Sounds of Capitalism: Advertising, Music, and the Conquest of Culture*. Chicago: University of Chicago Press, 2012.

Théberge, Paul, Kyle Devine, and Tom Everett. "Introduction: Living Stereo." In *Living Stereo: Histories and Cultures of Multichannel Sound*, edited by Paul Théberge, Kyle Devine, and Tom Everett, 1–34. London: Bloomsbury, 2015.

Tochilovsky, Alexander. "Albers in Command." *Medium*, January 28, 2015. https://medium .com/vvvvvv-studio/albers-in-command-b3184edd7746#.5lces2rwl.

Thomas, Robert McG., Jr. "George Wright, 77, Theater Organist with a Cult Following." *New York Times*, May 30, 1998. http://www.nytimes.com/1998/05/30/arts/george-wright-77-theater -organist-with-a-cult-following.html.

Tiegel, Eliot. "Entertainment Fields Sparkle with Diversity! Record Companies Emphasize Standard Sounds While Embracing the Big Beat." *Billboard*, December 16, 1967, M4–M5, M26.

Tuller, David. "What's New in Barbecue." *New York Times*, September 6, 1987. http://www .nytimes.com/1987/09/06/business/what-s-new-in-barbecue.html.

United States Holocaust Memorial Museum. "The 8th Armored Division." *The Holocaust Encyclopedia*, 2016. https://www.ushmm.org/wlc/en/article.php?ModuleId=10006149.

Urkevich, Lisa. *Music and Traditions of the Arabian Peninsula: Saudi Arabia, Kuwait, Bahrain, and Qatar*. London: Routledge, 2014.

Urry, John. *Consuming Places*. London: Routledge, 1995.

Urry, John, and Jonas Larsen. *The Tourist Gaze 3.0*. London: Sage, 2011.

"Uses designed by Acy Lehman." Fonts in Use. n.d. http://fontsinuse.com/designers/2119 /acy-lehman.

Vale, V., and Andrea Juno, ed. *Incredibly Strange Music*. Vol. 1. San Francisco: RE/Search, 1993.

Verkerk, Ruud. "Capitol of the World Series 10100-10199," *musiceureka* [blog], October 29, 2014. https://musiceureka.wordpress.com/category/capitol-of-the-world-series-10100-10199/.

Verkerk, Ruud. "Columbia Adventures in Sound Series," *musiceureka* [blog], October 29, 2014. https://musiceureka.wordpress.com/category/columbia-adventures-in-sound-series.

Welch, Patricia Bjaaland. *Chinese Art: A Guide to Motifs and Visual Imagery*. Rutland, VT: Tuttle, 2008.

Wharton, Annabel Jane. *Building the Cold War: Hilton International Hotels and Modern Architecture*. Chicago: University of Chicago Press, 2001.

Whitburn, Joel. *Christmas in the Charts, 1920–2004*. Menomonee Falls, WI: Record Research, Inc, 2004.

The White House. "Charting a New Course on Cuba." President Barack Obama Official White House website, 2016. https://obamawhitehouse.archives.gov/issues/foreign-policy/cuba.

Wilentz, Sean. *360 Sound: The Columbia Records Story*. San Francisco: Chronicle Books, 2012.

Williams, Mark. "Entertaining 'Difference': Strains of Orientalism in Early Los Angeles Television." In *Living Color: Race and Television in the United States*, edited by Sasha Torres, 12–34. Durham, NC: Duke University Press, 1998.

Williamson, Andrew. *The Golden Age of Travel: The Romantic Years of Tourism in Images from the Thomas Cook Archive*. Cambridge: Thomas Cook Publishing, 1998.

Winter, John. "Eames House." In *The World of Charles and Ray Eames*, edited by Catherine Ince and Lotte Johnson, 110–121. London: Thames & Hudson/Barbican, 2015.

Womack, Kenneth. "Dave Dexter, Jr." In *The Beatles Encyclopedia: Everything Fab Four*, 224–227. Santa Clara, CA: Greenwood, 2014.

ILLUSTRATION CREDITS

We thank the copyright holders for granting permission to reproduce the figures. Every effort has been made to track down copyrighted images in this book. Any errors or omissions will be rectified in subsequent editions provided notification is sent to the publisher.

Courtesy of ABKCO: Figures 1.1, 10.7

Courtesy of Celenese Chemical Company (permission to reproduce the *Music to Paint By* LP cover): Figure 1.10

Courtesy of Kodak: Figure 1.14

Courtesy of RCA Trademark Management, Technicolor SA (permission to reproduce RCA Victor and the Dogs & Phonograph): Figures 1.6, 1.15, 1.16, 1.17, 1.18, 2.2, 4.1, 4.2, 4.3, 4.4, 4.5, 6.3, 6.6, 6.7, 6.8, 6.9, 8.8, 8.9, 14.4, 14.7

Courtesy of Sony Music Entertainment: Figures 1.2, 1.6, 1.7, 1.10, 1.15, 1.16, 1.17, 1.18, 2.2, 2.4, 2.6, 2.10, 2.12, 2.13, 3.1, 3.2, 3.3, 3.4, 3.5, 4.1, 4.2, 4.3, 4.4, 4.5, 5.1, 5.2, 5.3, 5.4, 5.5, 5.6, 5.7, 5.8, 5.9, 5.10, 5.11, 5.12, 6.1, 6.3, 6.5, 6.6, 6.7, 6.8, 6.9, 6.11, 8.5, 8.8, 8.9, 8.10, 8.11, 9.4, 12.1, 12.2, 12.3, 12.4, 12.5, 12.6, 14.4, 14.6, 14.7

Courtesy of Universal Music Enterprises: Figures 1.4, 1.5, 1.8, 1.11, 1.12, 1.13, 1.19, 2.1, 2.3, 2.5, 2.7, 2.8, 2.11, 2.15, 2.17, 7.2, 7.3, 7.6, 7.7, 8.3, 8.4, 8.6, 8.7, 9.1, 9.5, 10.2, 10.4, 10.6, 11.1, 11.2, 11.3, 11.4, 13.1, 13.2, 13.3, 13.4, 13.5, 13.6, 13.7, 13.8, 13.9, 13.10, 13.11, 13.12, 13.13, 13.14, 13.15, 13.16, 13.17, 13.18, 13.19, 14.9, 14.10

INDEX OF LPS

INDEX